PENGUIN BOOKS

GOING SOLO

Merran White is a freelance journalist (*Cosmopolitan*, *SHE*, *marie claire*, *Time Out*), television researcher and inveterate budget traveller.

GW00578191

going
SOLO

The essential guide for

solo women travellers

Merran White

PENGUIN BOOKS

The medical information given in this book has been checked by an independent expert from the Travellers Medical and Vaccination Centre.

The author and publisher thank Australian *Cosmopolitan* magazine for allowing the author to use extracts from her article 'Working and studying overseas' in the chapter 'Work, study and doing business'.

PENGUIN BOOKS

Published by the Penguin Group

Penguin Books Ltd, 27 Wrights Lane, London W8 5TZ, England

Penguin Putnam Inc., 375 Hudson Street, New York, New York 10014, USA

Penguin Books Australia Ltd, Ringwood, Victoria, Australia

Penguin Books Canada Limited, 10 Alcorn Avenue, Toronto, Ontario, Canada M4V 3B2

Penguin Books (NZ) Ltd, Cnr Rosedale and Airborne Roads, Albany, Auckland, New Zealand

Penguin Books Ltd, Registered Offices: Harmondsworth, Middlesex, England

First published by Penguin Books Australia Ltd 1989
Second edition published in Australia by Viking 1997
Published in Great Britain in Penguin Books 1998
10 9 8 7 6 5 4 3 2 1

Typeset in Giovanni 10/12pt by Post Typesetters, Brisbane
Printed in Australia by Australian Print Group, Maryborough

CONTENTS

PREFACE

Since I was a little girl, I've dreamed of packing up my possessions, bidding farewell to my loved ones and travelling the world as a free spirit. At the age of three, in a fit of daring, I filled a small swag with essentials and set off down the driveway, bound for foreign parts. It was dark and cold and my courage failed me, but the desire for solo adventure remained.

My nearest and dearest did nothing to discourage these nomadic aspirations. Our family tree is laden with explorers, starting with great-great-great-great-great uncle Captain James Cook. My maternal grandmother was forever haring off on overseas adventures, often on her own. My great-aunt drove across West Asia, Nepal and India in the 1930s with a female companion after their male partners died of typhoid. My academic father spent one year in seven studying abroad, with us tagging along, and his interest in ornithology provided the perfect excuse to explore exotic destinations, from which he'd return with amazing stories about the giant spiders of the Amazon Basin, the nomadic tribes of the Sahara, the Mayan ziggurats, and the wildebeest herds of the Serengeti.

My first solo adventure was accidental but influential: on a two-month road trip across America, my family inadvertently abandoned me in the toilet of a gas station and drove off down the freeway. With a six-year-old's logic, I deduced that since I had no idea how to find them, they'd have little chance of relocating me. After the initial shock and the inevitable bout of tears, I sat down and took stock of my situation, realising that, for the first time in my life, I was truly alone in the world. It was a scary but exhilarating feeling – knowing I was thousands of miles from home, with no-one to look after me and only my own resources to rely on. To my surprise, it was a feeling I rather enjoyed.

By the time my distraught parents returned, I felt quite

composed and perfectly at home. In less than an hour, I'd made new friends (the garage attendant; a local shop owner); sussed out the available resources (my petrol-pumping mate had taken me to a nearby snack bar for some comfort food); found safe, suitable accommodation (the garage owner's home) and formulated a plan of action (to stay with the garage owner's family, attempt to fit in with the local culture and become an all-American girl). I'd been accidentally thrown in at the deep end and, instinctively, I'd swum. I'd experienced the heady thrill of being alone in a foreign land, living on my wits and learning to adapt to strange and challenging circumstances. I'd survived: I was proud of it. And I was ready for more.

Two decades passed before I had the chance to experience the world on my own, but the positive feelings that accompanied my first solo adventure never left me. And in the hundreds of female travellers who've told me their stories, solo journeying has inspired similar feelings. Most women are unsure, initially, about going it alone, but having taken the plunge, few of us regret the decision. Indeed, most wonder what on earth took us so long to get out there and do it.

Going Solo was written to inspire confidence, increase competence and instill courage, to give women the knowledge and the streetsmarts they need to make their solo journeys safe as well as stimulating, enriching as well as enjoyable. The new edition of *Going Solo* has been totally revised and expanded to include more detailed information about practicalities such as health, packing, accommodation and transport, more positive anecdotes, tips for older women, lesbians and women from ethnic minorities, up-to-date advice on cultures, customs and attitudes to women travellers, and more information about on-line resources and work/study options abroad.

This edition, like the first, is based not just on my own experiences but on those of many other well-travelled women. My interviewees included a businesswoman who spends over half of every year in Asia, a student who traced her family roots in Greece, a travel consultant who fell in love with Indonesia and its inhabitants, two sisters who went off the beaten track in China, a tour guide who travelled extensively in Africa, and a writer who followed the bohemian trail to Morocco. Because some destinations were more popular with the women interviewed than others, these places receive somewhat more attention in the text. The advice given and the insights to be gleaned from these women's stories can be applied, however, to solo travel in many overseas countries.

The new *Going Solo* is aimed primarily at the independent female traveller on a limited budget, but may also be useful to those women travelling in tour groups, on working holidays or on business. It is intended as a supplement to destination-specific guidebooks, not as a replacement for them.

It is my intention to allay your fears and empower your explorations. If you finish reading this book and decide that you're ready to take on the world, I will have succeeded in my task. The world needs more intrepid women out there. Be one of them. Bon voyage!

ACKNOWLEDGEMENTS

I wish to acknowledge STA Travel Pty Ltd for their financial and practical contribution to the updated edition of *Going Solo*, and for their long-term involvement with the *Going Solo* project. An international company with an ongoing commitment to helping women travel independently, STA initiated the first *Going Solo* book, and many of the quotes and anecdotes included in the new edition are from interviews with STA staff members of various ages and nationalities. Moreover, my own research could not have been undertaken without STA's generous donation of a round-the-world air ticket.

Many thanks, also, to IBM Australia, who loaned me a nifty Thinkpad 710C laptop computer for the duration of my round-the-world journey. Tucked into a corner of my daypack, IBM's tiny dream machine accompanied me on planes, trains, trucks and buses, into cafés, plazas and hotel rooms, up mountains and through jungles across more than two dozen countries. The Thinkpad allowed me to access city maps and local information, correspond with family and friends via e-mail, book hostel beds by fax modem, and write the first draft of the new edition of *Going Solo*. Without it, I can't imagine how this manuscript would have got out of my head and onto the page.

Thank you to all the women who contributed their travel experiences and tips for use in *Going Solo*, and to the representatives of the many female-friendly travel organisations who gave me advice and information about the needs and preferences of independent women travellers.

Special thanks to my husband, Richard, for his patience, support and love; to my inspirational parents, in whose world-wandering footsteps I followed; to my friend and mentor Elizabeth Parsons, without whose vision there would have been no *Going Solo*; and to my sister, Alison, whose unflagging encouragement and sheer hard work helped to make this book a reality.

WHY TRAVEL SOLO?

Once, only the most intrepid and affluent females jour-
neyed alone. Today, women are wandering the world in
ever greater numbers. We travel for all sorts of reasons – to
explore and experience new people, situations and cultures; to visit friends and relatives; to make the most of a
break between study and work; to discover ourselves; to
make a life transition, or just to have fun.

Whether we go alone by design or by default, it rarely
proves a mistake.

> 'If you gave me the choice of travelling alone or with
> somebody of like mind who wants to do similar things,
> I'd prefer to travel with someone. But there have been so
> many occasions when I've wanted to travel and there's
> been no-one ready to go to that place at that time. So I've
> not let it stop me.'

> *'Sometimes I travel alone because there isn't the opportunity to go with friends or boyfriends – their schedules don't coincide with mine – and sometimes I do it just because that's the way I want to do it. Either way, I've never regretted the experience.'*

Travelling alone means different things to different women. It's impossible to generalise about the sorts of experiences you can expect or how they'll affect you. But once you've acquired a taste for solo travel, you tend to go back for more.

It's easy to get addicted to the sense of freedom that comes from being in control of all your decisions: where to go, where to stay, what to do and how to pace yourself.

> *'I was 21 and I needed to do something on my own. I wanted to experience things, to survive by myself. The fact that you have to rely on yourself and be totally independent was what attracted me. I did it and the whole thing was fabulous.'*
>
> *'I only set out to do a six-month trip. I'd finished up a job and I'd decided to go to uni the following year. As it turned out, I wasn't accepted into uni in time to make appropriate arrangements. And I was having such a great time that I thought, "I'm learning more about myself and about life by being out here, having this experience, than I would if I went to uni." I ended up never going back home.'*

Travelling alone means you can be supremely selfish. You never have to consult or compromise. You don't have to plan your itinerary around anyone else's needs or schedule. You just pick up your bags and go.

> *'I went alone because I think you have fewer hassles that way. You don't have to worry about changing your plans or relying on someone else.'*

> *'I don't want to have to ask somebody else what they
> want to do, or if they'd be interested in going here,
> because I like to be spontaneous. If I get fed up with a
> situation, I just think, "Oh, today I'll whip off to
> Amsterdam", or whatever. I don't want to be obliged to
> anybody at all.'*

> *'When I travelled by myself, I had the freedom of doing
> exactly what I wanted to do. You're not committed – if
> you don't want to go in that direction or if you don't want
> to go out to dinner that night, you don't have to.'*

Having time to yourself is one of the unexpected rewards
of travelling by yourself: it may be the first time in your life
you've felt truly free from outside demands. Travelling
solo helps teach you to enjoy your own company and rel-
ish your solitude, rather than fearing loneliness.

> *'I went alone to Europe because there were certain things
> I wanted to see and I didn't want anyone else to tell me
> that I couldn't. I went for the independence of doing
> exactly what I liked, staying where I liked, spending what
> I liked.'*

> *'You learn to enjoy your own company and appreciate
> your own qualities, particularly when you work through
> something by yourself, and at the end of the day you can
> think back on it and say, "I really did it! I've done it and
> I'm here!"'*

When you travel without companions, you become more
outgoing and more approachable. It doesn't take long to
realise that friendly, interested people are everywhere,
eager to interact with you; that you're never truly alone
unless you choose to be.

> 'Travelling solo, you have more fun. You meet more
> people, because you've got to make the overtures, whereas
> if you're with someone, you tend to stick to your group
> rather than getting out.'

> 'I found I was far more open to meeting people because
> I was alone. You have to make an effort, but at least you
> can do things in your own time, at your own pace, and do
> what you want to do, not what they want to do. You meet
> people, spend a couple of days with them, and then go off
> and do your own thing.'

You find that other travellers can be great sources of companionship, support and information. Local people, too, are often exceptionally helpful and hospitable, especially to female travellers. If you're ill, in trouble, or need a bed for the night, somebody's sure to help you out.

> 'I was going to meet someone at the other end, but they
> weren't there when I arrived. I was a bit alarmed at first,
> but I found that I met people almost as soon as I got off
> the plane, and from that moment on I had support. The
> last thing I ever was was lonely. There were always people
> – more people because I was by myself. There's never that
> feeling of being totally alone.'

> 'I left Israel thinking I was going to be on my own, but
> I ended up with this horde of people. Travelling on your
> own is a myth – actually, you are seldom alone, apart
> from when you're in your bed, or maybe in your room.
> Even then, if you're staying in hostels, you're not on your
> own. Off I went on my big solo adventure, going to the
> Greek Islands on my own – then I realised that three
> Israelis would be meeting up with me two days later, and
> a girl I'd met on the kibbutz was meeting up with me a
> week after. So much for travelling on my own.'

More opportunities come your way when you're alone. You get invited to parties, asked to house-sit, given personalised tours, offered meals in family homes.

'Travelling alone, you meet local people readily – and because you're on your own, people are very receptive to you. They'll look after you: give you advice on transport, accommodation, things to see. It's fairly transient, but those experiences are really positive.'

'When you're on your own, you go out of your way more and you accept more invitations from people, both men and women. You become a little more careful, but then you also take opportunities you wouldn't take if you were with someone. Because that's how you entertain yourself and how you discover things. By going to places, going to parties and events and celebrations and local things.'

Being alone forces you to take the initiative and get involved. There's no-one around to cushion you from the culture, so your experience is one of total immersion.

'The good thing about travelling on your own is that you get more into the culture. The reason you're going to a place is to expose yourself to new things. One of the things you learn about is the geography, the culture and the people. But you also learn so much about yourself, by placing yourself in a strange environment.'

'Being in contact with different people, cultures, experiences, thoughts, concepts of time and place is the most mind-expanding thing. It's the best way to educate yourself, first-hand, as long as you're open-minded enough to take in the experiences. Many people travelling by themselves stick to the more secure options, and lose a hell of a lot.'

'After travelling with a man, I decided I should go off and do some travelling by myself. I noticed the changes immediately. I noticed a lot more. I had a lot more interaction. I got into a lot more adventures, doing things that I just wouldn't do if I was with someone and could hesitate and say, "Will we, won't we?" If you're on your own, it's completely spontaneous and you just think, "Why not?" You're free to choose your own course.'

You're more likely to try out new ideas and are more open to new influences when you don't have your usual networks around you.

'I know I'll miss out on a lot if I go with someone else. There are certain experiences I wouldn't have had if I'd had someone else there to rely on. When I travel, my mind's very open and I'll go anywhere. You read about places and you talk to people, but I like to form my own opinion. For years, I would never go to Bali, because I thought only yobbos went there. Then I went with a friend for a week and stayed on for five weeks by myself. You have to develop your own feelings and thoughts, and see it the way you want to see it.'

You can even find yourself becoming a different person.

'The great thing about being by yourself is that there are no presumptions. You can do anything you want. You can pretend to be one thing or another. You can do the most outrageous things and no-one else is going to know about it. Even if they did, you don't really mind.'

'I prepare my "act" before I travel on my own. I have an image of how I want to be and how I want to present myself – as a confident, go-for-it, slightly tough, fairly sophisticated person. And I live into that. It's easy, because there's nobody out there who knows me, who's *going to come along and put a pin in the balloon of that act. It's a wonderful opportunity to practise new ways of being.'*

'You're on your own in a totally different world, where nobody knows you. You can do anything, be anyone you want.'

Even experiences that may have been frustrating or frightening at the time can prove positive after the fact. Once you've travelled economy class across India, talked your way out of trouble in Turkey, coped with a crisis in Cairo, and survived Bali belly, you begin to believe that you really can take on the world and win. You feel like a survivor.

'I wanted to discover what I was capable of doing on my own. I've always been independent and I didn't know anybody at that stage who I wanted to travel with. But I also wanted to know what it was like to suffer and, through suffering, become stronger and more independent.'

Solo travel demands that you meet challenges, surmount obstacles, hone skills and survive crises. It forces you to rely on yourself, to test your limits and capabilities. It teaches you to be strong and flexible, resourceful and compassionate. The outcome is often a tremendous boost in self-reliance and self-confidence.

'You learn to rely on yourself. It makes you stronger. And less naive. You have to do everything for yourself – there's no-one to feed off. You have to organise it all, whereas if you're with someone you can take it in turns. And you learn to be more careful. Having to rely on your own devices, you grow up.'

'There's something about travelling on your own. It was exciting. I like living on the edge, not knowing what's

*going to happen from day to day. I was scared in one
sense, but on the other hand, it was a real buzz. The
unknown was both exciting and terrifying, and I thrived
on it – that sense of excitement and adventure and living
dangerously.'*

*'I'm more of a survivor now. I was a lot more confident
out there than I ever imagined I would be. I still get pre-
trip butterflies – even on my last trip around Australia,
I was nervous – but once I get out there, I'm fine. As soon
as I'm there and I've met a few locals, I'm off and
running. It's much easier than you think.'*

With no-one but yourself to answer to or fall back on, you
learn to make decisions, act independently, trust your
instincts, assert yourself, and get what you want. You learn
that it's OK to stand out in a crowd, to make mistakes, to
ask for help when you need it. You lose your fear of the
unknown, because you've experienced it and coped. Then,
the world truly becomes your oyster.

*'Travelling on your own is special. I like the thrill of it.
There's an incredible amount of freedom in saying,
"I want to do this" and doing it. And you're forced to
cope, you can't blame anyone else. The onus is on you to
look after yourself. It's a good feeling – to be in control of
your own destiny.'*

*'You learn about yourself. You get to know your
weaknesses and your strengths. I can't recommend it
highly enough.'*

Travelling solo can bring immense rewards. It broadens
the mind, heightens the senses, opens the heart, hones the
intuition and develops the person. Few other experiences
can change your life so dramatically, so constructively, so
pleasurably.

> *'I discovered things about myself I never knew existed until I was put to the test. I learned that I could basically do anything. I was much more alert to things, much more confident. The knowledge I gained was invaluable.'*

Too many women wait around for the 'perfect' travel companion.

> *'I went to get away on my own, to sort myself out. I would have liked to have gone with my brother, but he didn't have the money. Probably he isn't as adventurous a spirit as myself, either.'*
>
> *'I'd planned to travel with someone else and it didn't work out. A group of friends urged me to do it by myself. They said, "All you need is confidence – plenty of people do it." That encouragement was enough to set me off. As long as you've got a good head on your shoulders and are open-minded enough to truly experience the adventures that happen along the way, don't hang around for other people – just go for it.'*

Why wait for someone else to come along? You can be your own perfect travelling companion.

TRAVEL WITH A PURPOSE

Having a 'mission', something to accomplish on your travels, gives your trip structure and focus, and can help you feel more purposeful and secure. There are hundreds of things you can do to make your trip more than just a holiday.

You may decide to:

- ❑ do a live-in language course at a local university
- ❑ attend film school in New York, a yoga intensive in an Indian monastery, or flamenco masterclasses in Madrid

- sign up as a volunteer with an overseas aid organisation
- work as an English teacher in Asia
- trace your family tree
- learn to ski/scuba dive/ride a camel
- see every Rembrandt painting in Europe
- crew your way around the South Pacific
- visit your relatives in Cyprus
- write a novel set in an exotic place.

'Travel is a big deal if you do something extraordinary – it's your showcase. I trekked Everest and was really proud of that. I got altitude sickness and came down – but I made it to so many thousand feet and I was proud I got as far as I did. That was something special.'

'I went to Greece for three months: I had some family there and I wanted to spend some time with them, 'cause that's my background. I hadn't been back to Greece since I was two years old, so it was a once-in-a-lifetime thing for some of my relatives, and naturally, they made a big fuss.'

'One of my favourite places is the Austrian Alps – because they're picturesque, and because I love skiing. It's so invigorating. I would go off all day skiing – I didn't mind doing it by myself. I'd put my Walkman on and ski between villages, and stop and get a Swiss chocolate cake here and chat to someone there. It was fantastic. That's a selfish motive, I guess, for travel, but that's what I like doing. I get a lot of fulfilment out of skiing.'

'I'd always wanted to visit the Sinai, so I linked up with an American guy who was one of the volunteers on the kibbutz I was working at, hitched down to Eilat, then caught a bus to Mount Sinai. We climbed the mountain, up the 3000 steps of repentance, and spent the night in a

Bedouin cave. I had gloves, ski jacket, woollen socks, hat, and I've still never been as cold in my life. I don't think I slept all night. These little Bedouin guys kept on feeding me tea, and the cave was about the size of a café table. It took about a day to get up there, but I decided it was well worth it when I looked out over the mountainous desert in the sunrise. It was pretty special.'

'In Thailand, I attended a 10-day meditation retreat organised by a temple there for Westerners who were visiting. It was held on Koh Samui. They had signs up around the islands and I read one and decided to go along. It was one of the best retreats I've ever done. All the monks were Thai except for this one American guy who'd been with the temple for a number of years, and he did the lectures. It was an introduction for Westerners to the Thai Buddhist religion and culture. But it was largely a silent retreat, so it was very introspective as well. And the setting was fantastic. It was an unforgettable experience.'

SIMPLE SOLO TRIPS

If you're travelling alone for the first time, make it easier on yourself by:
- choosing a destination with which you're familiar
- visiting countries in which you have friends, relatives or work opportunities
- opting for a spot frequented by like-minded travellers
- following guidebook recommendations when planning your accommodation: that way you can be sure you'll meet other people
- travelling within cultures where attitudes to unaccompanied females are relaxed.

> 'If it's a choice of travelling solo and not travelling at all,
> I'd always go ahead and do it. If I go on my own, though,
> I always make sure I'm in a situation where I can meet
> people. I don't go anywhere too remote. You can only
> handle talking to yourself for so long, so it's good to pick a
> place where you know you'll get at least some interaction,
> even if it's just a lunch with people here and there.
> Meeting up with friends or relatives abroad is the perfect
> way, really. You get to be on your own when you want,
> and then you get to spend time with them and they can
> show you the local side of life.'

> 'I've always been really shy, I'm not an extrovert. That
> was why I had to have a job lined up for me when I first
> left, so I knew where I was going. I was a bit scared about
> how it was all going to work out, but travelling helped me
> see that I can certainly get by on my own, and enjoy
> myself – more, sometimes, than if I'm with someone else.'

Relatively 'easy' destinations for a Western woman alone
include Scandinavia, Europe, Canada, the USA, Thailand,
Bali, Kenya, India, Nepal, Japan, Australia and New
Zealand.

ONE WOMAN'S STORY

'I'd gone overland through Asia, Afghanistan and Iran,
when all that was open, with a friend. Then we got to
Israel and went our separate ways. I really loved it and
wanted to stay longer, and I was ready to travel by myself.

'For six months, I spent a lot of time on my own, on and
off – meeting groups of people, then doing stuff alone. It
was funny for me, 'cause I'm a real "people person" – I
love being around people. And suddenly, there I was, *not*
being around people, and really loving that. I still don't
know where that came from.

'I went to Indonesia, then India, and I spent lots of time in Europe. They've all been conscious decisions to be by myself. It's been fantastic for me. I love the feeling of being able to get up in the morning and think, "I want to do this", without having to consult anyone. I like the feeling that I've made all the decisions for the day, or the week – of where I'm going to stay, what I'm going to eat – and that I'm not relying on somebody else in case I'm a bit nervous. That I'm encountering the other culture and I have to work at it. I have to work really hard to not feel isolated and lonely, but to feel inspired and passionate about where I am.

'It seems like when you're on your own, you take the time to stop. When you're with other people, you tend to all bounce off each other and you miss the stillness. For me, travel was a lot about sitting, and observing, and being part of things I wasn't really part of but I *was* part of. I'd be sitting in a magnificent place or in a group of people, and I couldn't understand what they were talking about but I knew they were happy for me to be there, and I was happy to be there, so we just sat together.

'I felt stuff much more deeply when I was alone than when I was with other people. I'm not at all a religious person and I wasn't brought up with any religion. Yet I found myself walking through the back streets of Jerusalem and touching the walls and feeling where the story comes from. Thinking, I'm walking the same track that Jesus trod on with the cross, and whether I believe it or not, I am in a truly historical place. I really took it in. When you're with others, you kind of rush through those things and you're affected by what they're doing and feeling. It's not the same.

'I did things I never would have done if I was with other people. I did stuff for my mum, 'cause mum is religious: I went into churches and lit candles for her, and thought, "How would she feel if she was here?" I took the time to do that. I slowed every pace down, slowed what I was feeling down, so I could do things for her – and ultimately, for me as well. Now, they're very special moments that I cherish.

'Then there are the ridiculous things, like being ecstatic that you've caught the right train and you're actually in the right place, when you had no idea of what the sign above the train said. That sort of thing was really a buzz – it showed me I didn't have to rely on other people to get me through.'

'I found it hard to be as passionate about travelling with other people as I was on my own. When I was on my own, it was like there was another me. It was like a layer, a shell had come off and there I was, the person who I knew I could be, who I was able to be. I think when you go to another culture on your own, you can create yourself. You can actually be whoever you want to be.

'It may be that the person you choose to be is exactly the same person you are at home, and I probably was that, but I was also some other things. I was more insecure, but in a positive way. I didn't have to prove to anybody that I was me, and I was strong, and I was all these things. I just had to prove it to myself.

'I felt like all of my skin was alive. Every sense I had was alive. And that was because I wasn't having to trick anybody: there I was – actually doing it. It was absolutely fantastic.'

TO GO SOLO OR NOT TO GO SOLO

Travelling alone is a challenge that not all of us want or feel ready to take on. You may feel more comfortable journeying with a friend, partner or group, especially on your first trip to an unfamiliar or 'difficult' destination.

The people you travel with affect every aspect of your trip. So think carefully about what you want from the journey before choosing your companions.

TRAVELLING WITH ANOTHER PERSON

There are advantages to travelling as a duo that make it an attractive first-time option. First and foremost is the confidence you get from taking a friend along. But there are other benefits:

- You can give each other support and companionship, and share your excitement, emotions, experiences. Having a second perspective can make things more fun and less overwhelming.
- You can halve accommodation expenses and taxi fares.
- Another person means added security: you're less likely to get harassed if you're with someone; you can watch each other's backs and baggage.
- Each person brings different skills and strengths to the partnership (she speaks fluent Spanish, you're a brilliant map-reader). Your combined skills, if complementary, can make you a formidable team.
- Two people can share tasks, minimising the time and energy you need to spend queueing for tickets, buying necessities, finding accommodation.
- You can help each other through crises: if one of you is ill, the other can play nursemaid; if you lose your travellers' cheques, your friend can cover you till you get replacements.

'Travelling with someone has its real pleasures – you can relax. You can take it in turns: if you're tired, or just tired of making decisions, they can do a bit of the hard work for a while and you can just follow along. You don't always have to be thinking, "What street am I on?" or "Where am I going?" and all those practical things you have to be conscious of constantly when you're doing it alone. It's more comfortable. And you can share your pleasures and talk about things.'

'I am more adventurous when I'm with someone else. Taking a train off to an unknown destination, getting there at eleven at night, stuck without a hotel room and by yourself is quite frightening. It may be something you'll talk about later, but at the time it's nerve-wracking. I'd rather do it with someone else.'

'I think how well you travel together depends on how connected you are to that person, how similar your likes and dislikes are, and how you relate to them on a day-to-day level. I travelled with my sister in China. We were very close, and had much the same interests, too. I think if I'd gone without my sister, it would've been harder. There were times when I was finding it really difficult to get things done, and she'd pick up and be the dominant one and say, "OK, I'll go and organise this or that." And vice versa.'

'Travelling alone makes you far more aware of the things that are going on around you. But other people notice things you don't. So there are advantages on both sides.'

Travelling in tandem can make for a simpler, safer, more comfortable and less confronting trip. But it has its drawbacks, too. Accommodating another's needs and differences can at times be frustrating and inevitably involves compromise.

'Travelling with someone is like having lived on your own for two years and suddenly having to share a house. You have to give up your independence; you have to compromise your lifestyle and activities. When you travel with another person, you've got to be considerate of their needs as well as your own, and if those needs don't coincide – if you want to do something and the other person doesn't – it can get difficult.'

'I really enjoy old buildings and history and ruins. I never got into history at school. Reading about it, it could be just a story. But when you're actually there, and you see the ruins, and read the books and pamphlets, it makes so much more sense. It gets my mind going. To appreciate it, I have to put myself in the position of who would have lived there and what life would have been like for them at that time, and how it's evolved to its modern form. So I like to go to places and just sit there for hours, looking at the buildings and thinking about all that sort of stuff. You can do that better on your own. If you're with someone, you tend to be conscious of the other person, and they may not be having the same sort of experience or thoughts as you. They might just say, "OK, seen that!" and walk off. It happened to me when I was with a friend at the Forbidden City in Beijing. I found it so fascinating. You get this cassette you walk around with that tells you where you are and what you're seeing. But my friend wasn't interested at all – she was like, "OK, it's another Chinese building." We just about had an argument over it. I spent a whole day there – she walked round once quickly and left. That's why I like to go places by myself.'

'It's hard when you travel with someone who's looking for a very different type of holiday. They might just want to find a beach and lie down, or they want to find the grooviest bar, or they want to go to art galleries – but I'm not into suntans or drinking or art, so I don't want to do that. Often, I don't know what I want out of my holiday until I'm there, discovering the place.'

'If I do travel with somebody now, I'll always tell them that maybe it's selfish, but I want to do what I want to do and see what I want to see, and not be forced into a schedule by someone else. I like to set some clear ground rules very early on. I made a point of not travelling with a friend the last time, because I knew she was different to me, and I didn't want to jeopardise what I might do or people I might meet. You don't get a lot of chances to travel, so the quality has to be good.'

Male vs female companions

Women travelling with other women have certain advantages over mixed or male travel partnerships. Two women will often get offers of help and hospitality that wouldn't be extended to men. Females, whether alone or in tandem, are seen by many people as less threatening and more approachable than women accompanied by men. A man and a woman together will often be left alone by others – people assume you're a couple and that you want your privacy.

'When I travelled with another woman I made loads more friends – local people and other travellers. Both men and women were more inclined to come up and say hello to us, probably because it's easier to start a conversation with girls than guys: they're less intimidating. We got better service at restaurants, more free drinks in bars, and more invitations from locals – probably because of the 'flirt factor', but hey, who's complaining?'

Travelling with a same-sex partner has practical advantages, too: opposite-sex travel mates may find themselves having to sleep in separate dorms in hostels or occupy separate sleeping carriages on trains. Unmarried couples may not be permitted to take double hotel rooms, or even to eat or socialise together, in countries which have strict moral codes, and in some tribal societies, custom forbids men and women from doing certain things together.

'In Vanuatu, my husband and I often found ourselves separated because there were activities that females were prohibited from participating in, such as kava drinking. I understood that this was a tribal society, and that I wasn't being singled out – all the local women were in the same situation – but it meant I spent quite a few evenings on my own.'

A woman accompanying a man may find herself relegated to a 'back-seat' role, either because others (especially other men) assume that the male of the party is the decision-maker, or because the woman herself defers to the man.

> 'My boyfriend and I spent a month in Turkey, and
> although everyone was polite to me, they addressed all
> their conversation to him. I felt as if I was invisible: if I
> tried to put my opinion, the Turkish men would look at
> me as though I was some sort of freak. In some countries,
> it seems, it's still a case of women being seen but not
> heard.'

> 'I find travelling with other women more egalitarian –
> when I travel with a man, I leave more of the decision-
> making to him. It's not because I'm wimpy, but because
> men tend to assert their preferences more forcefully and
> are less flexible and accommodating generally. People say
> women are whingers, but in my experience, it's the men
> who get grumpy if they have to do something that doesn't
> interest them.'

Women travelling together arguably have more empathy
for each other's needs and feelings: you and another
woman are more likely to perceive certain things in a similar fashion. You're more likely to be in sync with each
other's mood cycles and to support each other appropriately in emotional crises. And another woman is probably
more inclined to sympathise when you're feeling premen-
strual and just want to take it easy.

> 'My girlfriend was great when I had my period and was
> feeling ratty and lacklustre. A guy would have just told
> me to get over it, but she fussed around, made me put my
> feet up and then went off on her own, leaving me by the
> pool with a book. She understood what I was going
> through – I didn't have to pretend to be all gung-ho and
> tough.'

If you're travelling light (or someone steals your backpack), you can share clothes and cosmetics with another
woman, too.

'The second day of our trip to South America, someone stole my pack off the roof of a bus. I only had my documents and what I was wearing – I lost my clothes, books, toiletries, everything. Luckily the girl I was with was about my size so I borrowed clothes from her till I managed to buy more stuff.'

The average male's habits and interests may not gel with women's, and this, too, can be a source of conflict. For example, men tend to be more interested in food, less in shopping and gallery-hopping. And you may find it simpler to sort out expenses fairly when you're sharing with another woman – splitting bills 50–50 with a hungry male usually disadvantages the female.

'I travelled with a male friend around Europe, and boy did I regret it. All he ever wanted to do was eat and hang around in bars. I had to drag him kicking and screaming to galleries, he got grumpy if I wanted to stop and take a photo, and he needed 10 hours' sleep every night. I ended up spending way more money than I'd anticipated on taxis, food and booze, and missing out on lots of the things I'd planned to do. I should have ditched him after the first week.'

Should we travel together?
To get the most out of travelling with a friend, it's important you plan a journey that suits both of you. Get together and discuss your travel plans thoroughly. Before you commit to travelling together, ask yourselves these questions:

❑ What does each of us want and expect from this trip?
❑ What are our respective budgets, and how do we see ourselves allocating them? Do we have access to extra funds if needed?

- What do we expect in the way of accommodation, transport, food and entertainment?
- What do we want to do and see? Where do we want to go? And how flexible is this proposed itinerary?
- How interested are we in meeting local people? Other travellers?
- Are we planning to spend all our time together, or do we want to take independent excursions? How much 'private' time do we need?
- Are we 'day' or 'night' people?
- Are we urban or outdoorsy? How much do we want to rough it? What risks are we prepared to take?
- Are we both independent types, or is one of us more likely to assume the role of leader?
- Do we have the ability to discuss disagreements in a constructive manner and find workable compromises?
- Are we prepared to go our separate ways, temporarily or permanently, during the course of the trip? Under what circumstances?

Conflict, communication and compromise

Before you set out, discuss how you'll accommodate different interests, needs and goals. Are your travel styles compatible? If not, can you make compromises that will satisfy both of you? How will you handle conflicts, crises or changes of plan?

> 'If I'm travelling with somebody, I feel like I have a responsibility to do what they want to do, and they feel the same towards me. Particularly if it's someone I don't know very well. You're forced to compromise.'

On a long trip, you're bound to have the occasional disagreement. Sometimes small things take on unforeseen significance: her habit of talking with her mouth full starts to drive you mad; his endearing vagueness turns into irritating dependency.

> 'I went to Thailand with a guy who had never been out of Australia before. He was a designer, very talented but completely vague and impractical. It was like taking a two-year-old on holiday. He didn't have a clue, he just tagged along. You couldn't rely on him to do the simplest thing without getting in a tizz or stuffing it up. If there was the slightest hitch in our plans, he panicked. He blew his budget because he hadn't estimated how much alcohol would cost him, then had to borrow from me so we both ended up broke. He was a nightmare.'

In new environments, people's personalities can transform in unexpected ways. The girl who was so sociable on home turf can become timid or dependent in a foreign country; the generous friend can turn into a tightwad, the happy-go-lucky guy can prove flighty and unreliable.

> 'My friend was great fun at home, but I guess I didn't know her all that well. When we got to Europe, she became really selfish and just went sex-mad. She'd let me make all the overtures, then once I'd established contact, she'd come along and flirt her arse off. She was really pretty, so it was easy for her. She never bothered to ask me whether I might have been interested in them. I'd make friends with a guy and she'd end up having sex with him – this happened about four times. Then she ran out of money from having blown it all on going out, so she ended up going to London to get work, and I went my own way. I haven't seen her since. Thank goodness. Six weeks of her was all I could stand.'

Try not to allow privacy conflicts, personality clashes and petty disagreements blow out of proportion and spoil your trip or your friendship. Take these positive steps to prevent problems from escalating:

❑ Have regular chats about how the trip is going. Be flexible, good-humoured and prepared to compromise. Work on finding win–win solutions.

'If you're on your own and something goes wrong, you think, "I did it, I'm the idiot", and leave it at that. But if there's someone else, you can sit there and attack each other. You have to get over that. Work it out, then drop it, so you can get on with having fun.'

'It's really important to sort out your disagreements as amicably as possible. If you have a falling-out, those negative feelings can reflect on how you see the country you're travelling through. It can make your whole trip a bummer.'

❑ Raise issues before they become resentments: if you're unhappy about something, or aren't getting your needs met, say so.

'Friendships end because of the stress of money, plans not going as you thought they would when you left, meeting someone else. When friends travelling together are pissed off, they take it out on one another. You've got to be prepared to learn a few home truths, to have frank, open discussions, or there's a good chance you'll end up having arguments.'

❑ Give each other space. Even when you're travelling with a close friend or partner, you need time alone, to relax, think and experience things for yourself. Don't crowd each other – you'll enjoy each other's company more if you're not together constantly.

'If you spend all your time with another person, you don't meet people in the same way. You don't meet as many

other travellers or gain the same depth of contact because
you have each other to rely on. You have to give each
other the time and space to go out and make your own
friends, have your own fun occasionally.'

❏ Make sure that each of you has opportunities to
   make decisions and act independently. If one of
   you tends to be a leader, the other a follower, take it
   in turns to choose the day's activity or make
   arrangements. That way, one person won't feel
   burdened by the responsibility of making all the
   decisions.

'I went away with a friend who was incapable of doing
anything on her own. She didn't know what was going
on, what to do in an unfamiliar place, she couldn't amuse
herself, she was too scared to go off sightseeing by herself.
I had to hold her hand the whole time. I got really sick
of it.'

❏ Act considerately. If you've decided to travel with
   someone, you have a certain responsibility to each
   other – don't go off for days with no
   communication, fail to turn up to a rendezvous, or
   fall in love and forget your travel partner exists. If
   you have a contingency plan to cover spontaneous
   changes of heart, it makes it easier on everyone.

'I'd arranged to meet up with a girl on the Spanish Steps
in Rome and I made a monumental effort to meet her
but she never turned up. I waited for two days for her at
the same spot, same time, but she never came. I was
devastated. I even phoned my mother in tears. If I'd
thought I was getting to Rome and doing my own thing,
I wouldn't have reacted in the same way. When you have
expectations and they're not met, that's when it's hard.'

'Your trip may have cost you a whole year's savings, so the last thing you want is to be stranded because your mate's fallen in love, or have to abandon someone you've fallen for because you don't want to leave your mate stranded. You need to establish some sort of balance between freedom and companionship, and have an "out" clause in case one of you changes plans.'

'I travelled with a guy through Indonesia. We said from the start that even if something went wrong between us, we'd still stick together for the trip, because we knew it was going to be a fairly rough journey and having the support of another Westerner would be good. We made that commitment to each other to start with, but it wasn't as though we relied on each other all the time for entertainment or company – we were quite free to do what we wanted within that framework. It worked well.'

Establishing independence

As you gain confidence, take day or half-day excursions on your own. If you want to shop and she'd rather visit a gallery, go your separate ways, meeting in the evening to discuss your adventures. If she feels like a night out and you're tired, stay in and write letters while she socialises.

'At first, I wanted to do everything together, because I hated the idea that I might pass on something that turned out to be an amazing experience. But I realised that I could go off and have an amazing experience of my own. Instead of tagging along with my friend, sharing her adventure, I could create my own. I had a lot more fun once I started thinking, "Now what do I want to do today?" '

Plan to take solo side trips, and organise to travel separately on some legs of the journey, one of you arriving a day or two earlier. Taking short trips alone gives you practice at making your own travel and accommodation arrangements, orientating yourself to a new place, meeting people independently. Have a firm arrangement to meet up again at a certain time and place, with a contingency plan or contact number in case one of you is delayed.

'I was lucky enough to be in a relationship where we had very different plans and gave each other the freedom to pursue them: I wanted to go to the Philippines, so I spent two weeks there, then went to India and met up with him. It's a real plus for a relationship and for a person to be able to say, "No, my plans are different from yours, and I'm going to pursue them on my own".'

SEMI-SOLO TRIPS

On your next journey, you may decide to plan an itinerary that incorporates both group and independent travel. You may feel most comfortable if you start off in company and go on alone. Or you may be happy to link up with friends or stay with relatives at various points during the trip.

'I was with people, then we went our separate ways. It was hard at first but once I settled in, it was all so simple. My confidence grew as I became better acquainted with the places and people around me.'

'I started off with a female friend. We travelled together for a bit and then she wanted to go to Greece. I had a passion for Spain, whereas Greece didn't do much for me, so I went to Spain, met some people and never looked back.'

'I would recommend solo travel to everybody – but that's not to say that everybody can do it first up. I did it when I

> *was ready enough to do it, and I got the confidence I
> needed from first travelling with other people. That gave
> me enough guts to keep going.'*

Some women travel alone in areas that are well-touristed,
then find companions or sign up with a tour group for
legs of the journey that encompass more remote or difficult areas.

> *'I find it's better travelling on your own and spending
> parts of the journey with people. Visit a relative, join a
> tour, link up with a friend. Or meet other travellers and
> hang out with them for a while, then separate and meet
> up with someone else. It's a lot less boring than travelling
> with the same person all the way.'*

> *'I like combination travel best. I travelled through Asia
> last year, supposedly alone. But I have friends who live
> in various spots: some I was staying with, and in other
> places, I'd stay in hotels and just visit. Some worked and
> some didn't; some had children, some didn't. I was doing
> my own thing during the day but I got to come home and
> chat to them about it at night. It was a good balance
> between being alone and not alone.'*

If you're planning a semi-solo trip, do some advance preparation to make sure you know where you're staying and
who you're linking up with, when, where and for how long:

❏   Find a friend who's willing to set off with you and
    part ways mid-trip, or who has to go home earlier
    than you do.
❏   Organise to spend some of your time on a group
    tour: do your research and make bookings before
    you go.
❏   Contact friends and relatives living abroad and see
    if they can put you up, and if so, for how long.
❏   Join a global network that helps you link up with

locals for visits or homestays: write to people who sound likely and see if they can put you up or show you around when you arrive.

Have contingency plans in case a companion doesn't show or you decide you can't spend two whole weeks with your Italian auntie.

> 'I went to Indonesia with a Balinese guy I'd been going out with. He had hassles and was unavailable for quite a few months, so I travelled on my own. You've got to realise that circumstances change and you have to be ready to alter your plans.'

> 'I'd agreed to travel with this girl who was coming over, but I booked my ticket and planned everything to be by myself. 'Cause everybody says "I'll come along" and then they pull out. If you have your attitude geared towards travelling with somebody, you're likely to pull out as well. It's better to think, I'll go by myself, and if somebody joins up with me, that's fine.'

But don't worry too much about the possibility of being left unexpectedly to fend for yourself. In most countries frequented by Western tourists, it's easy to find temporary travelling companions if and when you need them. In fact, it's way simpler than ditching a travel partner who's driving you mad.

> 'One of the beauties of travelling on my own is that I could choose my company. As long as it suited me and the other person, we'd stick together, but if there was any problem, or if I wanted to do this and they wanted to do something else, that was fine too. Then I was back to being my own person and doing what I wanted. I preferred that to having an obligation to stick with one person for a certain length of time and having things go wrong.'

> 'If you're on your own and meet someone going somewhere that interests you, tag along. If you travel with them for a few days and don't like them any more, just go your different ways. It's not like a commitment you've made before you leave, so you don't feel obliged to stay together. There are none of the hassles you have travelling full-time with someone else.'

TRAVELLING WITH A GROUP

If your time is limited, your destination remote, or you'd rather have someone else handle the details, travelling with a tour group is a practical option. Because everything's pre-arranged, you don't waste time or energy on boring bureaucratic details.

> 'Because I'd grown up outside the city and had never travelled, I took a group tour the first time I went abroad. I wasn't very sure of myself so I thought, "I'll do one of these tours and someone else can think for me".'

> 'I went on a trekking tour through Borneo. It's pretty untouched – not a place where it's easy to get around on your own, 'cause there's no public transport. So you really need to visit on an organised trip to make the most of it.'

On your first trip abroad, you may feel more comfortable travelling with a group under the guidance of someone who knows the territory. That way, you can get to know the culture gradually rather than being thrown in head first, you'll have fewer hassles from local men, and you're bound to meet like-minded people.

> 'If you're not sure about starting off solo, take a short tour to begin with. You'll probably meet up with people and then you can go off on your own. That's what I did in

Nepal. I met a couple of guys who ran small tours and
went on a cheap five-day rafting trip. It was mostly girls –
only three guys. We had a ripsnorting time: we'd get on
the rafts during the day and paddle up the river, and at
night we'd haul the rafts up onto the bank and all sit
around the campfire while the guys cooked up a meal.
Then another girl and I hired a porter and did a week's
trekking on our own.'

'I took a camping tour of Spain, Portugal and Morocco.
The group consisted of 15 females and two males –
probably because women often don't feel confident about
travelling through Morocco by themselves. Which is
exactly why I did it. I thought I might as well see the
place properly, without any hassles. We had nine days
there and most of it was free time. It was really good.'

'I left home with a friend but she'd arranged to meet up
with her boyfriend overseas. So I booked a Contiki tour
round Europe. It was OK for first-time travellers but a bit
too organised for me. The best thing was that I met a lot
of people. Afterwards, me and a girl I befriended on the
tour decided to travel together.'

'I saved some money in London, then went on a three-
week Transglobal tour to Egypt. We went places that as a
single white female, I would have been wary of visiting
alone.'

In some places, taking a package tour may be the most
economical, practical way to travel.

'Scandinavia is one place where it's economical to take a
tour. Even hostels are expensive, and once you add in
transport and three meals a day, it becomes obvious that
doing it with a group is the cheapest way. It's quite boring
up there on your own, too, so tours are more sociable. On

the tours, too, you can carry your own alcohol, because it's really expensive there. We stocked up on duty-free booze before the bus even left London, and had mulled-wine parties. Everyone had a ball.'

'In China, it's quite hard to get to places like the Great Wall on your own so you're best off taking a tour. You end up taking in a few other crappy places on the way, but you can't help that.'

Potential drawbacks to travelling in a group include lack of privacy, less control over decision-making and activities, less flexibility and spontaneity, organisational difficulties (and, in some cases, the tendency for men to dominate the group agenda) and reduced opportunities to make meaningful contact with local people. Tours can also be expensive, so make sure you're signing up for the sort of holiday you want.

'I took a Contiki tour of South-West America. It was a great way to see the countryside, and the accommodation was fine. You had to share with one or two other girls, but that was OK. And it was nice to have all the details handled. I got a bit sick of early rising and all the time spent sitting on the bus, but we did see some fantastic scenery. I didn't want to do all the group things that they'd planned – I'm too independent to want to do everything in a herd – but at least they gave us the choice. For me, though, the whole thing was too self-contained an experience, like going on a school camp. Most of the people on the tour were very young, most of them were from Australia, and they weren't really interested in getting to know the locals or finding out about places we visited. They were into getting drunk and getting to know one another. Whenever we had free days, I'd abandon the group and go out and do my own thing. It was the only time I got to meet local people.'

Women-only tours

Most tour groups try to get a 50:50 ratio between males and females. But if the idea of taking on the world with a bunch of macho males doesn't appeal, join one of the growing number of tours run exclusively for women.

These days, there are hundreds of well-run women's tours on offer, from rafting trips down the Amazon to tent safaris in Kenya, writers' camps in the Greek Islands to cooking tours of Europe. Women-only tours have a number of advantages:

❑ The atmosphere is generally congenial and comfortable.
❑ Relations among group members tend to be egalitarian. In all-women groups, your opinion is more likely to be considered in group discussions and decision-making.
❑ You'll get to perform a variety of activities, from changing a tyre to lighting a fire to washing the dishes – stereotyped sex roles don't determine who does what.
❑ You can learn new skills and take on physical challenges in a cooperative, non-competitive environment.
❑ You're free from male harassment.

If you're interested in finding out about organised travel options for women, get hold of a copy of Thalia Zepatos' *Adventures in Good Company: The Complete Guide to Women's Tours and Outdoor Trips* (Eighth Mountain Press, 1994). It includes information on cycling, canoeing, horseback riding, sailing, trekking, dog-sledding and rock-climbing tours, as well as programs for older women, women with children, lesbians and women with physical disabilities. It lists opportunities for cultural exchange, leadership development programs and spiritual journeys, and profiles over 100 tour companies that offer women's trips.

Choosing the right tour

Whether you decide to tour with a mixed group or a women's group, do your research. Before you book, get recommendations and shop around. Don't be afraid to ask questions, such as:

❏ What type of people will I be travelling with? How large is the group? Does it consist of people of different ages and nationalities or is it relatively homogenous?

❏ How much say do group members have?

❏ How flexible is the tour schedule? Will I be expected to spend all my time with the group or will there be opportunities to explore independently?

❏ Do I have regular duties as a tour member, such as cooking, cleaning or putting up tents? What are the rules and restrictions?

❏ What's included in the cost of the tour, and what will I be paying for separately?

❏ Do the designated activities appeal to me?

❏ What are the standards of accommodation, transport and food?

❏ How much opportunity will the tour provide for meeting locals and absorbing the culture?

❏ Have the organisers taken steps to minimise their negative impact on the peoples, cultures and environments they visit?

❏ What are the standards of safety and security? Where risky activities are involved, are the team leaders qualified?

❏ What is the company's track record?

Before signing up as a member of a mixed-sex tour group, you may also want to get answers to these questions:

❏ Will there be a roughly even balance of men and women on the tour, or is the group mainly males (or females)?

- ❏ Will the tour guide(s) be male or female? (In many cases, guides are male, but as more women gain the necessary skills and experience, we're seeing more females take charge of groups.)
- ❏ Have the organisers addressed the needs of female travellers?
- ❏ Are the activities, decision-making processes and division of tasks devised so that there are equal opportunities and challenges for both males and females?

PRE-TRIP PLANNING

Bureaucratic hassles, financial crises, dental emergencies and bungled rendezvous are situations every traveller wants to avoid. It's especially important to have your arrangements in order if you're travelling alone – because if something does go wrong, you'll have to deal with it by yourself.

Before you leave home, do your research. Have at least some idea about the climate, customs, laws and politics of the countries you'll be travelling through. Compile a list of contacts and plan a workable itinerary. Get your health, documents and finances in order, and pack everything you're likely to need. With the basics well organised, you can set out confident that whatever circumstances arise en route, you'll be ready to handle them.

GETTING INFORMED

The journey begins in your head. The more information you have, the better you can plan your trip. Get an idea of where to go, where to stay, what to pack, how to dress and what to expect by talking with people who've travelled recently through the areas you plan to visit, reading books and surfing the Internet for contacts and tips.

Travel information can be accessed from a variety of media sources: TV programs, newspaper and magazine articles, the Internet and CD-ROM. However, most of it fails to provide information relevant to solo women travellers.

Films and TV shows give tantalising glimpses of foreign cultures, but the view is often distorted, glamourised or sanitised. And travel shows can be misleading: when that female presenter appears to be alone, she's backed up by a (usually male) crew.

Travel articles in magazines and newspapers can help you get an idea of where you'd like to go, but supplement what they say with a dose of guidebook realism. Most are aimed towards short-term holiday-makers on medium budgets rather than to independent travellers.

Women's best bets for information that's relevant and useful are a good general guide, specialist women's travel books, Internet connections and first-hand stories and tips from returned female travellers.

Returned travellers

Other travellers, particularly women, are a great source of inspiration and information. Seek them out and ask them about their experiences. Most travellers love to recount adventures and pass on tips. The more first-hand, up-to-date information you can get about specific destinations – cultural differences, dress codes, local attitudes to women, safe areas, accommodation – the better idea you'll have about what to expect when you arrive.

> *'I knew where I wanted to go and what I was likely to find there because I have a lot of friends who'd already travelled extensively through South-East Asia. I set off with so many tips and addresses for accommodation and things I must do and see that I hardly needed a guidebook.'*
>
> *'In Peru, I decided to go to Mexico because of what I learned through other people. I was talking to someone about it and thought, "That sounds like somewhere I'd really like to go." Two years later, I did it.'*

Guidebooks and travelogues

There are hundreds of travel guidebooks currently available in English, each catering to a particular audience. Until recently, however, most of these guidebooks presented a predominantly male view of the world. Few directly addressed women's needs or concerns or listed women's services. The absence of answers to important questions, such as 'Can I buy tampons?', 'What will I wear?' or 'How do I avoid being sexually harassed?', left many women ignorant about what to expect, especially if they ventured off the beaten track.

Over the last few years, guidebooks have begun to take their female readers into account. Most well-known series, especially those aimed at independent budget travellers (such as Lonely Planet guides, Rough Guides, Berkeley guides and Time Out's city guides), now include cultural and safety information for female travellers and list women-friendly bars, hotels and services. The Virago women's travel guides offer a wealth of advice and information for urban destinations including New York, San Francisco, London, Paris, Rome and Amsterdam. *The Independent Women's Guide to Europe* is primarily a cultural guide but includes special tips for female travellers.

Read your guidebooks before you go – they're a fantastic source of information on culture and customs, give sound advice on preparation, and can help you plan where and how you want to travel, what you want to do and what to expect when you get there.

> 'I swear by Lonely Planet guides, although there is a danger of relying on them too much and never going outside of them. But to get some background on a place, find out how to get around – and for maps – they're great. If you meet someone going the other way, you can swap guides along the way.'

> 'My guidebook was like a bible, really. And I also talked to people from home who'd been there. I actually had a friend's old guidebook and they'd pencilled in where they'd stayed and how much they paid and where were good places to go to eat or go out. I read the guidebook, and since I only had about a month, I worked out where we wanted to go from that, and from talking to people I met. I decided not to go to Koh Samui because so many people told me it had become too touristy. Instead, I went up to Chiang Mai and to the islands on the west side. In hostels and guesthouses, there are always other travellers to advise you on everything from where to eat to which bus to catch.'

Don't get so dependent on guidebooks that you never venture from their recommendations and explore other avenues. Leave some room for spontaneity. Some of my most memorable adventures happened when I closed my guidebook and opened my eyes and ears to what was going on around me.

> 'I preferred to base my decisions of where to go and where to stay on my emotional response, rather than on guidebook information. I liked to get a feel for the place, the culture or the scenery or something, rather than following the tourist trail, going from one backpackers'

place to another. So I tended to go where my interests lay, or where people led me.'

There are a growing number of specialist women's travel guides, such as Jennifer Cecil's *Travelling Solo* (Harper-Collins, 1992), Maggie and Gemma Moss' *Handbook for Women Travellers* (Piatkus, 1995), or *A Journey of One's Own* by Thalia Zepatos (Eighth Mountain Press, 1996). The Feminist Press's recent travel series features women's poems, essays and fiction on topics relevant to the country in question, its people and culture. There are two initial titles, *Australia for Women* and *China for Women*, with similar books on Greece and Italy to follow.

Get inspiration from compilations of women's travel stories such as *Without a Guide*, edited by Kathryn Govier (Hungry Mind Press, 1996), *Solo on Her Own Adventure*, edited by Susan Fox Rogers (Seal Press, 1996), *Unsuitable for Ladies: An Anthology of Women Travellers*, compiled by Jane Robinson (Oxford University Press, 1994), *Passionate Quests: Five Modern Women Travelers* by Sonia Melchett (Faber & Faber, 1992), or *More Women Travel*, edited by Natania Janz and Miranda Davies (Rough Guides, 1995). Or delve into one of the numerous travelogues by solo adventurers such as Dervla Murphy, Sorrel Wilby, Christina Dodwell and Robyn Davidson.

Groups and newsletters

In the past few years, we've witnessed the inception of a number of specialist magazines and newsletters written by and for women travellers. Most include first-hand travel stories, contact details and useful tips from female travellers of various ages, interests and levels of experience. Write to the relevant organisation to obtain back issues or become a subscriber.

❏ *Maiden Voyages: The Indispensable Guide to Women's Travel* (quarterly), 109 Minna Street, Suite 240, San

Francisco, CA 94105, USA (ph 1-510-528 8425; fax
1-510-528 5163).
- ❏ *Journeywoman* (quarterly networking magazine), 50
  Prince Arthur Avenue, #1703, Toronto, Ontario
  M5R 1B5, Canada.
- ❏ *Smart Woman Traveler* (monthly), PO Box 770-227,
  Park City, UT 84060, USA (ph 1-800-250 8428 or
  1-801-269 9993; fax 1-801-269 9906).
- ❏ *Travelin' Woman* (monthly), Nancy Mills
  Communications, 855 Moraga Drive, #14, Los
  Angeles, CA 90049, USA (ph 1-310-472 6318; fax
  1-310-476 8389).

Organisations that foster global ties and link like-
minded people can be a great way to meet locals and
make friends. International organisations such as Women
Welcome Women can link you up with local people for
homestays and sightseeing or sharing information.
- ❏ Women Welcome Women is a global women
  travellers' network. It provides its members with a
  long list of women in countries all over the world,
  along with details on their professions, interests,
  language skills, ages, lifestyles and willingness to
  accommodate travellers. Once you're a member
  (membership of this non-profit-making
  organisation is very reasonable), you can write to or
  fax any woman on the WWW list and arrange a
  meeting or even a homestay.
- ❏ International women's groups, religious bodies or
  special interest groups may be able to help you to
  find suitable places to eat, stay and socialise.

Cyberspace connections
Travel is one of the fastest growing areas in cyberspace.
A browse of online services, the Internet and the World Wide
Web yields hundreds of sites geared to the independent

traveller and can put you in touch with potential friends and helpful contacts from all over the globe. The Internet can be used to scan maps, travel magazines and guidebook listings, give you up-to-the-minute local information, find you the cheapest airfare, connect you with women's groups, book a hostel bed, translate a phrase, find someone to practise your Spanish with or get you a part-time job.

Some online travellers' resources you may want to explore include:

❑ Guidebooks: Many of the major series can now be accessed via the Internet – Frommer's guides, for example, are available through America Online; the Mobil Travel Guides are on Prodigy.

❑ Travel books: Rough Guides' *More Women Travel* has an Internet site, as do Lonely Planet and Moon Travel Handbooks. Women travelling with children should check out the Penny Whistle Travelling with Kids Book web site.

❑ Travel magazines: Monthly issues of *Travel Holiday*, *Bicycling* and other travel-related periodicals are available through various servers. You can even ask magazine staff members questions by posting messages to their bulletin boards.

❑ Bulletin boards: Post queries about local events, accommodation, sights, nightclubs or weather, and get quick, up-to-date replies from people who've been there recently or who are living there now.

❑ 'Experts' forums: The Women's WIRE service on CompuServe occasionally hosts forums with female travel writers; guidebook writer Arthur Frommer holds monthly forums through America Online; and the staff of Weissman Travel Reports put out a monthly Travelers' Corner. Check the Women's Wire Web Directory for other relevant sites.

❑ Travellers' resource centres: Global Network Navigator's Travel Resource Center gives current currency exchange rates and has regular columns from travel writers worldwide (access via America Online). The CityNet, Tips for Travellers and Tourism Information: The World web sites are all useful sources of up-to-date info and tips.

❏ Access to global facts and figures, via the CIA World Factbook, US State Department Travel Warnings and Consular Information Sheets, The Electronic Embassy and the Perry Castaneda Library Map Collection sites, amongst others.

❏ Airline reservations: You can now access flight booking services such as EAASY SABRE Reservations System (the one used by travel agents and airlines themselves) via a number of service providers, to check routes, seat availability and fares, or even to book your own tickets.

❏ Foreign language sites, including Foreign Language for Travellers, the Yahoo! Language Index and Webcrawler's Language Index.

❏ Accommodation services: Try one of these web sites – the Internet Guide to Hostelling, Hosteling International, Hostelling International (two separate sites), Travel Connection Europe: Budget Accommodation, or the Travel Exchange: World-wide Home Exchange Club.

❏ Transport services, including the How to Travel Europe by Train and Subway Navigator sites.

❏ Current currency information, via the TraveLinks – Currency & Money Exchange web site.

❏ Travellers' health information, accessible through a number of web sites, including Centers for Disease Control: Traveler's Health Information; Moon Travel Handbooks: Staying Healthy in Asia, Africa and Latin America; Lonely Planet: Health; Medical College of Wisconsin: International Travelers Clinic; and Stanford Comprehensive Healthcare for International and Wilderness Travelers.

❏ E-mail (electronic mail): You can use it to

correspond with anyone, anywhere (including tourist bureaus, travel agents, hotels and home), provided they're hooked up to the Internet.

Valuable local contacts can be made with people all over the world via the Internet – browse the travel sections till you find likely sounding sites, or post your own notice calling for women who've travelled through or live in the countries you plan to visit, to set up real-time chats. On the World Wide Web, surf hundreds of fascinating travel-, language- and culture-related sites. For a start, check out some of these:

❑ Internet Solutions Rec.travel Library – one of the most extensive travel databases on the WWW. It's at http://www.solutions.net/rec-travel/

❑ The Infohub WWW Travel Guide, which details information on destinations, accommodation, transport and travellers' aid. It's at http://www.infohub.com/

❑ CityNet, a traveller's guide to over 1600 cities and 650 other destinations, at http://www.city.net/

❑ GNN's Travel Centre at http://www.nearnet.gnn.com/

❑ The European Travel Commission's web site of tourist offices in over 25 European countries. It's at http://www.GoEurope.com/

❑ Shoestring Travel, an 'e-zine' for budget travellers, at http://turnpike.net/metro/eadler/shoe1.html

❑ The Travelers' Tales Books: Women's Links web site, at http://amber.ora.com/www/oratt/webtour/womenlinks.html can give you information about accommodation and services for female travellers, plus other travel tips.

❑ Rough Guides' More Women Travel site contains stories from women travellers and information on over 60 countries. Access it at http://www.roughguides.com/RG_WWW/books/tbk_wom.html

❏ The Wayward Women site features women's travel
writing from the book *Wayward Women: A Guide To
Women Travellers*. It's at http://northshore.shore.
net/catalog/t/t7/3598.html

Many TAFEs and community colleges hold introductory
courses on how to navigate cyberspace and access the
information you want from the Internet. Sign up for one
of these. Or get a friend who's hooked up to the Net to
show you how to use it.

If you have a CD-ROM drive on your computer, you can
access some interesting information via multimedia data
(video footage, photos, music and talk, as well as text) on
CD-ROM. Travel CD-ROMs such as *Fodor's Interactive
Sports and Adventure Vacations* let you experience simulated
action-adventure trips. Get a feel for hang-gliding or
mountain climbing, the Andes or Africa, before you actually go out there and do it.

DECIDING ON A DESTINATION

For some women, choosing a destination is simple – we
have a burning desire to see Paris, visit the Galapagos Islands
or trek the Himalayas. For others, the choice can be overwhelming. Narrow down your options by asking yourself:
❏ How much time and money do I have?
❏ Do I have particular goals – diving the Red Sea,
visiting Tutankhamen's tomb, learning Spanish,
writing a novel, seeking out a long-lost friend?
❏ With which countries do I share common
languages?
❏ Are there places in the world whose culture, history
or art fascinate me?
❏ Do I have friends or family in foreign countries I
could visit?

- Do I plan to work or study while I travel? What skills do I have and where are they needed?
- What am I interested in doing on my travels – gallery-browsing, skiing, shopping, trekking, relaxing, voluntary work, meeting people?
- Do I want an outdoorsy or an urban holiday?
- What level of comfort, hygiene and security do I need?
- Am I prepared to make significant adjustments (in dress, behaviour, outlook) to fit in with a particular culture? Or would I prefer to go somewhere more similar to home?
- Am I prepared to take on a culture where women are treated very differently, or would this make me feel uncomfortable?
- Do I want to meet other travellers or get off the beaten track?

PLANNING YOUR ITINERARY

It's tempting to make overzealous travel plans that try to fit in everything, especially when it's your first big trip. Don't exhaust yourself by setting an unrealistic schedule – or go to the opposite extreme and see nothing but the hotel bar for your entire holiday. Practical travel planning involves setting a realistic agenda and pacing yourself.

- Don't try to do and see too much – a jam-packed itinerary can turn what should have been a pleasurable adventure into a gruelling series of barely-there encounters and tiring transits.

'When I took a Eurail trip around Europe, I had eight weeks and I wanted to see it all. It was such a whirlwind, so rushed. By halfway through, I was so tired that I just wanted to sit somewhere for a month and relax, and *think about what was happening. I had no time to assimilate what I was experiencing.'*

❏ Be realistic about how much you can see and do comfortably in the time and with the money you have available.

'The thing that made my year of backpacking around so special is that there was no set plan and no time limit. It didn't matter if what I wanted to do took a day or a month. Now when I go somewhere, it has a beginning and an end, so there's no way I can relax and get into it the same way. You have to schedule everything when you don't have much time.'

'I ran out of money halfway through my trip, which meant I had to go to London and get work so I could do the rest of the travel I'd planned. By the time I'd saved enough to go back to Europe, it was almost time to go home again. I seriously underestimated how much I'd spend. Next time I'll make sure I take more.'

❏ List your 'must-dos' and plan an itinerary that incorporates them, but beyond that, be flexible. Leave room in your schedule for spontaneous side trips, unexpected encounters and extensions.

'Once I decided I wasn't going to go back home, I was really relaxed about my schedule. I'd been in Thailand two months and loved it so much that I thought, I'm not ready to leave yet. So I went down to Penang, renewed my visa and spent another two months there. By that stage I'd decided to hang around that part of the world. I realise now I'm back in full-time work that it was such a privilege to be able to take that time out.'

'I don't believe in doing too much organising – maybe arrange the first few nights' accommodation, and that's it. Because opportunities come to you if you're flexible and open to them. Don't set goals too far ahead – if you arrange to meet someone on a certain date, at a certain place, too far in the future, it's really hard to stick to it.'

'Once you're over there, you get a feel for what you want. I booked a tour of Europe first up, thinking, "I'll do the tour and if I like a particular place, I'll go back to it by myself." I had a Eurail pass so I could do that but I ended up cashing it in, because once the tour finished, I decided I'd seen enough of Europe and would rather go to the Middle East and Africa. Those places were so close and I'd always wanted to see them: it seemed silly not to do it once I'd come so far. So I just changed my itinerary. It's a personal thing, I guess: if you like to be really organised, haven't got much time and just want to see A, B, C and D, my way of travelling wouldn't be sensible. You have to narrow it down depending on how much time and money you've got.'

❏ Pre-book the first few nights' accommodation and make sure you have any transport passes you need, but don't worry about having everything organised in advance. Generally, it's easier to book internal journeys when you get to the country concerned.

'I spent a month in China, which was the maximum-length visa I could get. I pre-booked the first few nights' accommodation and the rest of the time, just found my own. I used local transport the whole time – trains, buses and planes – and I organised it all while I was over there.'

❏ When touring through developing countries, plan a loose itinerary and allow plenty of time for travelling between destinations. Road transport can be notoriously unreliable, services are erratic, and delays and disruptions to public transport are frequent. You may find yourself slowed down further by extreme temperatures or an upset stomach.

> 'In China, I gave myself a week extra to allow for being stranded – because I was going to remote areas, I wasn't completely sure of the logistics of getting into and around places. But I didn't get stuck anywhere – it was surprisingly easy to travel there.'

> 'I went from Greece to Italy on a ferry, and there was a train strike at the Italian end, so I had to get on a bus. But there weren't enough spaces on the bus. I had to wait about 14 hours.'

❏ Give yourself time to orientate to one place before moving on to the next, and avoid taking long journeys back-to-back. If you only have a short time, it's tempting to try to squash in as many destinations as possible, but the two-days-per-city schedule is guaranteed to stress even the most experienced traveller. Accept that you'll enjoy it more if you don't push yourself so hard.

> 'I got so sick of travelling every few days, because it's time-consuming and tiring and stressful. You have all your stuff with you, so you can't really relax, and just when you get to know a place and settle in, it's time to move on.'

❏ Plan to vary the length of your stops rather than spending the same number of days in each place. If you like somewhere, stay longer; if it does nothing for you, move on after a day or two. You don't have to book every leg of the journey in advance.

'In some cities in Europe, I'd only spend a day, walking around and checking out a gallery or two and the main sights, then I'd catch the night train to the next place. If I got somewhere and really enjoyed it, I might stay a week. I stayed longer than I expected to in Spain and Morocco, but only a day each in Munich and Vienna. It was good to change pace like that.'

❑   Check the local calendar: in peak tourist season and during festivals, local accommodation can be fully booked; on some days of the week, galleries and museums close; on important religious holidays such as Corpus Christi, many shops and services shut down; on the eve of public holidays, transport can be crowded with local people leaving town.

'I arrived in Seville on the eve of Corpus Christi and all the hotels were full of out-of-towners. It was fine, 'cause I teamed up with some other girls and shared a room, but it would have been smarter to book in advance. The museums and most of the shops were closed, too. That was a pity, since I was only there a day.'

❑   If possible, divide your time between country and city touring so you get relaxing breaks and changes of pace.

'I divided my time between big cities and countryside. In cities, I spent a lot of time wandering around the back streets to see how people really lived, not just going to the touristy spots and tourist shops. I also made an effort to go off the beaten track and visit places where there were no other foreigners at all. It was really good to see the differences in lifestyle.'

❑   Don't try to plan everything down to the last detail – keep an open-minded attitude. Having too many preconceived ideas can lead to disappointment, and feeling compelled to stick to a schedule can prevent you from finding out what a place is really about.

'Travel with an open mind. You hear a lot about certain places and head off expecting to see fantastic stuff, and you get there and it just looks like the picture in the brochure, it's not anything special. But you've got to look past that. There's going to be something, somewhere, that excites you, even if it's not the reason you went. You discover other areas.'

'When I travel, I try not to have any preconceived ideas, not to build it up and get so excited about a holiday that when you get there, you're disappointed. Know about things, but let them take you over while you're there.'

GETTING HEALTHY

Before setting out on any long journey, make sure you're in optimum health. This is especially important if you're planning to visit remote or disease-prone areas, to travel in countries where sanitation and medical facilities are poor, or to undertake demanding physical activity.

Have full medical and dental check-ups, followed by treatment, if necessary, especially if you're planning a long trip or will be spending time in places that have poor-quality or expensive health care.

Well before your departure date, find out about any vaccines or preventative treatments you'll require from your doctor or Travellers Medical and Vaccination Centre. Once you've been vaccinated, get international health certificates to prove it (some countries refuse entry to those who can't verify that they've been vaccinated recently). Begin taking anti-malarial prophylactics for the prescribed period before entering a malaria zone.

Embark on a fitness program, especially if your trip will include strenuous activity such as trekking, watersports or long-distance cycling. You may also want to strengthen your system by taking vitamin, mineral or herbal supplements.

Ask your doctor or naturopath to provide you with typed prescriptions (including brand and generic names) for any medications you use regularly and will be taking on your trip. Some countries prohibit you from carrying certain medications unless you have prescriptions to accompany them; and if you lose your medicine, a legible prescription makes it easier to replace.

If you wear spectacles or contact lenses, see your optometrist for a check-up. Consider taking a supply of disposable lenses that you wear for two weeks, then discard. They're less of a hassle when travelling: they don't have to be cleaned, can be worn continuously, and if you lose one, it's not a drama – just pop in another.

Carry a pair of spectacles to use as back-up. Many people also travel with prescription sunglasses, although you'll need to keep a watchful eye on them (eyeglass chains are a good idea). Take a typed copy of your eyeglass or contact lens prescription in case you need replacements. You can buy contact lens supplies easily in Western countries but they can be scarce and expensive in much of the Third World.

Well before you go, book an STD test and Pap smear, and visit your doctor or family-planning clinic to discuss suitable contraception. Even if you don't plan on being sexually active, pack a decent supply of condoms – they can be difficult to find, expensive and of dubious quality, especially in the Third World (see pages 270–1).

ORGANISING YOUR FINANCES

Most travellers take a combination of travellers' cheques, cash (usually US dollars) and credit cards. If you buy travellers' cheques from a major company such as American Express or Thomas Cook, they're easier to replace.

Major credit cards are widely accepted throughout Europe, the USA, Canada, and any country with a well-developed tourist trade. You can use them to get cash advances from ATMs or banks, buy goods, and pay for tickets, car hire, hotel and restaurant bills. Credit cards give you a back-up source of extra funds, and your bills can be paid off regularly from home base by a reliable friend or family member with access to your savings. Credit-card holders may be entitled to additional benefits such as free medical insurance cover, cheap car hire or frequent-flyer points.

Discuss your travel plans with your bank manager and work out how you'll deal with ongoing financial commitments at home, funds transfers, credit-card payments and so on. Make sure you know who to contact and what to ask for if you need to access extra funds from abroad.

Tight budgets

Women can and do travel successfully on shoestring budgets. But if you're travelling on a tight budget, you'll have to be resourceful. This may mean eating at markets and street stalls, staying in hostel dorms or sharing hotel rooms with other travellers, catching local transport and picking up part-time work en route. If you've done your homework and know to cut costs without sacrificing security, this doesn't have to mean compromising your enjoyment or your safety.

Where possible, however, it's wise to have an emergency source of funds – even if this means you have to max out your credit card or borrow from family or friends. Being low on funds can lead you to do risky things that otherwise wouldn't be necessary. Read your guidebook and make sure your budget can cover you for at least the basics: food, transport, accommodation and the occasional unforeseen expense. If there's a possibility you'll run out of funds, arrange in advance to have someone standing by to pay for your flight home or tide you over till you can pick up a job.

If you're in a tight spot financially, you're more likely than a man to be helped out. Women present less of a threat and are more likely to arouse a protective response, so female travellers tend to get more invitations, offers of assistance and 'lucky breaks' (free meals, opportunities to stay in low-cost or no-cost accommodation) than men do. Sex or money are sometimes the ulterior motive, but many are genuine, no-strings offers.

> 'When I travelled around Japan, I didn't have much money – a couple of hundred dollars to last me two months – so I had to do things to economise. Japan's meant to be so expensive, but it isn't really, once you get into the local culture and eat the local food.'

In fact, women often cope better in 'strapped-for-cash' situations than men do. We tend to spend less on food than men, and many of us are skilful shoppers, good at hunting down bargains and negotiating favourable deals on accommodation and cab fares. But it's reassuring to have the security of knowing you have a stash of extra cash – or access to credit – so you can afford a comfortable hotel room or taxi home when you need one.

PUTTING DOCUMENTS IN ORDER

Make sure all your travel documents are up to date and in order. This is best done well in advance, especially if you need a new passport or a lot of visas. Have a number of passport-sized photographs taken, to use in visa applications, on International Driver's Licences, on transport passes, and so on.

Check with your travel agent or the relevant consulates about the regions you'll be visiting: what the current visa requirements are and whether there are any other special conditions affecting travellers. Allow extra time if you need a number of visas – most consulates have limited opening hours and you may have to leave your passport with them for up to a week while they process your application. Getting 'express' visas can be expensive.

If you're planning a big trip with an open itinerary, or wish to do repeat business in a particular country, get the most flexible visas you can: a year's multiple-entry visa gives you more scope than a two-week holiday visa. If you're hoping to work or study, you may need to apply for the appropriate visa.

If you're thinking of driving while you're abroad, get an International Driver's Licence and a list of road rules and service centres for the places you'll be visiting. If you're a student, get an International Student ID Card – it's useful for getting discounts and proving your age when going out to bars and clubs.

If you plan to use internal rail or air transport extensively, consider buying a discount pass. Don't wait till you get there – most discount passes must be purchased before you enter the countries to which they apply. If you'll be doing a lot of air travel, consider joining a frequent-flyer club – with the points you'll rack up, your next overseas ticket could be free.

Photocopy important documents and pack them separately. Leave a second set of copies with someone who can be contacted in an emergency.

GETTING INSURED

Insurance may seem like an expensive precaution, especially if you're planning a long trip, but it's worth it for the peace of mind it brings you.

'I didn't bother to get insured, because I was travelling on such a tight budget. It was stupid of me, really. As it was, I lost a few things and had to see a doctor once, which would've added up to about the same as what I'd have paid for insurance. And I was lucky – if I'd had an accident or lost my travellers' cheques, I would have been in real trouble.'

You may need to shop around to find an insurance package that suits your particular travel needs. Make sure you're covered for all the activities you're planning – some policies don't cover you for 'adventure sports'; others won't compensate you for motorbike accidents; and some refuse to allow pregnancy-related claims.

Most travel insurance policies will cover you for accidental death or injury under normal circumstances, reasonable expenses arising from non-self-inflicted illness, and loss, theft or damage not resulting from wilfully reckless or negligent behaviour.

Depending on your destinations and activities, you may want to look for a policy that offers you:

❑ a generous amount of travelling time with the option to extend your cover
❑ wide medical expenses cover (including dental and optical cover) and few health restrictions
❑ generous compensation for theft of luggage or documents
❑ compensation for loss of deposits and cancellation charges
❑ personal liability cover
❑ special cover for high-risk activities.

Read the fine print: most policies contain 'exclusions' – circumstances under which compensation will not be paid. Some only provide partial payments and you'll be required by most policies to exercise reasonable care and caution and to act in a responsible manner before and after the event from which any claim arises.

Note that most insurance companies won't compensate you for 'self-inflicted' conditions, such as drug-related illnesses or accidents, sexually transmissible diseases, pregnancy, abortion, the recurrence of a pre-existing medical condition, and accident or loss arising from knowingly participating in a 'dangerous' sport, competition or activity, from carrying out a money-making activity, or from negligence.

Try to get additional coverage if your policy doesn't cover expensive items (such as laptop computers or video cameras) or particular activities or hazards – don't just trust to luck.

If you're travelling to the USA, don't skimp on medical cover as hospital treatment there can cost a fortune. And if you plan to give birth while in a foreign country, check the terms of your policy carefully. Even though you're insured, your child, once born, may not be – and maternity ward costs can be astronomical.

Shop around till you find a policy that suits your type of travel, covering you for foreseeable difficulties but not requiring you to pay extra for activities or circumstances that are unlikely to affect you. When deciding on a policy, also take into account:

❏ whether the company's claims procedure is speedy and simple
❏ whether the company provides on-the-spot medical claims-settling and cash compensation arrangements
❏ fringe benefits, such as access to worldwide, 24-hour medical and crime 'hotlines' that give referrals and advice in your native language
❏ the business track record of the firm.

Leave a photocopy of your policy with a friend or family member back home, and carry all the relevant details with you, including serial numbers of cameras and equipment and the policy terms and conditions, so you'll know what's required if you have to make a claim.

GATHERING CONTACTS

Compile a list of contacts in the countries you plan to visit. Start a travel address book with contact details for relatives, expatriate friends, friends of friends, work contacts, addresses of recommended hostels or bars, organisations you wish to link up with, and so on. Where possible, phone or write in advance of your visit, especially if you're hoping to stay with people or obtain work on arrival.

KEEPING IN TOUCH

Draft at least a rough itinerary, with contact details wherever possible, and give copies to people at home who may need to get in touch with you while you're away. Include phone and fax numbers, e-mail and postal addresses where you can be reached at various times, if you have them.

Decide on a system for keeping in contact. You may wish to send weekly postcards, or phone or fax home at regular intervals giving updated information on your movements. People can write to you via poste restante (at the central post office in most cities and larger towns): tell them to print your surname clearly in block letters, as that is what the mail will be filed under. American Express offices will hold mail for card-holders, and for users of Amex travellers' cheques provided you can show them some photographic ID and travellers' cheques as proof.

These days, some travellers choose to keep in touch via a mobile phone. While this used to be prohibitively expensive, an internationally usable (and affordable) mobile phone is now available: consult your local dealer for details.

PRACTICAL PACKING

There's no big secret to sensible packing. Take only necessities – and be ruthless in deciding what's necessary. If you want a stress-free trip, travel light. You need to be able to pick up your stuff and go at a moment's notice – too much baggage is a psychological as well as a physical burden.

Lugging bulky bags tires you out and makes you vulnerable to thieves and dependent on porters. Ideally, you should be able to carry your baggage for at least a kilometre, negotiate stairs, escalators and train corridors, run with it if necessary – and have one hand free for handling documents and opening doors.

'Generally, I'm a very light packer, and I think it's the key to no-hassle travel. Especially when you are, literally, backpacking. You can always pick up cheap clothes along the way if you need anything desperately.'

> 'Don't overpack. I did the first time and I ended up
> shipping half of my stuff back. My backpack was just
> overweight. You don't need 10 pairs of shoes and dozens
> of books.'

> 'I travel very, very light. And the more you travel, the
> more you learn that that's a good idea.'

To work out whether you're carrying too much, pack
everything you propose taking into your backpack, travelpack or suitcase, then take the lot for a long, hilly walk. Do
it in the heat. Carry all your stuff up and down a couple of
flights of stairs. Take it on a bus ride across town. After a
few practice runs, you may revise your idea of what's
'essential'.

A general rule of thumb is to decide what you really
must take, then halve it. Impossible? Remember, no-one's
going to notice if you wear the same outfit twice, or 20
times, and most toiletries and basic items can be purchased en route. Still can't cull that packing pile? Consider
ditching these things:

❏   Electrical appliances, such as travel irons and
    hairdryers (and the power adaptors needed to run
    them), are heavy and bulky. Instead, pack
    crushproof clothes and get a wash'n'wear haircut.

> 'I was vain enough to take a hairdryer to Europe so I
> could do my hair before I went out at night. It was heavy,
> a hassle to pack, and I only used it twice in six weeks. If
> you really need to dry your hair, you can use hot air
> dryers in public toilets.'

❏   Extra books: Take one guidebook (or photocopies
    of the relevant pages from two or three guides), one
    or two novels, and a journal, if you like to keep
    one. Choose high-quality books with small print

that will keep you absorbed for longer. It's expensive to buy English books in most parts of the world, but you'll find second-hand bookstores and book exchanges in most cities and tourist areas. Or swap with fellow travellers.

> 'Books, yes. As long as you have one good book, once you've read it, you can swap it with someone else. I did have a journal to start off with, but I didn't keep it up. Life took over!'
>
> 'I always take a couple of good reading books: in Italy, I ran out of things to read, and English books are so expensive in Europe that I ended up reading anything, even the backs of train tickets. But you don't have to take a lot of books – you can always swap with other travellers.'

❑ Big towels: A small one, or a lightweight 'travel towel', does the job just as well, dries faster, is less heavy and takes up less space.

> 'The first time I travelled, I carried a big bath towel, it took up half my packing. I think that the biggest problem most people have is that they take too much. Especially when you're talking about Asia or Africa, the hotter climates. You really don't need to take much.'

❑ Camera gear: Unless you're a really keen photographer, seriously question whether your trip will be enhanced by taking your camera, telephoto lens or Handycam. Photographic equipment is heavy, easily damaged and attractive to thieves. Taking snaps tends to intrude on your experience and can annoy locals (many are sick of being treated as photographic subjects first, human beings second). Instead, buy postcards of the sights you visit, or get your photo taken in situ by a street photographer.

'Cameras tend to shield people from experiences. I travelled for a while with a guy who took a camera, and I swear he saw Indonesia through a lens, whereas I saw Indonesia. He got so focused on what would make a great photo that he forgot to experience what was happening at the time. I felt like saying to him, "Just put it away for a while and see what goes on".'

'It's nice to have photos – but within reason. You can alienate people heaps with a camera. People shy away from you – and you're intruding on them. Especially when you're taking photos of people who may be very poor, and proud, and who think, "Why do you rich Westerners want to take a photo of me in this situation?" It made me very uncomfortable. I think if you can't remember it in your heart and in your mind, maybe it isn't all that memorable.'

'In Peru, a friend and I had hired a car and driver to take us around, and at the first glimpse of some llamas and local people, we were out with the cameras. They came up and quite aggressively demanded money from us. It was very unpleasant.'

❏ Personal stereo system: Unless your journey includes long bus trips or you're addicted to music, you may be better off ditching the Walkman. Take along a favourite tape or two and ask people you meet to play them for you (bus drivers, hostel staff and restaurant managers are usually happy to listen to anything that's Western and new). A Walkman marks you as a tourist, and puts a barrier between you and your aural environment. A person wearing headphones is less approachable and more vulnerable on the streets. And carrying tapes means more weight.

> *'I'm not a Walkman person – I don't like being shut away like that. Even if I'm just going to sit on a bus, I like to hear what's going on. For me, that's part of the experience of being there.'*

❑ All but the essential toiletries, cosmetics and medicines. It's unnecessary to weigh yourself down with things that can be bought just about anywhere (such as shampoo, laundry powder, soap and suntan lotion). Unless you're travelling in remote regions, you're unlikely to need dozens of remedies.

> *'I know people talk about taking tampons, but you can get them just about anywhere now. As for shampoo and soap and all that stuff, buy it over there – it may cost a bit more, but it's better than lugging around kilos of cosmetics.'*

Once you've decided what to take, lay it out on the bed or floor. Then be ruthless about paring it down to the absolute essentials. When you've culled the pile, go out and buy or borrow some suitable luggage (see pages 82–6).

CLOTHING

Your travel wardrobe should be tailored to your destinations and likely activities. Think about where you'll be going and what you'll be doing before deciding what to include. Take local dress codes and climate into account. Choose clothes you feel good in. And be practical.

❑ Don't take too much: what you need for a six-month journey is much the same as what you'd take for a week's jaunt.

> 'I've always worked in the travel industry and travelled a
> lot. I used to go on work trips, say, to Queensland for four
> nights – and I'd come back and unpack this whole pile of
> things that I hadn't even thought of wearing. Now when
> I go away, I go with a big daypack. I know what I need,
> what I'll use, I'm prepared for everything, and everything
> is mix'n'match.'

- ❏ Choose clothes that coordinate: pick a colour
  scheme and stick to it (black and taupe, navy and
  tan with a splash of red . . .). Avoid white garments.
- ❏ Take local dress codes and climate into account: if
  the local people are strongly religious or traditional,
  they won't appreciate it if you wear skimpy shorts
  and tight tops. Dress neatly and conservatively and
  you'll not only feel more comfortable, you'll be
  treated with more respect.
- ❏ Make sure your clothes are crushproof (test them by
  balling a bunch of the fabric in one hand and
  seeing if the creases fall out).

> 'I never take anything that crushes, just the sorts of things
> that you can screw up into little balls and they never look
> creased, and that you can rinse out overnight. I'm no
> glamour queen when I travel – I don't take good skirts or
> clothes for going out in. I'm very down to earth.'

- ❏ Don't take anything that needs bleaching, ironing or
  dry-cleaning, takes ages to dry, or isn't colour-fast.
- ❏ Choose garments made from natural fibres (silk,
  cotton, lightweight wool) rather than synthetics,
  especially if you'll be travelling in hot and humid
  climates. Artificial fabrics don't allow your skin to
  breathe, so you'll feel sticky and smell sweaty.
- ❏ Opt for clothes that don't show the dirt. Plaids and
  prints are practical, especially on the bottom half;
  tops are more versatile in solid colours.

- Choose clothes you can combine in many different ways, and make sure you can layer them comfortably to adjust to changes in temperature. If you're taking four tops, make them a singlet, a T-shirt, a loose, long-sleeved shirt and a lightweight jumper or cardigan.
- Take loose-fitting pants rather than heavy, bulky, hard-to-wash jeans or stretch pants, especially if you're bound for the tropics or for conservative countries.
- Take full, gathered, below-the-knee skirts rather than form-fitting shorter ones. They're more comfortable, more conservative, and it's easier to conceal valuables underneath them.
- Pack a wool or cotton-knit cardigan or jumper rather than a jacket, unless you'll be doing a lot of urban travel, have business meetings to attend, or anticipate very cold weather. If you plan to travel in very cold conditions, take a lightweight, down-filled parka. Silk and angora are two natural fibres that provide lots of warmth for little weight or bulk.
- Include one outfit that's more dressy and conservative, to use in applying for visas, passing through customs, attending formal gatherings or applying for jobs (this could be a skirt or pants and top in a matching colour, or a simple but sophisticated long-line shift).

> 'If you're going on a working holiday or think you may want to pick up a job at any point, bring something decent to wear. When I got to Australia from Asia, I was used to living in sarongs. Just a decent skirt and jacket or something, to go for interviews, would have helped.'

- Don't take short shorts, miniskirts, midriff tops or bikinis unless your destination is a beach resort in a Westernised country. For other destinations, even in the tropics, pack loose, long shorts with pockets, modest one-piece bathing suits and loose tops – shirts and T-shirts – that cover your shoulders.

❑ A large scarf or bandanna can be used for a multitude of purposes: to cover head and shoulders (when entering churches or temples, or when out in public in Muslim countries); to keep your hair from getting blown around in open-windowed buses; to jazz up an outfit; to hold your pants up; to wipe hands; to carry fruit . . .

❑ Bring a hat, or buy one en route: it's essential to protect you from the elements. For hot weather, the most convenient type is the ubiquitous baseball cap (straw hats don't travel well – you're better off buying a cheap one at the beach and giving it away before you move on); for cold weather, a woollen beanie is warm and easy to stuff into your backpack.

❑ Make sure you pack comfortable cotton underwear in good condition. Three or four pairs of undies (a pair of boxer shorts doubles as pyjama bottoms), two bras, two or three pairs of socks and one pair of pantyhose should be ample.

FOOTWEAR

Unless you plan to take taxis or spend all your time by the hotel pool, comfortable footwear is crucial. You'll inevitably find yourself walking more than usual (even around cities, you could easily find yourself walking at least 20 kilometres a day), and there's nothing more debilitating and frustrating than sore, blistered, swollen feet.

Take high-quality, hard-wearing footwear that you've broken in before you go. Don't take more than two pairs (along with flip-flops) and wear the heavier pair in transit. Depending on your destination and activities, choose from:

- well-constructed, lightweight walking shoes or cross-trainers, for city and country walking (including short day treks) and clubbing
- comfortable sandals with wide straps, a moulded insole and heel support (slip-ons are harder to walk and run in), for warmer climates and beach resorts
- lightweight flip-flops (thongs, sandals), for beaches, hostel bathrooms, swimming pools, and wading through water
- light and comfortable dressy shoes, with a low, solid heel (loafers or court shoes are more practical and versatile than strappy stilettos, although they're heavier), if you'll be doing business, applying for professional jobs, attending formal functions or spending lots of time in cities
- lightweight, waterproof hiking boots (those with Gore-Tex uppers weigh less than leather ones), if you're planning serious trekking or mountain-climbing.

'I usually only travel with two pairs of shoes: a pair of sandals that are comfortable for day and look OK for wearing out at night; and, in hot climates, my runners. If I'm going somewhere less warm, I take rubber-soled canvas or leather shoes, 'cause you can wear them day and night.'

'I always take a good pair of walking shoes, and a casual pair of shoes for going out. I started off travelling in winter, so I had jeans and skivvies and a jumper, but once summer came I got rid of all of them. I'd bought a coat in an op-shop, so I took that back once it got warm. When I go to Asia, I hardly carry anything – 'cause you don't need anything. A sarong and a pair of shorts are the essentials.'

DRESS CODES

How you dress can be crucial to how you are received. In some countries, dressing inappropriately is likely to be viewed by local people either as an insult or a sexual invitation. Consult a good travel or cultural guide to the destinations you'll be visiting before finalising your travel wardrobe.

> 'When you're deciding what to wear, it's really important to be aware of local customs, and not dress in too overtly sexual a way. 'Cause you're just inviting attention that you may not want.'

When travelling outside of Western cultures, take clothes that are simple, comfortable and conservative. Loose, curve-concealing garments that cover lots of flesh are best. You may not wish to adopt the local dress, but if you want to avoid offending, make an effort to follow the principles behind it and aim for the same level of coverage. If local women, for example, wear long, flowing tunics over loose pants, you could wear loose cotton shirts and tops with baggy pants or a calf-length, gathered skirt.

> 'I took a pretty basic wardrobe: T-shirts, shorts (as long as they come to the knee), skirts, baggy pants. Loose, conservative clothing – stuff that doesn't show too much flesh.'

Women are expected to cover more of their bodies in Muslim countries than in Western ones. In temples and churches, and at religious ceremonies in many parts of the world, women dress conservatively and cover their heads, shoulders and legs.

> 'You have to dress conservatively in Egypt, and cover your shoulders when you go into mosques. As a general

> *courtesy to their traditions, do what the locals do and you won't get hassled.'*

> *'They'll often give you a sarong if you're going into a temple in Asia. Just make sure you're not wearing short skirts or shorts and cover your shoulders.'*

It's acceptable and common for women to wear pants in some places (Europe, the USA, China) but not in others (the Middle East, parts of Africa). In most conservative countries, shorts and skimpy beachwear may result in unwanted attention or give offence outside of tourist hotels and resorts.

> *'In the villages and remote areas in Asia, I had to dress more conservatively. In the touristy places, it's sad but true that anything goes – they're so used to it. That doesn't mean they like it, though. I wouldn't wear G-strings or tiny tops the way some of the girls did.'*

> *'I realise in retrospect that I was very naive and not at all prepared for what it'd be like travelling in Asia. If I were going there now, I'd be more sensitive to the culture. The way I used to dress was probably very offensive to them. I'd get around in little shorts and skimpy tops, and I didn't wear a bra normally. Everyone was too courteous and polite to say anything to me, but they probably wondered what the hell this creature was doing, not covering up properly. I realise now that to them that would have seemed incredibly provocative, because they cover up a lot more and they're not into seeing women flitting around like that. I felt that I was being myself and it was right for me at the time, but I wouldn't do it nowadays.'*

> *'I think local people in tourist areas have just got so used to tourists not being dressed properly that they don't react.*

Asia
India, Nepal, Sri Lanka

Throughout most of India and Sri Lanka, local women wear traditional saris, even in urban areas. In some of the hill areas and in Nepal, you'll often see locals in tribal dress, and women in the north-west of India wear *salwar-kamiz* (loose tunics and pants), as they do in Pakistan.

Women travelling in India, Nepal and Sri Lanka should dress to cover their legs, shoulders, upper arms and breasts. Full, midcalf-length skirts or baggy pants with loose cotton tops are appropriate and practical for hotter areas; you'll need a hat, ski jacket, jumper, gloves and hiking boots for the hill stations and the mountains. Take a wide-brimmed hat to beat the heat, and a headscarf if you plan on visiting Sikh temples.

'In India, if you didn't want to be harassed, you had to wear all these clothes. It'd be boiling hot and you'd have trousers down below your knees and a T-shirt on all the time, 'cause you can't bare your shoulders. I was like, "I can't wait to get to the beach!" '

Wear a modest one-piece swimsuit rather than a bikini, even at beach resorts – local women bathe fully clothed. And don't go topless: it's considered offensive.

'I went down to Goa, which is a Western hippie hang-out, and there were Western women there with G-strings on, sunbathing practically naked. You'd get busloads of Indian men – it was like a holiday camp for the Indian men. They'd walk along the beach, fully clothed, and

> *watch these Western women. They must've thought it so*
> *bizarre. Because in their culture, it's so different: women*
> *cover up neck-to-knee, even when they're in the water.'*

It's not worth bringing too much gear with you – you can buy Western-style casual clothes, saris and leather sandals very cheaply in most cities and tourist areas.

North-East Asia

In urban areas throughout most of China, Korea, Taiwan, Hong Kong and Japan, the majority of local women wear Western clothes and many pride themselves on being fashionable and sophisticated. In rural areas, particularly in China and Korea, locals dress in more conservative, practical clothes – loose pants and baggy tops or jackets or traditional tribal dress. Generally speaking, however, even in big cities like Tokyo or Shanghai, local women dress more demurely than their Western counterparts.

> *'In China, it's good not to wear anything too flimsy.*
> *I wore loose baggy pants and tops with short sleeves,*
> *and that was fine.'*
>
> *'The women in Japan, Hong Kong and Taiwan are so*
> *Westernised and fashionable, and in the cities in China*
> *and Korea it's going the same way. They're not outrageous*
> *in their fashion, though – most of them still look like*
> *demure little office girls. I felt like a slob in my*
> *backpacker gear. But there's certainly no problem with*
> *wearing Western-style clothes: everyone does it.'*

Women travellers can ensure they blend in by donning simple Western styles. Take plenty of layers for colder months and airconditioned areas, and wear a one-piece bathing costume rather than a bikini at beaches and pools in China and Korea.

South-East Asia

In Thailand, Vietnam, Myanmar (Burma), Cambodia, Laos, Malaysia, Singapore, Indonesia and the Philippines, many local women have adopted Western clothing styles, although they tend to dress more conservatively than the average Western woman. Traditional dress and sarongs are still in evidence in less touristed areas, but these days, even tribal women sport Western T-shirts atop their traditional skirts and headgear.

For women travellers, light skirts, sarongs, dresses or loose pants and blouses or shirts that cover the shoulders and upper arms are a cool, conservative option. In Muslim parts of Malaysia and Indonesia, and when attending traditional or religious ceremonies, dress more modestly and consider covering your hair.

'In Indonesia you don't have to dress terribly conservatively, although parts of the country are strongly Muslim. I wore T-shirts and long shorts or skirts: anything that comes to about the knees. But you don't have to wear anything on your feet. There's a lot more freedom in Bali, because the people are Hindu, not Islamic. You can walk around almost naked if you want to. But it's not a good idea. People will stare at you unnecessarily and you'll draw attention to yourself. All you need to do is wear a loose T-shirt and shorts. If you're inappropriately dressed, they tend to talk about you as opposed to talking to you.'

Avoid wearing shorts, tight tops or short skirts or bikinis unless you're at a tourist beach. Elsewhere, skimpy gear is bound to attract unwanted attention. It's better to wear a one-piece costume or bikini with T-shirt when swimming – local women bathe in their clothes.

'In Thailand, they don't like to see your belly button – it's considered sexual. So you should leave your bikini and midriff tops at home.'

> *'I met a girl in Jakarta who hated Indonesia and Indonesians, and she said that in the last place she'd been, they'd been throwing pebbles at her. But she was wearing short shorts and a singlet top. She wasn't enjoying herself because of what she was wearing. It's common sense.'*

Cheap Western clothing is widely available and you can get clothes tailor-made, particularly in Bangkok, for very reasonable prices.

> *'I had lots of clothes made for me in Bangkok – a female friend who's a dressmaker gave me the name of a good tailor, and I had three silk suits and two tops made to measure. It took two fittings, three days to make, and it cost about $300 for the lot, fabric included. I wish I'd got more.'*

When entering temples, you may be required to wear a temple scarf (on Bali), to cover your head, and/or to remove your shoes. You can usually buy or borrow scarves if you need them.

Africa

In much of northern Africa, Muslim traditions mean modest dress (see pages 76–9). In Ethiopia, carry a headscarf for visiting churches, warm gear for cold highland nights, and modest, non-skimpy gear for everyday wear.

In Nigeria, Western dress is common, especially in towns and cities, and locals, even Muslims, are generally tolerant of tourist attire. Here, and in Senegal and Gambia, traditional wraparound skirts or sarongs with T-shirts or loose tops are cool, acceptable options – avoid shorts anywhere but holiday resorts and beaches. In Togo, Ghana and Mali, keep your legs covered up in Muslim districts, but feel free to wear pants, baggy shorts and skirts in non-Muslim areas.

In Kenya, you can wear normal Western casual wear in more touristed regions, but dress modestly in dresses or skirts when visiting more remote areas (local women never wear pants, although T-shirts are common). In Zambia and Southern Africa, shorts should be avoided outside of tourist districts.

In Tanzania, Western attire is common in cities but you'll be stared at if you wear shorts or pants in rural areas. In Muslim coastal areas, local women wear full-length robes, so you should cover up too: dress in long skirts and wear tops with long or three-quarter-length sleeves. In more strongly Islamic Malawi, you'll be refused entry if you're wearing pants, and skirts and dresses must be knee-length or longer. It's advisable to bring warm gear if you'll be travelling during the cooler season.

> 'Most of the time in Africa I was out bush, so shorts were OK. But wear loose safari-style shorts with pockets. In Muslim areas, you have to wear long skirts rather than pants, and cover up more.'

South and Central America

Modern urban women dress in fashionable, sophisticated Western gear, and are not at all shy about flaunting body curves. In rural areas, you'll find many local women dressed in traditional attire. Since many local people are strongly religious, you should cover your shoulders and upper arms, and wear pants or skirts that reach below the knee when visiting churches. Jeans or pants and T-shirts are acceptable tourist wear, and bikinis and even G-strings are fine at beach resorts, but shorts may be frowned upon by people outside of cities. If you're going for a job, don't wear pants: it's not considered feminine. Bring or buy warm gear for highland areas and winter months, and don't forget a raincoat or anorak.

> *'In more remote areas, I wore the normal backpacker gear
> – T-shirts, baggy pants or mid-length skirts. In the resorts
> and cities, it's pretty Western. On the beaches, anything
> goes – in Rio, all the local girls wear G-strings and
> skimpy clothes, even on the street.'*

South Pacific

On more remote, less touristed islands, local women often
wear traditional dress or a combination of handmade garments and Western hand-me-downs. In towns and resorts,
locals generally wear casual but conservative Western
clothes – loose dresses, longish skirts and baggy tops or T-
shirts. Tourists wearing resort wear are tolerated, but you'll
attract less attention if you dress the way they do.

> *'I went all round Fiji and Vanuatu. I didn't see many
> local women wearing jeans or trousers, and there were no
> shorts or tight tops except on the Western tourists. In
> Vanuatu, all the women wear these awful handmade
> dresses, like babydoll dresses only long, called Mother
> Hubbard dresses. I couldn't bring myself to wear one of
> those, but I did wear long skirts and sarongs with T-shirts
> rather than pants or shorts.'*

> *'Although there's lots of Western influence, people are still
> quite traditional, especially on some of the more remote, less
> touristed South Pacific islands. On some islands, women
> wear pants, but most of them wear loose dresses. I saw lots
> of tourists wearing skimpy gear, but I felt more comfortable
> in a loose skirt or sarong and T-shirt, or in longish dresses.'*

Europe, the USA, Canada, Australia, New Zealand

In all but the most traditional rural areas, modern Western
dress styles are acceptable, although you'll get fewer hassles

if you save the sexy gear for nightclubs. Make sure you pack lots of layers for winter months, especially in northern Europe and Scandinavia, Canada and the northern and central states of the USA. You can buy fashionable clothes in most cities, although choice may be limited and styles somewhat dated outside of major metropolises in Eastern Europe, Russia and Scandinavia.

Bikinis are fine on beaches in almost all Western countries, but topless bathing is frowned upon in parts of the former Soviet Union and Eastern bloc, along less touristed parts of the Mediterranean coast, and on some North American beaches.

> 'In Northern Europe they're really liberal and you can basically wear whatever you want to. Once you get down around the Mediterranean, some of the issues of how to dress and handle yourself are similar to what you encounter in Asia. But I had few problems, 'cause I made sure I took the right clothes and knew what to expect.'

Islamic areas

Under Islamic law, women are expected to conform to strict dress codes. In fundamentalist Muslim cultures, Western women who don't dress appropriately may be subject to considerable opposition, if not outright hostility or harassment.

In recent years, a number of Muslim countries have experienced a rise in Islamic fundamentalism, accompanied by religious fervour, patriotism, strong anti-Western sentiments, and the re-adoption of purdah (wearing of the veil or clothing that conceals) by local women.

The Gulf States, Libya, Iran, the Middle East (including parts of the former Soviet Union) and Pakistan are some of the strictest Islamic nations in the world, and Western women are generally discouraged from travelling through these places alone. If you manage to get a visa for one of these countries, whether for work or as a tourist, you'd be well advised to take conservative, extremely modest attire.

Skirts and dresses should be midcalf or longer, pants loose. Take tops with very demure necklines and long or three-quarter-length sleeves, and wear a headscarf that conceals all your hair whenever you're out in public, especially in Iran, Libya and Saudi Arabia. You'll need a light jacket or cardigan to counter airconditioning and chilly desert nights. Don't even think of wearing shorts, bikinis, short skirts or tight tops unless you're inside an expat complex.

> 'I covered myself in all of the Arab states. I wore a floppy top, long pants or skirts and, at times, a headscarf. I followed what the other women were doing – if the other women were wearing that much, I'd do the same.'

> 'In the Middle East, I was watching a woman water-skiing and I thought, What the hell's she got on? It was like a wetsuit but it wasn't – it was a bathing suit that went from her neck to her wrists and down to her ankles. But that's how seriously they take it, and you have to respect those Muslim beliefs when you're travelling there.'

In Pakistan, Islamic traditions are strong in both cities and rural areas, and all but a few local women wear traditional garments known as *salwar-kamiz* (a loose tunic top over fitted pants). Most women wear the veil. You should dress similarly, in loose tops over trousers or longish skirts, and a headscarf. Make sure your shoulders and upper arms are covered, and don't wear anything short, tight or skimpy. Even a modest one-piece bathing suit would be too much for anywhere apart from a private home or hotel pool.

> 'In Pakistan, the women walk around covered from head to toe. I wore a long skirt, long-sleeved top and a headscarf and I still got hostile stares from men on the street. You have to be so, so conservative.'

Some Islamic countries are more relaxed about women's dress. In Algeria, Egypt, Tunisia, Morocco, Jordan and Turkey, modest Western clothes are commonly worn by urban women, especially younger, more sophisticated ones. Away from cities, religious traditions are stronger and people tend to dress more traditionally, but veils are less common – you won't see them at all in Turkey.

For tourists, Western dress is considered quite acceptable, although you're still expected to cover up. Midcalf-length, full skirts and baggy pants are tolerated everywhere, and headscarfs are a courtesy rather than a necessity. Leave the short shorts and bikinis behind – wear sarongs and T-shirts over one-piece swimming costumes, even at beach resorts.

'I was always told, "Wear something sensible and you won't get hassled", and that was my experience in Egypt.'

'In Tangier, I was persuaded by a hustler to buy a jehlaba, this caftan thing that covers up everything. He assured me that in Marrakesh, because it was in the south of Morocco, everyone would be wearing one and if I wasn't, I'd get hassled. So I bought it, but when I got to Marrakesh, no-one except the local women wore the jehlaba. It would have felt stupid to wear it when no other travellers were, even though it could have been seen as a mark of respect for the local women.'

Islam has had a powerful influence on Africa – especially the northern part of the continent. Generally speaking, the closer to Mecca a place is, the stricter the traditions and the more conservatively you'll have to dress. Read your guidebook for advice on specific areas, and follow the example of local women.

In many parts of Asia – including areas of Indonesia, Malaysia, India and the Maldives – Islamic traditions flourish. Here, however, they tend to be tempered by having to coexist alongside other religions and traditions. Islamic fundamentalism experiences periodic surges. Currently, Indonesia's Muslim population is in conflict with other religious factions, causing civil unrest, while in Malaysia, many of the younger local women, particularly students, have reinstated traditional Islamic dress as a statement of their beliefs, and now wear long dresses, head coverings, and sometimes even gloves.

Generally, Muslims in Asia wear modest clothing without veils, and are reasonably tolerant of tourists wearing Western holiday clothes, provided they aren't too revealing. Don't get around in shorts or beachwear away from the resorts, and observe local customs when visiting temples or attending religious sites and ceremonies.

TOILETRIES

It's tempting to take every haircare and skincare product you use at home. Don't – toiletries and their containers tend to be heavy and bulky. Only take essentials.

❏ Assume you can buy basics, such as soap, cleanser and shampoo, everywhere.

❏ Take products that have multiple uses rather than a whole lot of separate cosmetics (almond or jojoba oil, for example, works as a moisturiser, massage lotion, eye make-up remover and lip balm; lip-liner in a neutral shade is smaller and more versatile than lipstick).

❏ Before you go, streamline your skincare rituals and work out what you can do without. If you get a wash'n'wear haircut, you won't need to take as many hair-care products and can ditch the dryer.

❏ To save space, minimise weight and avoid breakage, buy trial sizes or decant toiletries into small plastic bottles with screw-on lids. Screw all lids on tightly and place items into a waterproof container (plastic ziplock bag, Tupperware dish), with bottles packed so that they stand upright when your bag is in the normal carrying position.

MEDICINES

If you plan to travel independently to remote areas or in developing countries where standards of medical care can be erratic, disease is prevalent and sanitation poor, you'll need to bring a more comprehensive medical kit than you'd need for a European jaunt or group tour. Carry any medications you use regularly, plus remedies or preventatives for common ailments. A good guidebook or a travellers' health centre should be able to advise you on what you need for particular destinations. (See pages 288–91 for more information.)

Put together a kit that's tailored to your needs and pack all items into a sealed plastic container with the internationally recognised Red Cross symbol on the lid. Also pack copies of prescriptions for medicines you're taking.

PRACTICAL BASICS

Items that can prove handy, if not downright indispensable, on your travels include:
❑ sunglasses
❑ Swiss army knife (with scissors, knife, bottle opener, tweezers and screwdriver attachments)
❑ plastic, sealable containers for holding medical supplies and toiletries (these can double as food storage containers en route)
❑ plastic spoon
❑ hardy, lightweight torch and batteries
❑ waterproof matches or lighter

- ❏ towel (if you're travelling super-light, take a hand towel, special 'travel towel' or even a nappy)
- ❏ sarong (a strip of fabric you can use as a dress, skirt, scarf or shawl, beach blanket, curtain, tablecloth, sheet, towel or carrybag): if you're going to the Third World, you can buy one cheaply almost anywhere
- ❏ length of clothes line or string, and pegs.

'I always take my sarong, because it's so versatile, and you can use it as a sheet. In lots of cheaper places, the sheets are synthetic, which I can't stand, so I use my cotton sarong instead. And if you need to, you can dry yourself with it, too.'

Comfort

You may need some or all of these if you plan to travel through remote regions, camp, or use hostel accommodation:

- ❏ sleeping sheet (silk is ideal if you can get one) for hot climates and hostel dorms
- ❏ sleeping bag (if you plan to camp out, trek, take airconditioned overnight bus journeys or travel in cold climates)
- ❏ a lightweight mosquito net (especially in remote regions or low-budget accommodation in malaria-prone areas)
- ❏ fold-up paper fan: great for stuffy rooms and insufferably hot train journeys
- ❏ eye mask and earplugs
- ❏ a cheap, waterproof watch with a reliable, built-in alarm clock
- ❏ compact umbrella or lightweight raincoat (useful in countries such as the UK, where it rains a lot, or during tropical monsoons).

Pastimes and icebreakers

A few well-selected items can help pass the time on long journeys, act as icebreakers, and cross language and cultural barriers. Consider carrying:

- ❏ games (backgammon, chess or cards)
- ❏ books (including phrasebooks)
- ❏ stationery (journal, airmail paper, pens, glue stick)
- ❏ photos of your family, home, husband and children, and of you doing things – to show to people you meet
- ❏ small gifts to give to people you meet (badges, pens, lighters, guitar strings, sunglasses, baseball caps, cosmetics, foreign postcards, T-shirts with English slogans)
- ❏ a wedding ring (or a cheap imitation): it can be used to discourage male suitors and assert your respectability. Leave heirlooms and valuable jewellery at home.

'I always kept diaries and wrote in them tips and good places to stay and people's addresses, and notes on things you'd never find out about here. It's good to read them back later.'

'When I travel, I keep a journal – or else I ask for my postcards back when I get home, because you forget things so quickly if you don't write them down. I read and wrote a lot on my travels. I always carried a book or my journal: it acted as a safety barrier in cafés or restaurants. I'd sometimes get asked to join a table, but if I didn't feel like company, I'd just open a book.'

LUGGAGE

Most people travel with two pieces of luggage, plus a money belt. More than this and your baggage becomes unwieldy and is harder to keep track of. Depending on your destination and activities, you may decide to take a backpack or travelpack (a backpack that converts to a soft-sided suitcase) with a detachable daypack; or a lightweight suitcase on wheels and a shoulder bag.

Backpack

This is the most comfortable, convenient baggage for people who have a lot to carry and is a must for serious walkers and trekkers. Backpacks distribute weight more evenly and allow you to keep your hands free.

When choosing a backpack, buy the best you can afford – it's worth it for the extra comfort and high-quality construction. Most major brands have models suitable for women: buy one with an adjustable frame, or opt for a smaller size. Some backpacks have an extra-wide, padded hip belt that distributes weight better and suits the female physique. Get the store assistant to adjust it properly and see how it feels when fully loaded. Buy with comfort rather than style in mind.

> 'I spent a lot of money on my backpack, because I knew I'd be carrying it around a lot, and I knew no matter how much I tried, it would end up full of stuff. I bought with comfort rather than appearance in mind, and chose a pack with an extra-wide hip belt designed for the female body. It was incredibly comfortable and easy to carry. Even when I could hardly pick it up, I could walk for kilometres once it was on my back.'

Backpacks have a few drawbacks: their straps can get tangled in airport conveyor belts and overhead luggage racks, they're an awkward shape, and belongings packed in external pockets are susceptible to thieves. Although most are made of hardy, waterproof material, they can leak along the seams, so you'll need to line your backpack with a bin-liner.

Travelpack

If your trip includes a combination of urban and out-doorsy destinations, travelpacks are ideal. You can tuck in the shoulder straps and convert your backpack to a soft-sided suitcase, which is simpler to stow, looks smarter, and is less likely to get damaged in transit. Most travelpacks come with detachable daypacks which you can use for sightseeing and short excursions.

A travelpack is great for travellers who don't want people to label them as 'budget backpackers'. You look far more respectable walking through customs or into a hotel lobby holding one of these than you do hauling a backpack.

'I usually travel with a backpack, but they're making these travelpacks so well nowadays that my next bag is sure to be one. I travelled with a friend who had one and I was really envious. Especially in cities and going through airports – I'd look all dishevelled with my battered old backpack, straps hanging out all over the place, and she'd tuck her travelpack straps in, zip it up and carry it like a suitcase. Very cool.'

Suitcase

If you'll be spending most of your time in one place and lit-tle time in transit, have a back problem that prohibits carry-ing a backpack, or are travelling on business, it's appropriate to take a suitcase. Suitcases that are small enough to be taken on as cabin baggage (Samsonite and Travelpro both make excellent ones), with sturdy wheels and retractable handles, are perfect – they can be wheeled through city streets, stowed simply on luggage racks, and checked on some airlines as cabin baggage. They keep clothes and documents well organised, they're hard-wearing and compact, and they look smart. Make sure your case can be padlocked and has a strap for attaching extra luggage.

'I have one of those great suitcases with wheels and a pullout handle, and I can't do without it any more. It depends where you're going, of course. I still backpack sometimes – if I were trekking in Nepal, I would – but in lots of places nowadays, I just don't think it's necessary.'

Daypack

Detachable daypacks are perfect for sightseeing, shopping trips and short excursions. Take one that's comfortable, strongly constructed and big enough to hold supplies for four or five days (water, camera, spare clothes, toiletries). A pack that attaches to your backpack or travelpack is useful if you plan to move around a lot on public transport.

If most of your trip will be spent in cities, or you're on business, you may prefer to use a shoulder bag. Choose one with zip fastenings that can be made secure with safety pins to deter thieves, and a long, sturdy strap you can wear diagonally across your body.

Money belt

Opinions differ as to what sort of document and money pouch is the best. Although security is your primary concern (it has to be difficult to steal), comfort and convenience are also important considerations.

Most women find that money belts worn around the waist or large concealed pockets sewn inside the waistband of skirts or loose pants are the safest, most comfortable and most convenient way to carry valuables. Round the neck pouches can be obvious and uncomfortable (especially when stuffed with travellers' cheques, passport, cash). They're more easy to spot and grab, and harder to get at without attracting attention.

Bumbags which fasten round the waist aren't suitable for carrying valuables but are fine for carrying petty cash, sunglasses, maps and the like. Fasten the zip with a safety pin to deter pickpockets in crowds.

How big?

Don't make the mistake of taking luggage too capacious for your needs. It's tempting, with all that extra space, to slip in extra items. Before you know it, your baggage has become a burden.

> 'I had the tiniest bag when I first travelled – I don't think I could ever manage to travel that light again. But it was great. When I see women hauling around huge backpacks, I think, "Why do they bother?" It's like carrying your whole house around.'

While it's good to have space for purchases made en route, it's better to pack a lightweight, fold-up carry-all or buy an expandable suitcase than to set out with an oversized bag.

Ideally, you should be able to take all your luggage as 'carry-on'. Travelling this light has a number of advantages:

❑ Your baggage never has to go in the plane's cargo hold, so it's less likely to get lost or damaged in transit.

❑ You don't have to wait around to retrieve it on arrival, so you can be first in line for taxis and money exchange counters.

❑ You're not dependent on porters (or anyone else) to carry your luggage for you.

❑ You can negotiate public transport easily.

❑ You can walk longer distances without tiring.

❑ You'll spend less on taxis and baggage lockers, and will have fewer hassles in transit.

❑ You can pick up your bags and go at a moment's notice.

PACKING

You begin to appreciate having a system after you've emptied your entire suitcase onto the floor of a crowded railway carriage in order to find your toothbrush. Organised packing makes for fewer hassles, losses and spillages, and a lighter load. Try these tips to help keep your things in order:

❏ Put stuff you use frequently in accessible places.

❏ Separate things in a sensible, systematic way (toiletries in the right-hand corner, underwear separate from outerwear, medical kit stashed so it's handy, books in a side pocket).

❏ Use the same internal system every time you repack, so you come to know exactly where everything is and can locate items efficiently. This saves you having to rummage noisily in the dark in hostel dorm rooms and minimises your chances of mislaying or losing things.

❏ Consider weight distribution. When packing a backpack, put heavy, often-used items (toiletries, towel, guidebook) at the top. Your pack, fully loaded, should sit close to your back and have a more-or-less normal centre of gravity.

❏ Don't attach things to the outside of a backpack – they're easily lost, attract thieves and add disproportionately to your load. If you must put extras on the outside of your pack, attach them to the top rather than the bottom.

❏ Make sure fragile goods are buffered (surround them by soft objects) and pack spillables in plastic to protect against leakage.

❏ Make the contents secure. Put towels and clothes on the outside (they are harder to slice through) or line the pack with newspaper. Only put stuff of little value that's easy to replace in outside pockets. Use combination padlocks to secure the zips.

Fold, roll or scrunch

When packing clothes, you can economise on space and keep clothes from creasing by rolling them. This method works well for pants, T-shirts, sarongs, jumpers and towels. Shirts, skirts and jackets are better interfolded and packed towards the top. Underwear and socks can be scrunched and used to fill corners and pad shoes. Pack garments in plastic bags to protect them and keep them organised.

LAUNDRY

When you're travelling with a skeleton wardrobe, frequent clothes-washing is a fact of life. The simplest way to deal with laundry is to put dirty clothes into a separate bag and wash them every few days in your hostel laundry tub or hotel sink.

Scrub your clothes while you're under the shower: it's the simplest way to keep yourself in underwear – a must if you're travelling light. You can buy soap or soap powder in sachets almost everywhere in the world.

Unless you've got a lot of clothes or can share a load with a friend, laundrettes are an expensive option, but once in a while, it may be worth it to get your things really clean. Use laundry services at cheaper hotels with caution – they may not get your clothes back on time or in good condition.

'I stayed in a budget hostel in Berlin, where I decided to wash my clothes in the machine. I put it on the "warm" cycle, and thought my woollen jumper would be fine, since I've often machine-washed it before. But it came out shrunken beyond recognition, the water was so hot. I was really upset. I heard later from some models that they never use laundries in Germany because German people don't think anything's really clean till it's been boiled and sterilised, so there's a good chance they'll ruin your delicates.'

If you're forced to travel with damp clothes, pack them towards the top in a sturdy plastic bag; better still, keep them in a separate pocket (some backpacks have a special waterproof compartment for wet items).

Generally speaking, you'll have to improvise when it comes to hanging out the washing. Your best bet is to pack a length of string or a special travel clothesline and a few pegs – you can't always find a clean rail or a spare hanger, especially if you're in budget accommodation.

Hanging stuff outdoors, on the balcony or out the window, isn't a great idea either: you either lose it or it's dirty and dusty by the time it's dry. And in some parts of the world, insects can take up residence or lay eggs in your drying clothes.

MENDING

Mending en route is simple: take along a small sewing kit with strong thread that matches the clothes you're taking, a couple of needles, a button or two, and a roll of double-sided tape (an instant fix for fallen hems and split seams). And remember that a stitch in time saves nine.

IN TRANSIT

Transits present particular problems for people travelling alone. You have no-one to watch your stuff while you check the platform number, use the toilet or buy a coffee; no-one to secure a seat for you while you supervise the loading of your baggage; no-one to share the task of finding your way around when you arrive, jet-lagged, in a new city; no-one to lean against while you're trying to sleep on an overnight bus. For these reasons, you need to be well organised and vigilant when you're in transit: that means whenever you're arriving, departing, travelling or waiting.

DEPARTURES

Departures can be smooth or stressful, depending on how you play them. By arriving at the last minute in a panic, you leave yourself frazzled and with little room for error. Take these steps to ensure that you make your connections without hassles.

When travelling by air:

❏ call the airline two days before departure to confirm your booking (and request any special provisions, such as vegetarian meals). Call again just before you leave for the airport to check that your flight will be departing on schedule.

❏ arrive in good time for all journeys. Not only does this ensure you'll get a better seat, it also means you'll have the time to deal with unexpected problems in a calm, constructive manner. If you're in a panic, you're more likely to lose something or attract the attention of thieves.

❏ have enough local currency on you to pay departure taxes, buy duty-free goods, and cover for unexpected costs.

When catching long-distance trains or buses:

❏ be there in good time. Don't assume that because you're in a country where things are somewhat chaotic, trains and buses will depart later than scheduled. Often, they leave exactly on time, and if your watch is five minutes slow, you could be left standing at the end of the platform as your train disappears into the distance.

❏ carry local currency. It's not uncommon for people to jump on a train with a Eurail ticket, only to find they have to pay a supplement to the conductor. If you don't have the cash, you could be booted off the train at the next station. A stash of US dollars could also come in handy if you need to buy a visa at the border or thank a local for a favour.

❏ have a bit of cash in small denominations to pay for food en route. Usually, long-distance buses make food stops, and most trains have a buffet car or walk-through food-and-drink seller. If you're buying food from platform vendors, it's best to have the correct change, as most transactions are made through the carriage window and stopping times can be short.

❏ don't assume a journey will take the scheduled number of hours. Expect delays and plan accordingly.

EN ROUTE

Keep tickets, passport, visas and other relevant documents handy but secure. Travellers' cheques and extra cash should stay in your money belt at all times. In your day-pack, carry all the things you may need on your journey. Your 'essentials' may include some or all of the following:

❏ guidebook
❏ phrasebook
❏ local area maps
❏ something to read
❏ camera
❏ Walkman and tapes
❏ eye mask
❏ Evian spray
❏ toothbrush
❏ hairbrush
❏ toilet paper or tissues
❏ contact lens cleaning kit and spectacles
❏ sunglasses
❏ motion sickness remedies
❏ vitamins B and C
❏ a cardigan or jumper
❏ a change of underwear
❏ a blow-up neck pillow
❏ a sarong or sleeping bag to cover you
❏ food and drink.

In-flight

On international flights, wear comfortable, crushproof clothing that's conservative enough to get you through customs and immigration smoothly. Kick off your shoes on long hauls (feet tend to swell), moisturise your skin, drink plenty of water (but go light on the alcohol – it's dehydrating) and try to get in a few catnaps. If you're in economy-class seats, cruise the aisle every few hours to get the circulation going in your legs. The hormone melatonin (available over the counter at health food stores in the USA but not in most other countries) may help you to sleep and is reputed to combat jet lag.

ARRIVALS

Customs and immigration

Even if it's 4 a.m. in Calcutta, it helps to look smart and alert when passing through immigration and customs. You'll make this procedure speedier and less stressful if you do the following:

- ❑ Freshen up and use the toilet before the plane lands.
- ❑ Make sure you're in the right queue, and have the relevant documents (passport, arrival card) ready for inspection.
- ❑ Answer questions clearly and simply – don't give complex explanations unless they're asked for.
- ❑ Once you've shown your documents to the authorities, stash them safely before you proceed to the baggage claim area or customs line.
- ❑ Declare all goods that require special customs clearance, and ditch 'contraband' food or items of little value if they're the only things you have to declare. Don't risk not declaring items listed on the customs form – if you're searched and they're discovered, you may be delayed, interrogated, fined or even charged.

Keep an eye on your baggage when arriving at any busy transport terminal: bags can be stolen from baggage carts or carousels (or swapped for similar luggage), and your valuables can be pickpocketed. Don't carry anyone else's bags for them, no matter how plausible their story seems. People have been known to use naive travellers as unwitting drug or contraband couriers, by persuading them to carry bags in which they've hidden illegal drugs, or by slipping such goods into their luggage. This is why customs officials usually ask whether you packed your bags yourself. Casual 'porters' and 'helpful' bystanders may offer to assist you with heavy luggage, then disappear with it, especially in crowded, chaotic environs such as transport terminals or taxi ranks.

> *The time when you're in the most danger is when you first get off a plane, and you're tired, you don't know the place and you've got too much baggage. I believe in having a specific number of bags, as few as possible, and in counting your bags.'*

Changing money

It's smart to have about a day's worth of local currency with you when you arrive in a new country, as it saves queueing at the exchange office. If you have to get cash on arrival, don't change too much – wait till you get into town and can shop around for the best rates of exchange. Make sure you have enough small change to use telephones, pay bus or taxi drivers and tip porters.

If there's an automatic teller machine at your arrival point, use it to access quick cash via your credit card. Most terminals handling international traffic now have ATMs that take major cards (and generally give you a better rate than exchange offices). You may also be able to change currency in notes at automatic cash exchange machines. Do whatever is simplest – your objective is to get your money and get out of the terminal with a minimum of queueing and fuss.

Getting information
Most transport terminals have an information office that can supply you with maps and transport timetables. Some also provide hotel listings, assistance in booking accommodation, and information about sights and tours. At smaller terminals, this office may be closed outside of normal business hours – which is another good reason for planning to ensure you arrive in the daytime. Even if you've pre-booked accommodation, it's a good idea to pay a quick visit to the nearest tourist information office to pick up local maps and information.

Finding accommodation
Most travellers recommend pre-booking at least your first night's accommodation in a new place. This is especially important if you'll be arriving after dark. As it's impossible to guarantee that your bus, plane or train won't be delayed, you have to assume that you could end up getting to your destination at night. It's reassuring to know in advance where you'll be going, and that a bed will be waiting for you when you get there.

'I always pre-book the first one or two nights in a new country, no matter what the cost. It's always going to be a bit more expensive if you book from home, but it gives you a lot more support, particularly if you're going to a country that's not English-speaking and you've never travelled before.'

'I have absolute rules: I never arrive in a city at night – you just don't, because you can't figure out where you are in the dark. If there's no choice, then I'll stay at the

> *closest hotel to the airport or the station, and I won't go*
> *out of it until it's light, so I can figure out where I am*
> *and get an idea of where I'm staying and what it looks*
> *like and what's around it and how it feels.'*

If you haven't pre-booked, use your guidebook, hotel touts, the recommendations of fellow travellers or the tourist information office to direct you to suitable accommodation. You'll need small change or a phonecard to ring around hostels and guesthouses. Have your phrasebook ready in case the person taking your call doesn't speak a common language – or get someone who does to make the call for you.

Keep an eye out for other travellers, especially women, at money-exchange counters and information offices – they're often happy to share the task of finding accommodation. Banding together with one or two others to find a place to stay can make the job simpler, safer and more economical. You save money on phone calls, can share a taxi to the hotel, and may decide to cut costs by sharing a room.

> *'If I arrived in a new city and hadn't booked a hostel bed,*
> *I'd usually try to team up with other travellers who'd*
> *arrived on the same bus or train. You can always spot*
> *them – they're the ones wandering around with*
> *backpacks, looking lost. I'd just walk up to them and ask*
> *them if they had a hostel booked: if they didn't, I'd*
> *suggest joining forces. I never had anyone say no.'*

If you don't have a place in mind, use your guidebook, or check out the offers of hotel touts who hang around major transport terminals in tourist centres. The establishments they represent are usually geared for independent travellers and competition keeps prices reasonable. Compare offers and ask questions before settling on one. Often, you'll get free porterage and hotel transfers as part of the deal.

'I had nothing organised at all when I arrived in Sri Lanka. I'd heard about one place that was a hang-out for backpackers and I'd got chatting to a couple of guys on the plane who said they were heading there too. When we got off the plane and started looking around, there were people there with minibuses, all prepared to take us. We got together and hired a minibus – we got ripped off, of course, but you don't know that till afterwards so it doesn't matter. We got driven down to the coast where we wanted to be, looked for guesthouses and stayed there.'

'I arrived in Bangkok and it was a bit of a shock. I'd never been there and all I'd heard were the horror stories, like that you're going to get your bag pinched. I caught a taxi straight to the tourist district – Khao San Road – and I was so tired, I stumbled into the first little guesthouse I saw. It was full, but the manager wanted to offer me his bedroom. He was just trying to get a bit of extra money, I think. It was foul. I thought, "God, is this what it's going to be like?" But I eventually found a decent room.'

ORIENTATION

How well you adjust to a new place depends partly on your state of mind. When you first arrive, you may be tired, jet-lagged, confused or anxious. It's hard to get orientated when you can't even think clearly. So it's a good idea to get to a hotel and make yourself comfortable. When you've rested, you can start exploring.

DEALING WITH CULTURE SHOCK

In a completely new environment, it's natural to feel a little fearful at first. Don't push yourself: it's fine to stay in your hotel and take things slowly for the first few days. Use the time to read your guidebook, practise the local language and talk to the hotel staff and fellow guests, so you know what to expect when you do venture forth.

'If I was feeling a bit fragile, I'd go to a tourist hostel rather than to the little place down the road that's very local and a bit less comfortable. Sure, you're more likely to get an "authentic" experience at the non-touristy place. But if you're not in the mood, you're not going to enjoy it anyway. So sometimes I'd just take it easy and do touristy things, rather than pushing myself. When I felt stronger, I'd do something more challenging.'

'It's important to have a room to freak out in, then collect yourself, and to be able to go out and hit the streets and know that your bags are OK and that you've got somewhere to sleep tonight, somewhere that you can go and hide if you want to. It's good at first to stay somewhere that's more aligned to the way you're used to having things – with a nice shower, and so on – than really roughing it. Hostels and dorms can be a bit intimidating, if you're not used to sharing or showering with other women. To have somewhere that provides those semi-home comforts helps you relax and guides you into negotiating and discovering everything else.'

If you're nervous about being on your own, take guided tours to help you get orientated; stay somewhere you feel safe and comfortable in, and find companions to go out with.

'If I was going to a heavy Muslim country on my own, I'd book into a really expensive hotel where there aren't going to be cracks in the walls and men aren't going to be lying under the room looking through the floorboards. Then I'd go on tours booked through the hotel. If you're in that sort of situation, you need to do it in a way that enables you to feel OK.'

Do things to help you de-stress – go to places where you feel comfortable and do activities that help you to relax.

'I always find a swimming pool and do a few laps. It helps to clear my head. If you're in a hot climate, it also cools you down so you're less likely to feel frazzled.'

'I like to wander around galleries and museums. They're quiet, relaxing, you don't get hassled. Cafés are sociable and safe. Tourist bars are pretty relaxed and they're a good place to meet people if you want to go out at night.'

'I use the hotel's gym facilities. In Korea, they have fabulous scrub baths attached to the hotels. So I'll go there and have a spa and scrub and massage and sauna, maybe a facial. And I always go to the supermarket when I arrive in a city and buy some fruit and some water.'

'You can get a massage everywhere in Bali, in fact, you'll be hassled to have massages. I never used to accept. But one time, I was feeling a bit tired and stressed so I decided to have a foot massage. This guy massaged my feet for 45 minutes, and it was just heaven. It was the best way to unwind.'

'When I get stressed, I just close the door and read a book. If I'm feeling vulnerable, I just won't go out. But that doesn't happen very often.'

If you still feel anxious and uncomfortable after you've been in a place for a week, consider changing your plans – linking up with another traveller, signing up with a tour group, or going somewhere else altogether. There's no point in staying somewhere if you're really not enjoying yourself.

'There are places in the world I'd never travel to on my own. I spent a few days in Pakistan that were horrendous. I had done everything: I'd covered myself so only my hands and face were showing; I even wore a scarf. But

> *the men in Pakistan had a real hostile, angry feel, like it
> didn't matter how I dressed or who I was with: if I was a
> woman and I was Western, that was enough to condemn
> me. It's that myth about Western women: that you have
> to be either a mother or a whore. It was the most
> terrifying place I've ever been. You really feel it, and it's
> so hard to deal with. Having people hate you for no
> reason apart from the culture that you're born into is
> really hard stuff to overcome, especially when you're on
> your own. I just had to remove myself from it.'*

FAMILIARISING YOURSELF

Guidebooks are a great way to get the lowdown on a place
before you arrive – most give information about history,
culture, customs and dress codes, transport, accommodation and entertainment, and they often include useful
annotated maps.

Other travellers are a wonderful source of up-to-date
info and tips. Often you'll meet people who've just been
to the places you're planning to visit: ask them for advice
on accommodation, restaurants, 'must-do's', meeting
locals and getting around.

> *'I was forever meeting people who'd just come from where
> I was going, and I'd always ask them where they'd stayed,
> and what were fun things to do, and what the best
> restaurants and nightclubs were, and what the scams
> were. I used to write it all down in my journal, like an
> alternative guidebook.'*

Once you arrive, tourist information services can help you
find what you're looking for around town. As well as street
maps, pick up transport maps and timetables, sightseeing
tour brochures, shopping and services guides and accommodation listings.

Hostel and hotel staff can be fonts of local information. Ask them for recommendations about where to eat, where to go out, safe and unsafe areas.

'In Rome I stayed at a private hostel run by an expat Australian woman. She was fantastic – she had maps and transport timetables and cultural information brochures and details about local tours. Anything you could think of asking her, she knew about. It made it all so easy.'

'I use the information in guidebooks, at tourist offices, in railway stations to make sure I know where I'm going. And if I don't know, I won't go off without asking someone, like a hotel staff member or fellow traveller, for guidance. In India, I asked women on the trains whatever I wanted to know.'

Expats, too, can be valuable contacts and allies. Because they were once strangers to the place themselves, they're often sympathetic to your situation. They can help you get a handle on the culture, show you around, take you out and introduce you to local people.

'I found expats the best way to get an "in" with the locals, because they usually speak the local language, know a lot of local people and have a good idea of what's going on around town. They can explain local customs, tell you about scams and things to watch out for, and take you to places you'd never find by yourself. The expats I met were full of advice and they were usually happy to introduce me to people. They never seemed to have ulterior motives either – they didn't hassle me, even the men.'

GETTING YOUR BEARINGS

Reading a map is a fast, effective way to orientate yourself in a new place. As soon as you can, get hold of a detailed local map and study it. Note main roads, public transport routes, districts, landmarks and places of interest. Mark your hotel, public transport terminals and places you want to visit on it. Use the map to work out how you'll get to the places you're interested in.

> 'I carry a map, and as I go through the city, I mark where I am. Whenever I go somewhere I get the driver to show me on the map, and put a cross on each place I go, and at the end of the trip, I have an annotated map. I take it back the next time and add more things.

Develop an 'inbuilt compass'. Even in cities, you can use compass bearings to point you in the right general direction. If you know you have to head roughly north to get to a particular monument, you can use the sun's angle to guide you even if you're not sure of your exact location. That way, you don't have to check your map continually and can take intriguing shortcuts without losing your direction.

> 'I usually spend the first day in a new town orientating myself with visual cues, particularly if the place is hilly. I go out on the first day and locate north, south, east and west, and get visual pointers – sites, locations, monuments – things like that to orientate myself by.'

Church steeples, TV towers and tall buildings make great vantage points. Climb to the top to get an overview of the territory. Check out the way main thoroughfares carve up the city and try to pinpoint the location of your hotel, the station, the nightclub district, the major sights, and so on.

> 'Whenever I got to a new city, I'd go to the top of the tallest church spire or skyscraper I could find and have a look around. It was the best way to get an overall perspective on a place. The best one is the TV tower in

> *former East Berlin – I spent two hours doing the 360-degree panorama and working out where all the different landmarks and districts were. It was fantastic. By the time I came down, I felt as though I knew the whole town.'*

Before you set out for the day, list the places you want to go and ask a hotel staff member to write equivalents in local script beside each of them. You may want to mark each destination on your map, too. Then you can use the 'point and ask' method if you need to guide a cab driver or get directions.

> *'I always got a map first thing, and asked people to mark my hotel, the nearest bus or train stop and the places I wanted to see onto it. If I passed a good shop or gallery, I'd mark that on it too. It helped me locate places more easily when I was out and about.'*

It's also handy to carry the address of your hotel or hostel with you – it's surprising how often travellers forget the name or location of their accommodation.

> *'Once I went out with a group of people from my hostel, and I decided to go home early. I didn't have the hostel address on me, and I realised I had no idea where it was. I got into a cab and just said to the driver, "It's sort of around here." He was really nice and drove me around the area till I found it. After that, I always carried the hostel address around with me.'*

Using public transport can be a quick way to orientate yourself and get a feel for local life. You'll see more and get a better idea of a city's layout if you travel on buses, trams or above-ground trains, but in many modern metropolises, the underground is the most efficient way to get around. In sprawling cities like London and Paris, many tourists find it easier to learn the metro system, surfacing only when they reach their stops, than to tackle chaotic above-ground transport.

'Japan's public transport is really easy and safe, and not as expensive as I thought it'd be. I was staying with friends who were living in Tokyo, but every day I'd go off on my own and do things, like catch the underground. The signs are written in English so I found my way around without any trouble.'

'In London, I went everywhere on the underground for the first few months, because the roads are so chaotic that the tube seems faster and simpler than going on the buses. Once I got to know the place, I realised how close together some of the underground stations were. I hadn't really had any idea.'

Take yourself on a walking tour – self-guided or organised – to help you get orientated. While you're walking, note distinctive landmarks (buildings, church spires, towers, bridges, statues, shopfronts, railway stations) and geographical features such as hills or waterways. Use the landmarks to help guide you back.

'I usually catch a taxi around town, or take a guided tour, so I at least have an idea of where I am. Once you know your way around a city, you feel much more confident and that makes you less vulnerable.'

Get in the habit of looking behind you when you turn a corner, and fixing a mental picture of how the same intersection looks when approached from the opposite direction. When in doubt, duck into a shop or doorway to check your map. Don't drag it out on every street corner: it makes you look lost and vulnerable, and brands you as a tourist.

> *'I try to go without a map because you're a sitting duck
> every time you stand on a street corner and pull it out.
> Not only does it make you look like a tourist, but people
> can jostle you and steal your bag or come over and try to
> pick you up at those times, too. If I have to stop and look
> at a map, I try and do it discreetly.'*

If you can't find a street sign, continue in the direction you
think is correct for another block or two. If you still can't
confirm your bearings, re-check your map or go into a
shop or hotel for help.

> *'Don't be somewhere you've no idea about; don't stand on
> a street corner at night with your map open. It's really
> dumb – like you're waiting for someone to come up and
> say, "I'll help you." You should go into a café, buy a
> coffee, put your map on the table so you don't attract
> unwanted attention. Having the guy in the café help you
> is completely different to putting your fate in the hands of
> an absolute stranger.'*

Street numbers and signs

Where streets are planned on a grid system and houses are
numbered consecutively, locating a specific address is a
relatively simple matter. In places such as Japan where
streets are not named and house numbers bear no rele-
vance to geographical location, it may not be so easy. Get
detailed instructions ('Take the third lane on the left after
the church, halfway down, next to a grocer shop. It has
green shutters and a red door') if there's no 'official'
address.

> *'In Korea, the houses on the streets aren't numbered in
> sequential order – so 23,396 is next to 14. You have to
> know by people's descriptions of the buildings. And people
> you're meeting have to come out and stand on street*

> *corners to make sure you find them. They do it in Japan, too. So you've just got to have the address with you, and some sort of written instruction about where you're wanting to go. You think how many times you get into a taxi in your home city and the driver doesn't know how to get to where you want to go. Try that in a country where the taxi industry is only three years old.'*

In countries that don't use Western script, deciphering signs can prove impossible. If you'll be spending some time in a place, it's worth learning the numbers and alphabet in local script. When setting out, have any addresses, bus routes and destinations you plan to visit written clearly in local script (or at least take along a phrasebook that includes them): it makes asking for directions or briefing your taxi driver simpler.

ASKING FOR DIRECTIONS

Remember to introduce yourself politely before requesting directions. It helps if you have your destination written in local script, or a map. (Ask the person to point out the correct route or mark the destination with an X.) If you don't share a common language, a phrasebook can be helpful.

It's always a good idea to ask more than one person for directions. In some countries, people would rather give wrong directions than admit they're unable to help you, or they feel bound to agree with you: to avoid this problem, ask 'How do I get to . . . ?' rather than 'Is this the right way to . . . ?'

Shop and hotel staff, police and taxi drivers can generally give reliable directions (although cab drivers will often assure you it's easier to catch a taxi than to walk). In the street, approach women or family groups rather than men to ask for directions. If you go to a man for help, you may end up with an unwanted 'guide'.

'I orientate myself by talking with locals. I touch base with locals wherever I go. I'll walk into a bar, a service station, a restaurant, wherever. I go in with the attitude that I know what I'm doing, even when I don't. I pretend I know where I'm going and what I'm doing for the next three days. I tend to ask more point-to-point information, not give the impression I have no idea where I am. That's a security measure.'

'A couple of times I got very ambiguous directions, but I think it was because the people directing me were so laid back they were practically asleep. It was like that in Australia and Fiji. You just have to ask a few people – eventually someone will be able to give you clear directions.'

GETTING AROUND

Every country's transportation system has its strong points and its weaknesses: service, reliability, comfort and safety vary widely from place to place and between various modes of transport. You'll save time, hassles and money if you sort out the options available and work out how to negotiate the system early in your trip.

'I used buses rather than trains for long journeys in Thailand. I caught a train from Bangkok to Chiang Mai but I decided to take the bus back because the train was so hopeless. It was really slow, hot, and at one point, it actually broke down.'

'Around Asia, I found trains more reliable: at least you're on a set track, so you know where you're going to end up. Buses sometimes veer off in directions you're not expecting them to go in.'

Guidebooks give basic transport information but timetables, fares and routes change often: get current details from local transport offices or tourist information counters. You may decide to pre-book journeys on popular routes to avoid queueing and to ensure that you don't end up in a third-class seat on a long overnight haul.

If you plan to move around a lot, a special transport pass (such as Eurail), valid for a fixed period or number of journeys, can save you untold time and hassle, and often guarantees you a reserved seat. Whether or not you'll save money depends on the distance you plan to travel within the specified period, what class you'll be travelling in and how many of the places you want to see are covered by the relevant transport network. A good guidebook or your travel consultant should be able to give you the necessary information.

Around town, make it easier on yourself by having destinations written down, carrying a map and phrasebook, observing what other commuters do, and being prepared to ask for help.

URBAN TRANSIT

Chaotic traffic conditions, incomprehensible signs and 'flexible' timetables can make negotiating urban transport a daunting task. Even finding the bus stop can be difficult

– let alone working out which bus to catch. Methods of payment can also be confusing. Are you required to buy tickets before boarding, or do you pay the driver or conductor? Is exact change required at automatic ticket machines? Do you have to punch your ticket as you enter the subway, on boarding, or not at all?

To make things simpler, have small change handy, especially when doing short hops around town. If you're uncertain of the correct fare, ask the driver. To get the hang of automatic ticketing systems or local etiquette, watch what others do and follow suit.

If you plan on using urban transport intensively, find out about special deals: buying a weekly rail/bus pass or a book of metro tickets saves you time and money. Students, pensioners and children with appropriate ID may be entitled to concessions. Guidebooks and transport office clerks can give you information about discounts: don't forget to ask when you're buying a ticket.

'I used public transport in cities all over Europe. It was a good way to get a feel for local life, and it was usually pretty straightforward to figure it out. You just have to be prepared to ask people, and make a few mistakes. But you get the hang of the system pretty fast, and after a few days you feel like a local.'

Security on urban transport

Public transport in cities and larger towns is often crowded and thieves can take advantage of the crush to pick your pocket or swipe your handbag. Be alert for pickpockets at peak periods, on tourist routes, on escalators and while boarding or exiting in a crowd. Stash your valuables and hold your bags in front of you.

'Once when I was getting on a train, someone pushed me and ripped off my bag. The time you're most vulnerable

Men sometimes use crowded transport as an excuse to 'inadvertently' rub against or grope women. Avoid sleazebags by positioning yourself next to women wherever possible. If someone does grope you, assert yourself: tell your harasser to desist, 'inadvertently' push him out of the way, or complain loudly so the whole carriage hears about it.

In cities at night, buses, trams, share-taxis or cabs are usually safer modes of transport than train or metro. If you do travel on trains late in the evening, choose the compartment that adjoins the guard's van, a crowded carriage, or one in which other women are sitting. If someone unsavoury gets into your compartment, be prepared to switch to a safer one.

Fare evasion

On transport services where machines have replaced ticket collectors and conductors, it can be tempting to ride without a ticket, claiming ignorance if accosted. Transport services in cities with heavy tourist trade (such as Paris, London and Prague) have taken to using roving ticket inspectors who issue on-the-spot fines to fare-evading tourists. Be warned.

'In Prague and Budapest they're really big on catching tourists who ride without tickets. The system in both places is that you buy a ticket beforehand and punch it into a machine when you board, and there's no conductor to check it. A lot of tourists don't bother punching their tickets, but you do risk getting fined. I got my tickets checked twice in three days by plain-clothes inspectors in Budapest – it's not worth the risk.'

Share-taxis and minibuses

Where public transport systems are inadequate, private
operators tend to fill the gaps with alternative means of
getting from A to B. In developing countries, these can be
anything from shared taxis to minibuses, to a space in the
back of a pick-up truck or covered van that may also be
transporting goods.

Share-taxis and similar forms of transport work to different systems in different places. Some have set routes
with designated stops; others will pick up and drop off
passengers at any point along a set run, and still others
vary their route to suit the people on board. Most share-
taxis don't follow timetables – they set off as soon as
they're full. If you're in a hurry and the driver is waiting to
fill the last space, you may be able to get him to leave by
agreeing to pay the extra fare yourself.

'On the island resorts in Thailand, everyone travels in
these covered utes. They have signs saying which beach
they're going to and you just hop in the back of the one
you want. You pay a set amount and everyone squashes in
together. They load up in the centre of town and then
drive directly to the destination. Sometimes they'll pick up
locals on the way, so there'll be people hanging off the
back and out the windows. If you miss the bus, there's
always another one along soon.'

'On Bali, they have shared minibuses called bemos and
you pay a set amount and they drop you off where you
want to go. It's cheap and simple.'

Fares may be fixed, or may vary according to your destination (and your naiveté). Watch what locals pay. If the amounts given vary, ask the driver. Have small change handy.

Sometimes, as a woman, you'll be offered the privilege of sitting up front with the driver. This can be a more comfortable way to travel, especially if it's cold or raining, but it's not as fun, or as sociable, as travelling in the back with everyone else.

> 'Around Vanuatu, the only means of transport is in minibuses or trucks with wooden benches in the back. As a woman, I usually got offered the seat up front with the driver, but I never took it unless it was raining, 'cause it was more fun sitting in the back with local women on their way home from market, and schoolkids, and young guys from the villages. We'd chat and sing and muck around all the way. It was a really uncomfortable way to travel, but it was a great way to meet people.'

Taxis

For speed and convenience, cabs or the local equivalent (rickshaws, three-wheeled 'tuk-tuks', horse-drawn carriages) are the obvious choice. In most Western countries, taxis are metered, but in the developing world, taxi meters may be faulty or nonexistent. In that case, you'll have to agree on a fare beforehand. To do otherwise is asking to be ripped off.

Guidebooks usually give estimates of fares from various arrivals points to the city centre or tourist district. Expect fares to be higher in the evening, to and from the airport and if you have lots of baggage. If possible, ask a local how much he or she would expect to pay, then offer that amount.

Security in taxis

In some cities, unlicensed cabs operate alongside official ones. They're usually cheaper but they're often shonky operators. You're safest sticking to licensed taxis.

> 'New York, London, Rome, Paris – they all have shonky taxi drivers. In London, the minicab drivers, who are usually fine, use private cars, and you hear stories of men posing as minicab drivers and abducting single girls coming out of nightclubs. "Black cabs" are safer.'
>
> 'In New York, cab drivers sometimes use offsiders to rush you into their cabs. Rome's the same: they have hawkers who'll come up to you in the taxi queue and say, "We have a taxi around the corner, you don't have to stand in this queue. Come with me, I'll get you a taxi straight away." It can be safe but it can be a scam.'

While taxi drivers are unlikely to harass you, it's not unknown. Minimise your chances of getting into trouble by:

❑ phoning for a cab or catching cabs from public places (outside tourist hotels, restaurants or clubs) rather than hailing them on the street
❑ knowing where you're going, or at least bringing a map along so you have an idea of direction and distances
❑ opting for licensed cabs rather than private operators, especially when travelling at night
❑ sharing a taxi with someone else who's going in your direction
❑ being polite but not overly friendly to the driver
❑ noting the driver's licence or ID number in case you want to make a complaint later.

Negotiating fares

For many modes of transport, fares are not fixed and, unless you have some idea of what the going rate is, you could end up being substantially overcharged. Don't stress out about this – accept that you're likely to be charged the 'tourist rate' on the first few journeys.

Guidebooks often give advice, but rates change. Ask locals what they consider to be a fair amount, and use that as a guide to what you should pay. Make sure you've agreed on a fare before you set off – it's much harder to dispute it once you've accepted the ride.

When negotiating a fare, particularly in Asia, don't lose your cool or raise your voice. What the potential driver sees is a hysterical Western woman behaving very rudely. Drivers may become more stubborn the more you harangue them. Remember that no driver is obliged to take you, just as it's your right to refuse to be taken. Be firm but polite and if you can't agree on a price, wait for another taxi or minibus rather than getting into an argument.

LONGER JOURNEYS

For longer journeys, the mode of transport you choose will depend on your budget, the time you have available, your destination, scenic attractions, comfort and safety concerns. Read guidebooks, consult transport information staff and talk to other travellers before you decide which way to travel – it could make a big difference to your comfort, safety and enjoyment on long trips.

Crowds and comfort

Everyone's comfort requirements are different – what one woman needs to make her journey tolerable may seem like unnecessary extravagance to another. In the developing world, cheaper forms of transport are usually crowded and lack the comforts most Westerners take for granted. Don't expect cushioned seats, buffet cars, airconditioning and clean toilets. Yet journeys distinctly lacking in luxury often turn out to be memorable, thanks to the fact that they give you opportunities to interact with local people.

> *'In India, I got so much friendly hospitality on transport. I used to travel second class because it was cheaper, so I'd meet a lot of local people. Once when I was on yet another 10-hour train trip to wherever, I was in a compartment with a family – mum, dad and the kids. They had these little tins of food – one was rice, and one was curry and so on – and they insisted I shared with them. They were so hospitable. They'd offer you anything. In return, I'd take a photo and send it back to them a couple of months later. There were genuine people who were really nice.'*
>
> *'I was on a train in China, travelling in what they call "hard seat" class – it's a very basic sort of carriage with a hard board seat and there are people everywhere. A guy got up out of his seat to let me sit down, and as we went past part of the Great Wall, he showed me things about it. Even though he couldn't really communicate, he was very friendly. He definitely wouldn't have given up his seat for a guy.'*

How well you cope with less-than-comfortable budget travel conditions depends partly on your state of mind. If you're feeling robust, friendly and accommodating, and you're prepared to squash in good-humouredly with everyone else and answer a barrage of curious questions, you'll be fine. But if you're stressed out, exhausted, ill or longing for privacy, travelling on the cheap can be more trouble than it's worth. Sometimes it's a smart move – for your health, safety and peace of mind – to splurge on a sleeping berth, an airconditioned coach or an internal flight.

To help make sure that long-haul trips are enjoyable and hassle-free, it's important that you plan a sensible travel schedule, book the safest, most comfortable forms of transport you can afford, and prepare appropriately for the journey.

- ❏ Work out which modes of transport are the most appropriate for your needs, schedule and budget. Consider comfort, reliability, safety, sociability, scenic attractions, facilities (such as toilets, sleeping provisions, airconditioning), cost and convenience. In some countries (such as India), trains are much the best option; in others (such as Spain), express buses are generally a faster and more comfortable way to get around.

- ❏ Where possible, book your seat in advance, and arrive early to secure it. In some countries, a reserved ticket doesn't guarantee you a seat – you may have to fight for your right to sit in it.

- ❏ Avoid travelling in peak periods. Around cities, time your journeys so they don't coincide with rush hours. Avoid leaving town in the early evening or at the start of a weekend – transport will be full of commuters and roads will be crowded with traffic.

- ❏ Remember that in rural districts in Third World countries, transport into and out of town can be crowded on market days.

- ❏ If your luggage will be difficult to access during the journey, retrieve everything you're likely to need before it's loaded.

- ❏ On overnight journeys, consider booking a sleeping berth. If you're sitting up, take something to use as a pillow and some sort of covering (sleeping bag, coat). A window seat means you've got something to lean your head against, whereas an aisle seat lets you stretch your legs.

- ❏ On day trips, ask your driver which side of the bus or train gets the best views and seat yourself accordingly. Also take the sun's angle into account – you may be cooler and more comfortable if you sit on the side that gets more shade.

Security in transit

Theft is common on some forms of public transport. You're particularly likely to run into this type of hassle at stations and on overnight hauls. Take these precautions to make transits safer and less stressful:

❑ Keep valuables under your clothes, and sleep on your daypack.

> 'You can't travel long distances without falling asleep. I slept with my money belt on, put my bag underneath my knees, and slept curled around it. You've got to do that, whether you're male or female. If you're Western, you represent the good old dollar.'

❑ Line your backpack with newspaper or dense items such as towels and clothes to make it difficult for bag-slashers to extract anything from your luggage.
❑ Padlock your pack to the luggage rack or seat, especially if you plan on leaving the bus (or train compartment) or on sleeping.
❑ Don't accept food (or drink or smokes) from strangers, unless you're pretty sure it's a genuine, safe offer. Instead, take your own supplies (and offer them around if you want to meet people), or claim you're not hungry.

> 'I met a great French family on a train on the way from Spain to the south of France. They had all this wine and cheese, and I sat down with them and ate and drank and chatted.'

❑ To avoid being pestered, sit near women, families or other travellers rather than next to men.

> 'Travelling on night trains was a bit of a hassle – I always seemed to end up in a carriage with a whole bunch of guys. It made me feel insecure. I'd just move so I was

sitting next to a family. Or I'd ask the conductor whether I could change carriages. I never thought to ask in advance.'

❏ Don't disembark en route unless others are doing so, too, and find out from the driver how long he or she plans to be there for – stops can be very short and you might be left behind.

❏ Don't be persuaded by a fellow passenger to take an alternative route: even if the advice seems genuine, it's better to stick with your original, safe plan.

'I got talking to a Thai soldier on a long-distance bus, who persuaded me – in perfect English – that if I got off where he did and took a local bus, I'd get to my destination more quickly. I took his advice, because lots of local people were transferring at that point and it seemed safe enough. But it wasn't. The minibus ended up going to a military compound, where the soldier dragged me off with him. I protested but none of the locals would intervene, so I was forced to go with him. He kept me locked in his room for two days, raping and bashing me, before I managed to escape through a window and catch a local school bus out.'

❏ At stations, wait in first-class or women-only waiting areas if they're provided, or sit near other women or families, and keep your bags close to you at all times. If your wait is a long one, check your bags into the luggage room or put them in a locker.

'Although I tried to be aware, I got my backpack ripped off in London, waiting for the bus to Portugal. I just went to get a cup of coffee, and two seconds later I turned around and it was gone. It was just by chance that this guy saw someone pick it up and chased him down the road, and I got it all back. You've got to be so aware in stations.'

❑ If you find yourself in an overcrowded carriage with rock-hard seats or don't feel comfortable about the company, ask the conductor whether you can be transferred to a first-class compartment or at least to a different seat. Offering extra money can work wonders, even if the train's supposed to be full.

'If the carriage was too full, I'd just move – there's usually another seat somewhere, or you can politely ask someone to swap with you. It's easier to do on trains, 'cause you can always ask the conductor to transfer you.'

❑ If you're fed up with crowds, splurge on a first-class seat or sleeping berth. For some trips, air travel may be almost as cheap as ground travel, especially once you add up the incidentals.

'On a ferry from Corfu to Patras, I'd booked a seat and had planned to sleep sitting up, but I ended up paying extra to stay in a cabin, 'cause there were a whole lot of dodgy-looking people sitting near me and I was scared if I fell asleep, I'd wake up and find all my stuff gone. I asked the purser and he found me a berth in an empty cabin.'

❑ Schedule journeys so you arrive before nightfall, or at least while there are still women on the streets, especially if you're unfamiliar with the place or haven't arranged accommodation.

'Generally I travelled during the day and would try to arrive at a reasonable hour and have an idea of where I was going to stay. It's safer and less stressful that way.'

❑ Space your journeys to allow yourself time to relax and recuperate. A succession of long trips in cramped, overcrowded, uncomfortable conditions is no fun at all.

❑   Especially in developing countries, expect delays
     and disruptions, and try to keep your cool when
     they occur. It's frustrating, but it's all part of the
     travel experience.

> 'I had a transport mix-up in Greece where I had to wait a
> whole day for a bus because there was a train strike. It
> was so frustrating I ended up having a bit of a cry. You
> can laugh it off if you're with someone, but if you're alone
> you tend to get a bit sorry for yourself. And usually you're
> too exhausted to see the funny side of it. You're tired and
> dirty and you just want to get there.'

> 'You don't have a schedule in Africa – it's like, "We'll get
> there when we can." Once, we had to cut in and around
> a whole tree – it had fallen over the road and was too big
> to move, so we had to get out there with machetes. And
> we had to literally rebuild one bridge, because it had
> totally fallen apart.'

Women-only facilities

In most Western countries, women's waiting rooms and
segregated train compartments were phased out decades
ago. But in some parts of the world, such facilities still
exist. In Islamic countries and those with a colonial her-
itage, such as India, you'll find special provisions for
women travellers: women-only sleeping compartments,
reserved seats on trains and buses, segregated waiting
areas and even separate ticketing queues.

Women-only facilities in developing countries can be
crowded, and children, who often travel with their mothers in women's compartments, can be noisy companions.
Using women-only facilities has its advantages, however:
you're not going to get hassled by men, your baggage is
safer, and you get to meet lots of other women.

Booking tickets

Wherever possible, reserve a seat or berth ahead of time. Booking in advance makes sense even if you have an air or rail pass. You can't count on getting a sleeping berth or even a seat at the last minute, especially on popular routes.

In most parts of the world, computerised systems have streamlined transport ticketing procedures and reduced the likelihood of mix-ups, but in developing countries and small towns, booking systems may be less reliable. Transport offices in cities are generally the best places for making or changing reservations. In some places, you may even be able to book and pay for tickets by phone, using your credit card.

When booking in person, be prepared to queue, sometimes for long periods. In India, there are separate (usually shorter) ticket lines for women – take advantage of them. Come armed with relevant information (destination, preferred time and date of departure, class, berth requirements, and so on), written in the local script. Bring cash, Eurail or other passes, student ID and a phrasebook.

If your itinerary is more or less fixed, book a series of journeys in one go to save yourself time and hassles.

'From Germany, I made a string of Eurail train reservations for destinations all over Europe, with a minimum of fuss. The girl behind the desk spoke perfect English and was using a hyper-efficient, state-of-the-art computerised system. It's made the whole process so simple. There's no penalty if you re-book or cancel, so it's OK to change your plans. I prefer doing that to having to book tickets separately for each leg of the journey. Booking tickets is so difficult and time-consuming in places where people don't speak English or where the system's chaotic.'

Plane

Where time is a factor and budget allows, air travel is the obvious choice for long hauls. It can also be cost-effective on shorter hauls. Sometimes it's your only practical option: island-hopping, for example, is only possible by air or boat – and sea travel can be uncomfortable, slow and erratic.

> 'These days, I don't like the time spent getting to places and I have more money, so I tend to fly between destinations. Travelling with a backpack, taking it on and off buses and trains – I'm not into it any more. I'll still go trekking, but I'll pay a porter to carry my bag.'
>
> 'In the South Pacific, flying is often the most practical way to get around the islands. Boats might only go once or twice a week and schedules are a bit erratic. And if the sea's rough, it's not much fun. It's quicker and simpler to fly unless you're on a really tight budget or have lots of time.'

In many countries, you can cut the cost of internal fares by using a traveller's air pass. Passes must usually be purchased before you enter the country, and may limit you to certain flights, destinations and dates. Ask a travel agent or consult a guidebook before you leave.

Make sure you request a non-smoking seat (many international flights still allow smoking on board). If you're flying in daylight over scenic attractions, a window seat can make the journey more interesting. Request vegetarian food if you're unsure about the state of your stomach.

Train

Most countries have both local and express services. Express trains are faster and generally more comfortable, but they're also more expensive – even rail-pass holders may have to pay a supplement – and you'll meet fewer locals. Trains generally offer a smoother, safer ride than buses, but in developing countries rail travel can be slow, stops interminable, and carriages hot and crowded.

If you can't travel in daylight hours (or want to save money on accommodation), shell out the extra for a sleeping berth or couchette on an overnight service. Even the most basic berths are a more secure and comfortable way to travel than sitting up all night. Sleeping compartments are often sex-segregated, particularly in countries with strong Muslim communities. If they are mixed, women tend to look out for one another. Request a berth in a compartment with other women when you make your reservation.

For security, ask for a top bunk rather than a lower one. You'll be less vulnerable to thieves, groping hands or curious eyes, although you'll also be hotter. On some trains, you may be able to lock the compartment door (use a plastic bag tied around bunk-base and door handle if there's no functioning lock). Locking the door's a good idea: it keeps intruders from hassling you or stealing your valuables during the night.

> 'I didn't feel the need to travel in women-only compartments in India. My girlfriend and I used to get sleepers and they were usually in a mixed carriage. You had to look after yourself and your things. I'd put my stuff somewhere and tell my friend, "I have to go to the toilet", or "I'm going to have a cigarette, but I'll be back", so she could watch the valuables. You get people who'll try to touch you because they think "You're Western, you're easy." Sometimes you'd wake up and there'd be a hand on you. We used to get top bunks so we were out of the way, but we never got much sleep.'

'Tourist-class' seats and sleeping compartments on popular routes are usually packed with other travellers, and things can get very sociable. It's a good way to make friends, acquire information and accommodation tips, or hook up with temporary travel companions.

> *'I shared a sleeping compartment with a couple of American girls on the overnight train from Tangier to Marrakesh. When we arrived, I asked if they'd mind if I stayed with them till we found accommodation. They were quite happy about that. We shared a cab to the tourist office, got our maps and found a cheap hostel on the edge of the marketplace.'*

On some train journeys you may be required to relinquish your passport to the conductor – it's probably as safe as hanging onto it yourself. Keep your valuables secure, preferably on your body and under your clothes, when travelling, especially on long-haul or overnight trips.

> *'Some of the overnight trains in Europe have a reputation for hassles. I heard more than one story about people being ripped off on the trains in the south of France and Italy – people would come into the compartments, spray some sleeping drug in the air, then rob everyone's valuables. I also heard about hassles and theft on the night trains through Poland.'*

If you plan to do a lot of train travel in a short period of time, it's economical and practical to buy a discount rail pass. Check out the various alternatives – some passes will suit your needs better than others. You'll probably be required to buy the pass before entering the countries for which it's valid and to specify dates in advance. Students may be eligible for further discounts: make sure you carry an International Student ID Card.

> *'I took full advantage of my month's travel on Eurail. It saved me a lot of money, especially in Scandinavia. I also saved on accommodation 'cause I took a lot of overnight trains between cities. On more scenic routes, I travelled during the day. It was a really peaceful way to see the countryside, and most of the trains in Europe are very comfortable.'*

Even with a rail pass, you'll need to make advance reservations on popular routes, and may be required to pay supplements on some services (such as rapid intercity expresses) and to reserve a sleeping berth. You'll need to get your pass stamped and dated by the conductor on each journey. Once you've made a certain number of trips, or once a specified time period (usually between a week and three months) has elapsed, your pass is no longer valid. If you lose your rail pass, it may be impossible to replace it or get a refund on it, so keep it safe.

Bus

Buses often take more direct routes and service destinations not covered by the rail network. They can be a cheap, convenient way to travel. Bus travel has its drawbacks, however: hazardous roads, chaotic traffic conditions, maverick drivers, badly maintained vehicles, too little – or too much – airconditioning, lack of on-board toilet facilities, and cramped, crowded conditions.

To make your trip as safe and pain-free as possible:

❑   Book a seat on a tourist-class 'luxury' coach for long journeys, especially in tropical countries.

'Because I was on a really tight budget, I caught normal local buses around Asia: I never went for the airconditioned tourist coaches. It was hot, and very cramped, and you sit where you sit for 12 hours, but I had no problems. You just settle down and get used to being there.'

❑   Arrive early to secure your seat, even if you have a reservation.

'On buses in Asia, I used to put the backpacks under the coach and my friend would rush on and get us seats, because often they'd have overbooked and there'd be

people sitting in the aisles for 16 hours. I remember leaving Chiang Mai, and the only seat left was next to a window that was cracked, and I kept thinking, I'm going to be trying to sleep and it's going to break and I'll get my neck slashed. But I guess it's all part of the adventure.'

❑ Bring adequate supplies of food and water – you may have difficulty finding hygienic, palatable provisions at road-stops.
❑ Carry a neck pillow, jumper or cardigan, sarong or sleeping bag and an eye mask and earplugs, if you have any intentions of resting.
❑ Watch your luggage if it's being loaded onto the roof of the bus – it may be worth tipping the guy who loads and watches it a little extra to encourage him to safeguard your belongings. Keep valuables and necessities for the trip on your person.
❑ If you suffer from motion sickness, try to secure a seat in the middle section of the bus (it moves around the least), especially on journeys featuring mountain passes and winding roads.

'I felt very safe travelling around Greece on public transport, although it can be hard getting around on non-airconditioned buses in 35-degree heat. And there are really windy roads, especially on some of the islands. It was a bit scary, and made me feel a bit queasy.'

❑ Know the route, any transfer points, your destination and the estimated time of arrival – it's easy to miss your stop and the driver won't necessarily remind you. When in doubt, ask fellow passengers or your driver to help you out. If you have your destination and transfer points written in local script, you'll find it easier.

'When I was catching the bus around Greece, I had to change about four times, and I didn't speak the language that well, so figuring out where the buses were going, or where to catch them, was a hassle. Sometimes I'd have to walk from one end of a town to the other to change connections. The fact that I was a young girl made the locals far more sympathetic. They were unhelpful initially and then when they realised I was a girl on my own, they felt sorry for me and helped me.'

❏   Befriend fellow travellers or friendly locals (preferably another woman or a family) so you've got someone to help watch your gear and to alert the driver if you fail to re-board after a particularly short stop.

'In China, people who spoke English were always so keen to come up and talk to you and practise their English, that sometimes you really had no choice but to trust people who offered to help you out. My sister and I took a five-hour bus trip in this 1940s bus, and it was packed, there were chickens and wildlife – just amazing. None of the people on it spoke any English, except one guy, who found me and said, "Where do you want to go?" I wanted to go to this mountain monastery and he spoke to one of the guys on the bus and then told everyone where I wanted to go. After that, everyone looked after me the whole time. If I went for a break, they'd get their watches and do a little mime about when I needed to be back at the bus, and made sure that I was there, and that I knew what was going on. When there's a huge language barrier, you have to put your faith in people and hope they'll do the right thing by you.'

'It's good to have someone else with you in transit – to mind the baggage, find the next bus terminal with, talk to. I didn't have any bad experiences doing that when I travelled.'

Buses without on-board toilets can make things difficult for women on long journeys. Often, buses make food stops or roadside breaks in places where there are no toilet facilities and nothing for women to duck behind. The best option is to bring your own toilet paper and wear a long, loose skirt while in transit, so you can relieve yourself without immodest displays of flesh.

Boat

Boats can be a cheap and, weather permitting, pleasant way to travel. In some places, they're the only way to reach your destination. Costs range from thousands for a cabin on a luxury cruise ship or charter boat, to a few dollars for a fishing-boat transfer or ferry ride.

Check out local passenger services. Tourist information offices and guidebooks can tell you which operators are the most reliable, but schedules change frequently so you'll have to contact the relevant shipping lines for information about current fares, schedules and services.

Local ferry services that take cars, cargo and passengers can be a cheap and convenient way to travel. On popular routes and in tourist areas, these often run regularly, and on-board services and facilities are usually reasonable.

'I caught a ferry from Tokyo to the islands – it was so cheap and not too uncomfortable. A Japanese student told me about that option: they tend to be the ones who do the budget travelling in Japan so they know all the tricks.'

Cargo boats sometimes take passengers: you'll need to allow plenty of time, and may have to hang around the docks trying to organise a passage. Conditions may be spartan and you'll find few women on board, but you're unlikely to come to any harm.

If the boat is small, the journey long or conditions look like they might be rough, bring remedies for seasickness.

If you feel queasy, go on deck and get some fresh air. If you still feel nauseous, go ahead and throw up: you're less likely to feel seasick once your stomach's empty.

> 'I took an overnight boat between two of the main islands in Fiji. Everyone was bunched in together in one big room, and there were only about three small mattresses to go around 40 or 50 people, so most people just sat up in these old reclining seats. It got really rough, and people were staggering around. I was seasick and hadn't brought any remedy, so I just went up on deck and threw up overboard. I felt heaps better after that, but it was a long and uncomfortable night.'

If you have sailing experience, can cook or are willing to work hard for little pay, you may be able to get a free passage by signing on as a crew member on a yacht or charter cruise vessel. This can be a leisurely and sociable way to travel, provided you don't get seasick and don't mind living at close quarters with your companions.

Make sure the vessel is seaworthy, the captain is competent, and your conditions of employment are clearly understood before you leave port. If you can, meet the crew before sailing. If you're the only female on board, you may need to establish some ground rules. It can be difficult to escape unwanted attentions when you're stuck out at sea, so make your intentions clear from the outset.

> 'I worked my way across from the south of France to Miami by getting a job as a chef on one of those luxury cruise boats – the sort owned by rock stars and society people. It was quite easy to score a position 'cause I'd worked in some good restaurants in London, and had a few contacts in yachting circles through my brother. I didn't have to cook anything very fancy, because I was just cooking for the crew the owner had hired to sail his boat back from Europe to the USA. Everyone on the boat

ROAD TRAVEL

Hire cars

In places where traffic isn't too chaotic, hire rates and
petrol prices are reasonable and roads are navigable, hiring a car offers you flexibility and freedom. Make sure the
car is equipped with a local street guide or good, up-to-
date road maps and a spare tyre repair kit. In the USA,
many hire companies throw in a car phone at minimal
cost – it's worth taking up this option for peace of mind
(they're great in an emergency or if you get lost).

When hiring a car, have your International Driver's
Licence and credit card on you. Check the policy for hidden costs or omissions and the vehicle for existing damage
and driveability. Make sure you have third party and prop-
erty insurance even if your travel insurance covers you for
road accidents.

'I hired a car in LA, and just cruised around and did the
LA thing – shopped on Melrose Drive, went to clubs and
bars and restaurants and beaches. Took the freeways.
I used a tiny map to get around but I never seemed to get
lost. The freeways are so well signposted, as long as you
know where you're headed. I got the option of having a
car phone for an extra $3, so I took it. Not because I had
anyone to call, but in case I broke down somewhere dodgy
and had to call for road service. I didn't end up needing
it, but I did have a few funny car incidents.
    'I had to turn off the freeway one time to get petrol,
and I ended up in a gas station where I was the only

> *white girl – there were black and Latino and Mexican*
> *guys leaning out of beat-up cars, and I couldn't get any*
> *petrol out of the hose. I went in to the guy behind the*
> *register and said, "I'm sorry, I don't know how to get the*
> *gas out, I'm from Australia." He laughed and said, "In*
> *LA, you pay for the gas first." That was typical LA.*
>
> *'Another time, I wanted to window-shop on Melrose*
> *Drive, but I couldn't find anywhere to park. I ended up*
> *spotting some reserved parking spaces behind a café, so I*
> *went inside and asked the manager if he'd mind if I used*
> *the space for a short time. He was great, and said, "Park*
> *all day if you want to." So I did. By six the shops were*
> *closing and I returned to the car to find it wouldn't start.*
> *I went back to the coffee shop and the owner said, "No*
> *problem, I have jumper leads – I'm just finishing up: have*
> *a coffee." So I did, and we got talking, and by the time*
> *he'd shut up shop, we'd decided to have dinner. We went*
> *out to start my car, and when I turned the key this time it*
> *just started. Strange.'*

In many parts of the world, chaotic traffic, hazardous roads, limited fuel outlets and poorly maintained vehicles can make driving difficult. Even in countries where conditions are simpler, driving yourself can be costly – and stressful.

> *'In Bali, I hired a jeep for a few days. It was a scary place*
> *to drive – the traffic is so anarchic. I nearly had a few*
> *stacks because the direction of the traffic would suddenly*
> *change without any warning signs. And the roads were*
> *full of bikes and kids and dogs and people doing*
> *unexpected things. You really had to keep your wits about*
> *you. There was no chance to stare out the window – you*
> *had to keep your eyes on the road every second.'*

In many countries (Bali, India, Nepal and Thailand, for example) it's almost as cheap to hire a car with a driver as to drive one yourself, and in most cases, this is the better option. Not only do you get a guide, you get someone who knows the local roads and rules, and you're free to gaze out the window rather than having to dodge motorbikes, kids and chickens.

If you want to go off the main public transport routes but can't afford car hire rates, band together with other travellers and share costs and driving. You'll find share-ride notices on the walls of many hostels and tourist restaurants, or in English-language tourist publications.

Motorbikes

One of the most common causes of injury to travellers is motorbike accidents. Mopeds and motorbikes can be a cheap and convenient option but it's not advisable to hire one unless you're somewhere where the road conditions are good, traffic is minimal, or you have some experience with bikes (riding and, preferably, fixing them). If you hire a bike and are unsure of your skills, try to take less crowded, chaotic routes, travel slowly and only ride during daylight hours.

Make sure you take out insurance cover when you hire a bike, and read the fine print of the agreement. Note, too, that many travel insurance policies don't cover you for injuries or damage resulting from motorbike accidents.

Accidents and road hazards

Before you decide to drive, it's wise to know what you're letting yourself in for. Read your guidebook, or talk to locals about road rules, etiquette and what to do if you're involved in an accident.

When driving in any foreign country, be especially careful. Don't drive if you're intoxicated – even if you're just going from the pub to the beach at the end of the road in a sleepy resort town. Allow extra time to compensate for the fact that you're driving an unfamiliar vehicle on unfamiliar roads, and dealing with a whole new set of road rules that may include driving on the opposite side of the road than the one you're used to.

If you do wind up in an accident involving another vehicle, try to avoid getting into an argument. Be polite, calm and apologetic without admitting liability. Injured parties may be angry and unreasonable, and language difficulties can further complicate matters. Stay as collected as possible and seek support.

Even if the accident wasn't your fault, it may be difficult to prove this unless you have witnesses, and you can't assume that locals will take your side. Call the tourist police, and try to engage the sympathy of others on the scene who can act as negotiators (and, if necessary, interpreters).

In some countries, particularly non-Western ones, you could be in a vulnerable position – you're a foreigner to start with, and you may have unwittingly broken cultural laws (such as running over a cow in India) as well as road rules. Road rage is a growing phenomenon in the UK and USA, so don't push your luck if you tangle with a vehicle or anger another driver in one of those countries.

In the USA, you need to be wary of would-be carjackers who cause minor accidents deliberately in the hope that motorists will stop and get out of their vehicles to inspect the damage. If you're nudged or rammed by another car on an American road, especially at night or in an unsafe district, don't stop: drive towards a crowded area or a police station. Hire cars are particularly vulnerable to this sort of attack, so don't leave evidence of the car's origins sitting on the dash.

Security in and around cars

When approaching your car, especially in public car parks, take the following precautions:

❑   Check around and under your vehicle as you approach it, and check the back seat before getting in.

- Stand slightly away from and at a 45-degree angle to your car while unlocking the door, and scan around you.
- Lace your car keys between your fingers so you can use them as a defence tool if necessary.
- When driving around cities, lock your doors, and don't open passenger windows or fully wind down your own.
- Don't stop to exchange details if someone bumps your fender late at night – instead, note the license plate and drive on.
- If you're followed, drive to a police station or public place and wait till the car following you goes away.

> 'When I was in LA, I stayed in a hostel on Venice Beach, which is a really funky place full of skaters and street stalls and open-air gyms and tourists. I hired a beat-up car for about $15 a day and at night, I went out to clubs. I went to about a dozen different nightclubs and no-one gave me any trouble. Most of the people I met were friendly and the sleaze factor was lower than I expected. The only problem was with parking the car: I sometimes had to park a couple of blocks from where I was going. That was scary, especially late at night – it seemed like every guy I passed on the street was loitering with intent and there weren't many women out after midnight, either. I just walked fast and didn't talk to anyone. I'm still here.'

HITCH-HIKING

Hitching always carries an element of risk. In some countries, it's a relatively safe and accepted practice, but there are always exceptions. Scandinavia, Japan, New Zealand and parts of Europe are reputed to be hassle-free places for hitch-hikers, but any place can be risky if you're unfortunate and get the wrong driver. In isolated regions with no organised public transport system, hitching a ride may be the only practical way to get from A to B. If you do decide to hitch-hike, find a partner to accompany you and take sensible precautions to minimise your chances of getting a bum ride:

- ❏ Travel in daylight hours.
- ❏ Wait for lifts in safe areas, preferably where there are people to witness you being picked up. Petrol stations and roadhouses are good bets, because you can ask diners if they're going your way and you have a safe and comfortable place in which to wait for a ride.
- ❏ Have a map, and know where you're going and what route you need to take to get there.
- ❏ Bring appropriate clothing, a sign and adequate provisions – it could be a long time between meals.
- ❏ Get people to drop you off at roadhouses or in towns, rather than out on the open road.
- ❏ Choose your lifts judiciously – don't get in if you don't like the look of the vehicle or its occupants.
- ❏ Get out of any vehicle as soon as possible if you feel unsafe or uncomfortable.
- ❏ Let someone know who you're going with and where you plan to end up (even if it's only the guy in the gas station).

'I'd never hitched in my life and I probably wouldn't do it again, but a girl I was with had hitched a lot. We'd been working in Austria, and she'd take day trips to Salzburg or Innsbruck. There were certain places where she wouldn't do it, but she said that with two of us, we wouldn't have a problem. I thought I'd give it a go, so I did and it was very easy. We were lucky 'cause the people we got as lifts were friendly. We got one lift with a Turkish truck driver from the Austrian border to Belgrade – an overnight journey. When it got dark, he stopped and said, "I'm going to sleep in the truck and go on to

Belgrade tomorrow morning. If you want, you can sleep in the truck, too." We didn't have much money, so we decided to do that. It was a big truck: there was a bed in the front and one up the back, and then the two seats. He fed us Coke and chocolate before we went to bed and then again when we woke up. He was great. The next day, we went on to Belgrade and he dropped us off. We got good rides, but I wouldn't do it again. You hear so many stories. I didn't feel safe.'

'When I was working on the ski fields in Italy, the only way to get from my village to the nightclub area was to hitch. So every night, a girl I worked with and I would stand in the snow and put our thumbs out. We never had any trouble until one night when I was practising my Italian and was a bit sloshed, and I said the word funcula – which means fuck – instead of fredo for cold. The driver slammed on his brakes and I thought, "Omigod, I've said something wrong." Once I explained myself, he calmed down.'

'A girl I met and I tried to hitch a couple of times in New Zealand. On our way out of Christchurch, we didn't have much luck. In the end, the police picked us up and said, "Do you want a lift to the city limits?" By that time we'd decided to catch the bus, so they drove us to the bus station. On the North Island, though, we didn't have a problem: we hitched up there and did some whale-watching, then caught the cheap shuttle bus back.'

'A girlfriend and I hitch-hiked around Scotland, from Edinburgh up to Inverness. They're so friendly up in Scotland, it's simple to hitch-hike – you just put your little sign out and loads of people stop to give you a ride. One guy picked us up and took us to Glasgow, but first he gave us a city tour and took us to lunch, then dropped us at the door of our hostel and said, "Have a nice day." He was in the car with his children and their nanny and everything, so there was no sleaze.'

'Anywhere in Israel I wanted to go, I'd hitch. I got told off one day by one of the kibbutznik, for hitching by myself, but I never had any trouble. You had to check the car number plates: if it was a yellow one, it was an Arabic car and if it was white, it was a Hebrew car. You had to be a bit careful of who you hitched with. But because so many soldiers hitch around Israel, people are used to it, and I didn't get harassed at all.'

'After working in northern Japan, I took a boat to the southern islands because I wanted to get to somewhere warmer and I'd heard that's where the hot springs and mountains were. I met a couple of Japanese students on the ferry who said they'd heard of lots of people hitching and that it was safe. So I just started doing it. One of the first things I did on arrival was to buy a road map, and got someone to annotate it and translate a few things, and make sure the routes I was proposing to take were the right ones. And I think I just had guts. I spent a month hitching around, surviving by the seat of my pants, from one day to the next. I wouldn't hitch in many other countries, except perhaps New Zealand or Scandinavia. But in Japan, it was amazingly easy – I even got invited to stay with people who gave me lifts.'

'I was in Tokyo and some friends went away for a few days to the country, hitching. One of the girls, an American, had to get back to Tokyo early so she left the group and hitched back by herself. She ended up getting a ride from hell: she came out of it, but she was battered and beaten and raped. And we all thought Japan was so safe. I guess you can be unlucky anywhere.'

Share rides

There are safer ways to organise a cheap lift than hitching. In Europe and the USA, consider registering with a share-ride company: for a small fee, they'll match you up with a driver going your way. You pay part of the petrol costs and may be expected to do some of the driving.

Check hostel notice boards and tourist papers for ads about share rides. Or post a notice yourself, advertising for companions to share hire car costs. You may be able to pick up safe lifts by asking around at campgrounds.

'You can pick up lifts from campgrounds, and it's safer because you get to meet the drivers beforehand. In Africa, there was a truck at one of the campsites I stayed at, and it was heading south as I was, so I gave the guy some money and got a lift right down from the north-east coast to Harare.'

'I travelled in outback Australia for three months. I started in Broome and went across the north-west, which is quite remote. I did a lot of it by getting car rides with people I met in hostels. I ended up joining some people I met who were helping out as cooks on a tour. They had their own four-wheel drive so I hopped in with them for part of the way. I tended to land on my feet. And people in remote areas tended to take me under their wings. They probably wouldn't do it for a guy.'

Consider driving yourself – in America, many travellers use the 'Auto Driveaway' system. You get to drive a new car from coast to coast, paying only your fuel and food costs – the company gets their cars delivered coast-to-coast for free. The system operates mainly between major cities such as New York, LA and Miami, and there are conditions attached (you usually have to cover a distance of 400 kilometres a day) – but it's a cheap way to cross the country, and certainly beats sticking your thumb out on the roadside and flagging down a random passer-by.

ACCOMMODATION

In cities, large towns and tourist centres, you'll usually find a wide range of accommodation: hotels, youth hostels, YWCAs, convents, college dorms, government-run hostels, guesthouses, campsites and traditional-style lodgings. In remote regions, you're unlikely to have much choice about where you stay, but there's nearly always someone willing to accommodate a stranger. To find a place that suits you, consult listings in guidebooks, get recommendations from fellow travellers, or ask locals for tips on arrival.

'In China, I used the Lonely Planet guidebook and it was fantastic. The advice it gave on styles of accommodation gave a pretty accurate indication of what places were going to be like. In Beijing we stayed in a hotel the guidebook recommended, in a really good district: it had lots of public transport, buses into the city, there were *good restaurants around it, and heaps of travellers, and the accommodation wasn't too bad.'*

'The one time I didn't have a guidebook, I was in a small place in Indonesia where everybody knew somebody who had a warung, or a hotel, or a brother whose cousin worked somewhere you could stay, and everyone could tell you about a place to eat. You just had to ask. They're concerned about you travelling alone as a woman, so they don't want you to go to somewhere dodgy – they either want you to go to a relative's place on a recommendation, or they'll try to direct you to something a little more expensive than you'd normally pay.'

Tourist offices tend to direct you to 'tourist-class' hotels and may not carry comprehensive listings of budget accommodation, but they can be handy if you're stuck.

'When I arrived in London, I hadn't made prior bookings. I just turned up at the information office at Gatwick Airport and asked. They had rooms listed. It's the same in most cities around Europe. They have to be organised, because they have such a high turnover of tourists.'

'I arrived in Berlin once, very late at night, and I hadn't been able to book a room. The tourist information office was closed so I went to the woman at the transport information counter at Bahnhof Zoo station and asked her whether she thought I'd be safe sleeping in the station. She took one look at me and said, "Why don't you stay at the station mission, just around the corner?" I said, "Are you sure? I don't want to take a bed away from some homeless person." She said, "No, the women's dorms aren't full." So she took my arm and led me around the corner to this soup-kitchen-like place with about six dorm rooms. I shared a room with one other woman. She was asleep, and she had on about 20 gold chains. Presumably she was

wearing them so nobody could steal them in the night. She was snoring when I came in, with 15 cigarette butts in an old food container next to the bunk, and breath that stank of garlic. But the sheets were clean and the bed was comfortable and it was really cheap, so I wasn't complaining. In the morning, I ate breakfast with a bunch of refugee families from eastern Europe and Russia and Turkey who'd also stayed there. That experience wouldn't have happened to me if I'd been a guy – they just would've said, "Go sleep in a park".'

If you're pre-booking, or aren't sure whether the place is suitable, only pay for one night's stay. Then if you're not happy, you can look for an alternative the next day.

'When you read the guidebook and you haven't been somewhere, it's all hocus-pocus until you've seen the place. It's trial and error. You just have to pick somewhere that sounds OK, that's in a safer part of town, and go there. If you don't feel safe or confident, just stay one night. No-one's making you stay longer. And ask other people – they will often say, "Oh, I stayed there, it's crap", or "Come to this place, we're going here", and you can follow their tips.'

'You don't want to land up somewhere in the middle of the night and have no idea where to stay. It happened to me in Paris. Luckily, at the airport, some people told me there was a reservations system in Paris – you could call them and they'd guarantee to find you a bed for a reasonable price. So I rang them and it was great.'

TYPES OF ACCOMMODATION

You won't always be able to find a room that meets all your requirements, but having an idea what you're looking for helps. Ask yourself:

- Do I need a room to myself, or am I happy to share?
- Do I want to meet other travellers, or would I rather get off the tourist trail and get to know local people and customs?
- How important to me is comfort, cleanliness, security, a view?
- Do I want to be central, close to the sights, or away from noise and bustle?
- How important to me is access to public transport?
- Do I need child care or business facilities?
- Do I want to self-cater, go out for meals or have some or all meals at my accommodation?

Hotels

For women on business, a modern hotel is the most practical option. You'll find five-star hotels in most big cities and tourist centres, equipped with business facilities and time-saving services. If your budget is limited and your aim is to experience local culture and meet people, you'd be better off in a hostel, guesthouse or homestay. But it might be worth splurging on the occasional up-market hotel room if you feel run-down and in need of some extra comfort.

'I like staying at hotels, because you have more privacy. A lot of times, I would decline offers of staying at people's homes because I wanted to be on my own, to do whatever I wanted. I wanted to be able to get up at five, or order Vegemite toast at two in the morning, which is something you can't do if you're staying with other people. I love being on my own.'

'The first night I arrived in Bangkok I couldn't get anywhere, so I went to a pretty exclusive hotel and stayed there one night. It cost more than I'd usually spend, but it was safe and comfortable, and it shows you how other people travel.'

'When you're backpacking it's logical to stay in hostels, but if you only have a short break, and you're going for a holiday, you may decide to go up-market. Now I'm working and have less time and a bit more money, I tend to stay in hotels, in a different style of place. I've got quite sick of that, though. Staying in hotels you become a lot more isolated, because they're not natural meeting points. You don't meet people the same way you do if you stay in hostels and backpacker guesthouses.'

Hostels

If you don't mind sharing facilities and sacrificing privacy, a hostel is a good option. Hostels are great places to meet fellow travellers, share tips and information and find temporary travel companions. There are over 5000 official youth hostels in around 60 different countries, and most give discounts and preferential bookings to International Youth Hostels Association (IYHA) members. Most don't have age restrictions and, particularly in Europe, you'll find travellers of all ages sharing youth hostel dorms.

Most hostels have separate dorms for men and women, but even where sleeping quarters are mixed, you're unlikely to get pestered. Pilfering can be a problem, however, so lock your stuff in your backpack and sleep on your valuables, or use the hostel safe.

'On my first trip, I stayed in hostels – pretty scummy. In the hostels in India, I really had to watch my stuff. And there was one place in London where a lot of nefarious characters came in and out. I almost got robbed while I was there. I stayed in cheap dives that you wouldn't want your mother to know about – really dreadful places. Wonderful places, too – seedy but interesting.'

'Youth hostels are great because you meet lots of backpacking-type people with the same spirit, and lots of *other people on their own. For a single person, hostels really are the way to travel: they're cheap, and you get heaps of information from other travellers. It's not second-hand or out-of-date information, they've probably just done it a week ago.'*

'Rent is very expensive in Hong Kong, so you can work and make enough to stay there but it's hard to save. At the start, I hung around Chung King Mansion, which every tourist knows. It has about 18 storeys and four or five lifts within the building, and inside there are food halls and sweat-shops, with all these guesthouses in between. They cram them in: space in Hong Kong is a problem. The dorms were all full and you literally had two square metres to yourself and then your bed. The dorms weren't segregated – it was everyone in together. In the end, I took a room by myself in another guesthouse, 'cause I thought I'd go crazy once I started work – I need my privacy and to be at least able to sleep properly. It tends to get a bit noisy in dormitories. Then I was lucky to link up with some English guys who were there long-term and had rented a flat. I ended up sharing with them.'

Family-run guesthouses

If you want a comfortable, stress-free environment and a balance between privacy and sociability, try a family-run guesthouse or traditional inn. They're often run by women, you get home-cooked meals, there are opportunities to meet both locals and fellow guests, and you're generally made to feel safe and comfortable.

'Guesthouses are a safe bet for women on their own. If you can get a women's dormitory it's great, because you get to meet lots of women. Although sometimes it's nice just to have your own space, your own room.'

Religious institutions

If you're after peace and quiet, an ashram or convent might be more your style. They're usually clean, cheap and safe. You'll have to be prepared to rise and turn in relatively early. Curfews can make them an impractical option for women who like to stay out and sleep in late.

'I stayed in a convent in Italy, in the suburbs of Rome. It was very peaceful and the nuns were sweet, and everything was scrupulously clean. It wasn't a place I'd want to stay for long, because it was out of the centre and you had to go to bed pretty early, but it was great for when I first arrived.'

'I spent some time on an ashram in India. It cost virtually nothing, and although the facilities were pretty basic, it was clean and had a really safe, pleasant vibe.'

College and university dorms

During semester breaks, you can often find cheap accommodation in dorms or private rooms at colleges and universities. College dorms aren't always central and security can be a problem on sprawling campuses after dark, so check the location before you book. Advantages include access to sports and other facilities, and contact with fellow travellers and local academics.

'In Europe, I tended to stay in university accommodation. I'd arrive at a university and ask if there were any vacancies, and usually, during the summer months, there were places you could rent. At that time I was studying politics, so it really helped me. I met lots of interesting people, especially in Eastern Europe.'

Campgrounds

Camping out has many attractions – scenic locations, fresh air, cheap rates, free facilities (laundries, pools, videos) and the chance to meet people in a healthy, relaxed environment. Although your belongings may be less secure, there are few reports of women being harassed in official campgrounds. The presence of family groups and fellow budget travellers means they're generally safe and sociable places to stay. Local tourist information offices can usually provide you with lists of campgrounds in the area.

> 'You find a lot of people at campsites. I did a lot of onsite things, and you meet people and get pally with them. I'd just go on my gut feeling, and I never turned out to be wrong. You click with someone, inevitably, and often arrange to meet them further down the line.'
>
> 'In Africa, I'd always get to a campsite and meet other travellers there, and I'd talk to them and say, "How'd you get here, and where did you stay, and have you had any trouble, or been anywhere great?" I got a lot of good information that way.'

Women-only accommodation

If you want a total break from male scrutiny, and a friendly, safe atmosphere, consider staying in women-only hostels, hotels or YWCAs. The gay travellers' guides listed on pages 335–6 can help you find lesbian-run, women-only and gay-friendly hotels throughout America and Europe. Outside of the West, you'll just have to go with your hunches.

HOMESTAYS

If you want to meet local people and participate in the daily life of a community, consider a homestay. Living with a local family, especially in a culture very different from your own, may mean making significant adjustments to your lifestyle, behaviour or dress codes, but there are many benefits.

- ❏ You'll get to know local people in a relaxed environment where there are numerous opportunities to interact.
- ❏ You'll be more likely to meet women (especially in traditional societies, where women are kept out of public life).
- ❏ You'll find out more about the place and those who live in it.
- ❏ You'll get the chance to participate in the daily work of the community, to make a contribution that's not merely financial.
- ❏ As 'part of the family', you may be invited to events, gatherings and celebrations that most tourists never have the opportunity to see.
- ❏ Security problems and harassment are highly unlikely to occur – most host families are protective of their guests.

In many countries, it is possible to arrange an extended stay at reduced rates in a family guesthouse. Or organise to live with a local family – many families are happy to give up a bed or a room to a single female traveller. International homestay organisations can help to link you up with suitable families and arrange your stay.

'When I was 19, I went to Japan for a year. I'd organised to spend the first two weeks in a homestay in Kyoto. I'd done my homework and got some information from the Japanese Consulate – that made it easy to arrange. The family I stayed with was great. I met people through them, and ended up staying with another family, relatives of theirs, in a little fishing village in northern Japan. I decided to stay on in this guesthouse in the village,

*working, for about four months. I turned 20 while I was
there, so they threw me a coming-of-age party. They have
one every year in each prefecture, with about a thousand
guys and girls who are coming of age. They dressed me up
in a kimono and all the traditional gear. I was the guest
of honour; I had to make a speech and I ended up on the
local news. I was the only white person in the village.
That sort of experience was what made it for me. I didn't
want to stay in that normal, "teaching English" scene
that a lot of people get stuck in. You don't really get a feel
for the culture that way, and you meet up with other
foreigners rather than locals. I took a Lonely Planet guide
with me, but I honestly don't think I used it once.'*

If you don't have accommodation teed up in advance, ask
locals for advice on who might be willing to billet a traveller. It's usually easier to do in small towns and villages.

*'I planned where I was going to go, and in places where I
had relatives I knew where I'd be staying. But in places
where I didn't know anyone, there were always some
people who were renting out rooms, or I'd go to the tourist
information centre and they'd tell me about places I could
rent out. Accommodation is very easy to come by in
Greece, especially on the islands. Lots of local people rent
out rooms in their houses.'*

*'I stayed with the family of a Portuguese girl I met on a
train and had the best time. I met so many people and
really got to know the Portuguese people rather than
staying in touristy hotels and only meeting other
travellers.'*

Make it clear that you're willing to pay your way and help
out with chores or childminding. Speaking a little of the
local language helps, but it isn't essential.

Before you decide on a long-term stay, make sure you

and your hosts agree on terms. Will you have your own room, or share a room or a bed with family members? Will you cater for yourself or join in family meals? What contribution will you make to chores and expenses? It's a good idea to start off saying you'll stay for a week: this gives both parties an 'out' clause if it's not working out. You can always extend your stay if everyone's happy with the arrangement.

You may be considered a 'guest', but you'll get more out of the experience if you give something back. Make a contribution to the domestic chores, child care and day-to-day expenses. Offer to teach English to the children, or cook the occasional meal. Don't abuse the hospitality of poor hosts with generous hearts by overstaying your welcome or failing to pay your way. If your hosts are poor but refuse to take cash, reimburse them in kind (with non-perishable food items such as flour, rice, coffee, tea and sugar or practical gifts). Even if they can afford the expense of a guest, repay their hospitality with gifts or treats.

Organisations that help to arrange homestays include:

❑ the Friendship Force, which arranges two-week homestays in over 50 countries to promote world harmony. You pay your own transportation costs and expenses but accommodation is free. Contact Friendship Force, 57 Forsyth Street NW, Suite 900, Atlanta, GA 30303, USA (ph 1-404-522 9290).

❑ the Experiment in International Living Federation, which has two dozen member organisations globally, and will arrange one- to four-week homestays in 16 countries within Latin America, Asia and Europe. Fees vary depending on the destination and length of stay, with an average cost for a fortnight's stay being US$600–US$800, not including transportation. Contact The Experiment in International Living Federation, PO Box 595, Putney, VT 05346, USA (ph 1-802-387 4210 or fax 1-802-258 3126).

❏ the World for Free organisation arranges short homestays in 32 countries for members. Contact Seidboard World Enterprises, PO Box 137, Prince Street Station, New York, NY 10012, USA (fax 1-212-979 8167 or e-mail mykel@wps.com).

❏ Insight Nepal gives you the opportunity to stay with Nepalese families and learn Nepali, teach English or go trekking. Contact Naresh Shrestha, Insight Nepal, PO Box 6760, Kathmandu, Nepal (ph 977-1-418 964 or fax 977-1-223 515).

Home exchanges

If you're planning to spend most of your time in one country, consider exchanging accommodation with somebody who's planning to visit your home town. Other people's places usually come furnished and you may even get the use of the owner's car.

Some organisations that help set up home exchanges are:

❏ Homelink International, which has offices in a number of English-speaking countries, including the UK, the USA, New Zealand and Australia. Contact them at 34 Franklin Street, Maldon VIC 3463, Australia (ph 03-5475 2829; fax 03-5475 1078).

❏ WorldHomes Holiday Exchange – this Canadian-based company can fix you up with holiday homes in a variety of destinations. Write well in advance of your trip to 1707 Platt Crescent, North Vancouver, BC V7J 1X9, Canada (ph/fax 1-604-987 3262).

❏ Vacation Exchange Club, at PO Box 650, Key West, FL 33041 (ph 1-305-294 3720; fax 1-305-294 1448).

❏ The Invented City, at 41 Sutter Street, Suite 1090, San Francisco, CA 94104 (ph 1-415-252 1411; fax 1-415-252 1171; e-mail invented@aol.com).

Staying with friends or family overseas

It's great to catch up with loved ones and visit long-lost friends, and it can be reassuring to stay with people you feel close to. They're usually thrilled to have an overseas visitor and will often go to great lengths to make you feel welcome. In turn, you may have to make some adjustments, especially if you're staying with older or more conservative folk.

'Sometimes staying with my Greek relatives was a bit much. I wanted to go out and do my own thing every day, and they weren't used to girls being so independent, especially in the villages, where it's still about girls growing up and getting married. I'd want to go off and catch public transport and see ruins and they were really uncomfortable with that. It was like, "What if something happens to you – what are we going to tell your parents?" I was continually having to say, "I'll be OK!" And they'd be stressed all day while I was out. Going out late with friends would also make things a bit tense. But despite our differences, it was wonderful to get to know my extended family.'

'A friend had given me an address of some people to stay with on Mykonos who didn't know me from a bar of soap. She'd sent them a letter to say I was coming and would need a place to stay. When I rang them, they said, "Oh, you're a friend of so-and-so's, come down, come down!" I assumed they'd got the letter but they told me later that they didn't: they just loved having visitors. They were very friendly. They were so used to having people come from overseas and stay: it was no big drama. I couldn't believe it.'

Even though friends and family may be loath to accept any contribution to expenses, try to be a good guest. Help with the household chores, participate in the family's social life and behave in a manner which is appropriate to the culture. Take your hosts out sightseeing, to a concert or to a fancy restaurant – it's surprising how often local people don't do those sorts of things themselves. Give a thoughtful gift. Take photographs and send them duplicates. Make sure that when they remember your stay, they remember it with joy.

> 'At first, I was worried I'd be a burden on the friends I stayed with overseas, but they were used to having visitors and were quite happy about it. Often, they'd take me to sights – castles and monuments in their area that they'd never actually been to themselves – and say, "We're really glad you came, because it's given us an opportunity to go there ourselves".'

AVOIDING HARASSMENT AT YOUR HOTEL

While physical harassment of women in their accommodation is rare, staying in a place with a predominantly male clientele – especially if you have to share bathing facilities – can make single females feel uncomfortable and ill-at-ease. Tiresome situations – persistent stares and conversational gambits from men – tend to be more prevalent in male-dominated, conservative societies, where hotel owners, staff and the majority of guests are likely to be male, and where Western women tend to be objects of curiosity.

If you feel harassment could be a problem, make it clear from the outset that your room is your own and that you don't want to be bothered. In communal areas, read a book, write postcards or sit next to other women to discourage advances.

In countries in which it's common for women to travel unaccompanied, hotel owners have begun to recognise women's needs for privacy and freedom from male harassment. You'll now find women-only floors and facilities in many bigger hotels.

Most hotels are safe – if they weren't they'd lose business. But men can be mighty persistent, and managers aren't always vigilant about protecting female guests. Coincidentally or otherwise, most reports of nocturnal hotel-room 'visits' come from women travelling in Indonesia, Thailand and Egypt.

If you're nervous about intrusions, lock or barricade your door before you sleep, and don't leave windows open if they're accessible from the street. Don't sleep naked, and keep a torch under your pillow or leave the bathroom light on. If anyone does try to enter your room, don't be afraid to yell for assistance. And consider changing accommodation if you're worried about hotel staff, other guests or general security.

While you'd be highly unlikely to wind up in a hotel doubling as a brothel, it makes sense to steer clear of down-market hotels in red-light districts, which are often frequented by men. Opt instead for family-run establishments or tourist hostels.

> 'I tend to go for safer areas when looking for accommodation, and I look for places where other travellers are staying. I don't stay at the more remote places when I'm on my own, at least not until I've established my whereabouts.'

NEW CULTURES, NEW CUSTOMS

When you travel, you make a tacit agreement to live by the laws and customs of the countries you visit. Fitting in may mean making substantial changes in your attitudes, actions, dress or lifestyle. But if your intention is to experience new cultures rather than running roughshod over them, some degree of assimilation is necessary. You don't want to lose your identity (or your integrity), but neither do you want to offend your hosts.

MINIMISING CULTURE SHOCK

Do your homework before you go – that way, you're less likely to make a fool of yourself or insult someone out of ignorance. If you know people from places you'll be travelling to, talk with them about what life in their home country is really like. Read up on the cultures you plan to visit: learn as much as you can about their history, traditions, customs, politics, religious beliefs, taboos. Ask returned travellers for tips on behaviour, dress and communication.

> 'It's good to read about local cultures while you're there. While I was travelling in India, I read novels about India which went into the whole culture and caste system and history – they were great for getting insight. And Lonely Planet guidebooks, always.'
>
> 'You have to adjust to a different culture; you can't want everything to be the way it is back home, because it's not. You have to accept that people are different, that cultures are different, and if you can't take what they're giving and just experience it all, you may as well stay home.'
>
> 'Greece was my first trip out of Australia and it was a real culture shock. Even though I'm from a Greek background, it's still very different – they sleep in the afternoons, they speak much faster in their own culture, and they're more protective of women. You have to get used to it. I didn't really know what to expect – in hindsight, I wish I'd read up on it more.'

As well as the basic information given in travel guides, consult specialist books on cultural differences. Especially good are Elizabeth Devine and Nancy Braganti's guides to local customs and etiquette: *Traveler's Guide to European Customs and Manners* (Meadow Brook, 1992), *Traveler's Guide to Middle Eastern and North African Customs and Manners* (St Martin's, 1991), *Traveler's Guide to Latin American Customs and Manners* (St Martin's, 1989), and more. Or check out Roger E. Axtel's entertaining and informative guides to cross-cultural behaviour, customs and language, such as *Do's and Taboos Around the World: A Guide to International Behaviour* (John Wiley & Sons, 1993) and *Do's and*

Taboos of Using English Around the World (John Wiley & Sons, 1995), or Stuart Miller's *Understanding Europeans* (John Muir Publications, 1996). If you're going to Asia, try *Traveler's Guide to Asian Culture* by Kevin Chambers (Meadow Brook, 1989).

EXPLODING MEDIA MYTHS

When people from different cultures meet, they often bring with them misguided notions about what life in the other culture is like. Thanks to the global exportation of American TV shows, big-budget Hollywood films and, of course, pornography, people in non-Western countries can easily form the impression that all Western women are like the ones they see on 'Baywatch' or 'Dynasty': wealthy, glamorous, sexually available, aggressive and promiscuous.

> 'I try to dress and behave in such a way that I don't encourage that myth about the sexy, blonde beach girl. You see a lot of female travellers, especially at the resorts, who dress straight out of "Baywatch", or worse, and then flirt with the local men. It's just encouraging them to view Western women in the worst possible way. I think if you're going to kick up your heels you should try to do it discreetly. The more conservative the culture, the more careful you have to be about how you come across in their eyes.'

Counteract misleading media images by giving the people you meet real facts about life in the West. Once they realise you're nothing like the spoilt sex-bombs from TV soaps, they may start to question the stereotype – which is a good thing, and makes it easier for the women who come after you.

'When they heard that I was married, and a professional working woman, rather than some hippie-dippy tourist out to get drunk and get laid, people treated me with more respect.'

'In a lot of the Asian countries, they just don't get this thing about single women – they think if you're not married, there's something wrong and you've been hard done by. They don't see singleness as a positive, they see it as a terrible thing. I hope that by talking with the women I met, I was able to change their outlook a little. Because you know that they'll go back to their villages and their small family units, and talk about how they met a foreign woman and she was travelling on her own, and she was doing it because she wanted to. Whether it has any impact, I'll never know.'

'On some of the less touristed islands in the South Pacific, they're really naive about life in the West. They think it's all fantastic, and if they could only get to somewhere like Australia or America, they'd live happily ever after. It's hard to explain how things really are, but if you try, I think it helps everyone's understanding.'

Remember that your ideas about people from other cultures may be similarly skewed by things you've seen on TV or read about in the press. Keep an open mind.

'I was sure I was going to have my bottom pinched by Italian stallions, that Spanish men were unbearably macho and that I was going to be sexually harassed in Morocco. Yeah, I had to deal with gutter-crawlers in Rome, and hustlers in Tangier, and adorably macho men propositioning me in Spanish bars. But I didn't have any more trouble in any of those places than I get on the streets of Sydney, Australia.'

Showing – and getting – respect

You may be worried that as a Western woman alone, you won't be respected by the locals in some countries. How you're treated will depend to a large extent on how you behave, and whether you respect the people and customs of the countries you visit. Even if other tourists are dressing and acting as they would at home, it doesn't mean you should follow suit. Observe local customs, dress modestly and act appropriately, and you're more likely to be treated with courtesy and respect by locals of both sexes.

> *'I think it's an insult to the women of the country you're visiting not to try to follow the rules. And to dress or behave at odds with those rules is asking for people to look at you in a different way. Not that I'm saying it's asking for trouble, but it's asking for different reactions than you might get if you dress and act like everyone else. It's not a difficult thing to fit in with whatever culture you're travelling in. And it makes it so much easier to get along with the local people.'*

LOOKING AND LISTENING

Wherever you are, you'll find it easier to fit in if you develop the habit of listening before you speak and watching before you act. Carefully observe the social interactions going on around you, noting all the details. Model your actions on those of the local women. Attempt not to interrogate the people you meet, and try to become part of the group rather than the 'foreigner', the centre of attention.

> *'Once, this girl I'd met when I was staying in a little Greek village was taking me to see some of the local sights. As we walked through the village, there were people sitting on their porches and balconies all around,*

and she was saying hello to everyone she passed. After a while, she nudged me and said, "You have to say hello to everyone; otherwise they're going to think you're strange." At first, I found the idea of saying hello to total strangers really uncomfortable. But by the end of my stay, I got used to it.'

'When I get to a place, I like to sit down somewhere with a coffee and watch local people going about their daily business. You pick up a lot just by sitting, listening and watching what's going on around you.'

Gestures

Get to know the proper greetings and appropriate forms of address. Do people bow, shake hands, hug, kiss, or do something else entirely? Greetings may differ depending on the age, class status, religion or sex of the people involved. You may greet people differently in business, social and family situations. In cultures that revere their elders, you need to be especially respectful and formal when meeting or addressing anyone older than yourself. If in doubt, use the most polite form.

Gestures are a useful way of getting your meaning across when there's a language barrier. But they can mean very different things to people from other cultures. Using inappropriate stances or gestures can lead to misunderstandings or unwittingly cause offence. Make sure you know what you're communicating before relying on non-verbal cues, and avoid giving misleading signals.

Roger E. Axtel's book *Gestures: The Do's and Taboos of Body Language Around the World* (John Wiley & Sons, 1991) can help you to avoid embarrassing errors. When all else fails, smile: as Axtel points out, it's the only one of the thousands of physical signs humans produce that is universally understood.

'It was the small things that really made the difference – a smile just got you a thousand places. You need the utmost patience, and time. One time I was in this hotel, and the airconditioning and all the lights went down, and they were down for hours. I had the devil of a time trying to get anyone to fix the airconditioning or the lights, even to get a candle. I couldn't get anywhere by just speaking normally to the management on the phone, so I ended up going down and standing in the lobby, pantomiming bumping into walls and drawing pictures of candles, and so on. They thought that was hilarious, and I got a candle straight away.'

'I was in a carpet warehouse in Tangier, and the proprietor took me up to a little room to see a Berber woman weaving a rug. I watched her for a while, and played with her daughter. She couldn't speak any English, but she nodded and smiled at me occasionally, and I smiled back. It was such a brief encounter but I will always remember it.'

'On a couple of occasions, I met up with people whose English was very dodgy, as was my Japanese, and it was just by drawing pictures and pointing that we communicated. But sometimes, there's an understanding even when there's a language barrier. I think it's partly in the body language – if you give good vibes to someone, they tend to give good vibes back to you.'

Group etiquette

Ask for advice if you're unsure of how to behave. In a group situation, the simplest, friendliest way to make sure you get it right is to ask a woman sitting near you if she'll act as your mentor/guide. Follow her lead, and before doing anything you think might be a breach of etiquette, seek her approval with a questioning look: if she indicates that it's OK, you can go ahead.

> 'I was staying with a local family in a small village in the South Pacific island of Tanna. I was lucky enough to be there for an important circumcision coming-of-age ceremony and the villagers asked me to participate. The village women took me off and we all dressed up in traditional gear – the grass skirts, the flowers in the hair, painted faces, everything. At the ceremony, the men and women sat separately and had their own dances. I hung back a bit because I wasn't sure what to do. Then one of the women took my hand and made me follow her. After that dance was over, she kept hold of my hand, and stayed with me all evening as a self-appointed guide. She was wonderful.'

CROSSING LANGUAGE BARRIERS

Even if your knowledge of the local language extends only to a few words, your effort to speak it will be appreciated. Have a phrasebook handy so you can hold a rudimentary conversation. It's an especially good way to meet local women, who are less likely than men to speak English.

> 'It really helps if you make an effort to speak the language. There's this big fallacy that the whole world speaks English, but it's not true. Or they don't speak it to the level at which you want to converse, anyway.'

> 'It's easier to meet locals in the Philippines or Sri Lanka or India than in other parts of Asia, because they often speak English even in small villages. Whereas in Thailand, that's not the case. Even if you try to speak to people, it's that much harder when there's a language barrier. Learn at least a few phrases in Thai and use your phrasebook. It's very much appreciated.'

'I had a phrasebook but minimal Spanish, and that was a shame. I do think if you're going to spend any length of time in a country, you should do a language course. If you can speak with and understand the local people, it adds so much to your experience.'

'I always try to know some good words and expressions in the local language. The first Mandarin I learnt was "What a fabulous outfit." The next thing I learnt was "No, no, it's a long road to go", because for some reason, as soon as you say that, people say, "Oh, you speak very good Chinese." Learn a bit of slang, and some local gestures. In Cantonese, when you say "very good", there's a particular gesture that locals use to accompany it. You pick up things like that.'

'I spoke a little Japanese, and met lots of locals, especially uni students, travelling around Japan. I'd link up with them, because often they were wanting to practise their English. And I'd practise my Japanese on them. They'd help me to write things in Japanese and give me tips on what transport to catch and where to go.'

Conversational rules

Some people eat in silence, others converse during meals. In some cultures, long silences are not considered rude or embarrassing, so just sit comfortably – don't feel compelled to rattle on, just to fill the gaps.

'On Vanuatu, in the South Pacific, people speak very quietly, especially after a few bowls of kava. In the villages, everyone sits around in the dark and sometimes no-one will say anything for ages. They're quite comfortable with it, but it takes a little getting used to.'

OBSERVING PERSONAL SPACE

Make allowances for differing 'personal space' requirements. Whereas people brought up in Britain or Australia
usually like to keep about an arm's length apart while con-
versing, especially with strangers, people from Middle
Eastern or Latin cultures tend to move in close. It's easy to
misconstrue this as a personal or sexual intrusion,
whereas it's more likely to be a cultural thing.

> 'I found the men in Morocco unnerving at first because
> they stood so close to me when we talked. It feels like a
> sexual intrusion, but it's actually the way they converse.
> I would find myself leaning back to get away from them.
> I'd have to explain that I was from Australia and didn't
> feel comfortable standing so close to people. They'd back
> off, but then they'd start inching closer again. It was a
> continual battle over personal space.'

PACING YOURSELF TO SUIT THE CULTURE

In many countries, people live a lifestyle that isn't domi-
nated by efficiency, speed and business hours. It can take
a bit of getting used to, but fuming in frustration over
what you perceive as slowness or rudeness is unlikely to
get you far.

> 'In Indonesia, they live by what they call "rubber time", so if
> you say you're going to meet for a coffee in the morning, they
> might turn up at lunchtime. You have to be prepared to sit
> there and not stress out. Take your watch off. I don't wear a
> watch over there. The locals gauge time by the sun. There
> was one time in Sumatra when I ordered lunch, and lunch
> didn't come till about four o'clock in the afternoon. It turned

out that she'd had to go out to the avocado trees and get her husband an avocado; in the meantime I had about four coffees and entertained myself. You learn to be patient, because things do take so long.'

EATING IN COMPANY

If you're invited to a family home for a meal, make sure the household can actually afford to feed you before you accept. At the very least, bring along a gift (perhaps a bottle of wine, or non-perishable food items that they may have difficulty obtaining).

Observe correct eating etiquette. If you're unsure, watch what others do.

❏ In some places, it's polite to finish everything on your plate. In others, clearing your plate indicates to your host that he or she has failed to provide sufficient food.

❏ In some countries, you're expected to scoop food up with your hand and eat with your fingers, in others, you may be expected to eat with unfamiliar utensils, such as chopsticks.

❏ In countries where the left hand is used for washing after going to the toilet, avoid using that hand for handling food or drinks.

❏ If food is set out in bowls and shared, it's polite to take only a little from each bowl, and to take food from the side of the bowl that's directly in front of you rather than reaching over to get the tastiest morsel on the dish.

❏ It's not essential to belch to show your appreciation, even in countries such as China where this is an accepted practice. It's just as good to show your appreciation by thanking the host, commenting on the unique flavour of the dish, or asking for the recipe.

FESTIVALS AND CEREMONIES

If you are invited to attend a festival, celebration or traditional ceremony, find out beforehand what's involved – don't just turn up. You may be expected to bring a gift or offering and to dress appropriately. At some religious festivals, for example, you may be required to wear a special 'temple scarf'; at other ceremonies, women are not allowed to attend when they're menstruating. Ask a local for advice on dress codes, offerings, behaviours and restrictions.

Don't join in traditional or religious rituals unless you're specifically invited to participate. Even then, be careful to do only what you see other women of your age doing, or you could unwittingly break a taboo or offend the gods.

> 'We were usually in shorts and T-shirts, because we spent most of our time at resorts and beaches. But if you're going to visit temples, you have to dress correctly, be aware of the traditions. You have to appreciate what everyone's doing around you and try to do the same.'

COPING WITH CURIOSITY

In remote regions and places where there are few tourists, expect people to be curious about you, and accept their inquisitiveness with good grace and humour. Rather than being defensive, attempt to satisfy their curiosity and answer questions openly.

> 'Travelling across Zaire, local people thought it was a novelty just to see white people, and would come up to you and stare. They were so curious.'

> 'In Asia, local people always come up to you and say, "Where are you going? Do you know where you're going?" You get a bit fed up with them after a while

because they want to talk to you all the time, but it's a good way to start a conversation. If you don't want to talk, you just have to be polite and say, "Thanks, but I think I can do this on my own".'

'China was a totally inquisitive society – they were fascinated with the way you looked, how you dressed. The fact that I was a smoker was a constant source of amazement for everyone, 'cause women just don't smoke over there – let alone roll their own. They're just completely fascinated by our culture. I was asked a lot of questions about how I lived, what was different about Australia compared to China. It was hard to explain the differences but I tried.'

'In villages I got a friendly reception. People kept their distance, because they're generally a bit unsure about you, but they still came over. They have what's called "staring squads" in China – I'd read about it in books but couldn't comprehend the full meaning of it till I got there. I'd be standing somewhere watching someone making noodles, or eating in a restaurant, or writing a letter, and before I knew it, there'd be 20 people standing around, watching what I was watching. They stand quite close to you but it's completely non-threatening – they just want to watch you.'

'I travelled alone quite a bit in the Philippines, where the local people are very, very friendly. They'd always say hello and "How are you?", even in passing. The next thing they'd always ask is "Where is your companion?" or "Why are you by yourself?" They seemed to find it extraordinary that I was on my own. I guess it's because in their culture, they like to share all their experiences with somebody.'

Allow people to touch your hair, laugh at your pale skin, try on your funny hat, listen to your Walkman. You're doing the same thing to them, when you take photos, marvel at their traditional clothes, act as voyeurs to their lives.

'In villages in Asia, the kids would always crowd around me, asking questions and wanting to look at my camera and my clothes and everything I was carrying. I didn't mind it – I used to practise language with them and teach them English. You had to watch that they didn't take advantage of you – they often ask you to give them money or your watch – but it was lots of fun.'

'I visited a remote hill tribe on the border of Thailand and Burma where they didn't get many Western visitors. I wanted to take a photo of this kid, but he looked very unsure about the whole thing. So I went over to him and showed him the camera, and let him look through the lens. He loved it – he was fascinated. I don't think anyone had ever shown him how a camera worked before.'

'I know that on my own I'll get hassled, poked and stared at and giggled about. There's nothing you can do. It's not that you're exposing yourself to danger, it's just that you're such an oddity in other cultures.'

If it all becomes too much, claim tiredness, go to your room and close the door, rather than losing your cool.

'In Indonesia, you're surrounded by thousands of people. It can be frustrating, 'cause sometimes you just want to be alone. That's when I close the door to my bedroom.'

'Indians are so curious it drives you mad. There are so many people, and they're always touching you and following you and asking you questions. They don't mean any harm, so I tried to be polite and take it all in a good-humoured way, but it can get very wearing. Sometimes I just had to escape to my hotel room, turn on the fan and chill out.'

ACCEPTING HOSPITALITY

In many countries, hospitality to strangers is considered a virtue, and people will often go to great lengths to make you, the visitor, feel comfortable and welcomed.

'Indonesian women are really generous and warm and they'll do anything for you. There's such a huge gap between their lifestyle and ours, but it doesn't make any difference. They do stuff for you because that's the type of people they are.'

'I met some really hospitable people in Australia. Two guys I met in Cairns told me if I was stuck to give them a shout – I'd only known them a week. I actually stayed at their house a couple of nights when I was broke. I'd also met two Irish girls in Cairns, and even though I only talked with them for a short time, they invited me to stay at their place in Sydney. So once I'd stayed with the guys for a few days, I stayed with the Irish girls. I was there for a couple of weeks without paying them anything, until I got a job. I ended up moving in and we became the best of friends. It was really good of them to do that for someone they'd known for 10 minutes.'

'When I was hitching round Japan, families would often pick me up, and we'd get talking, and maybe the kids would know a few English words and I'd know a few Japanese words, and they'd invite me home for dinner. Their hospitality was amazing.'

'I flew into Jordan and got dropped at the El Al office, and there was a gorgeous woman in the office waiting to find out about flights. We got chatting and she said, "Come and have some food at my house", so I went back there and it was absolutely heaven on earth. She and her family were so welcoming.'

In places where people are poor, this kind of hospitality can cost them dearly, so it's important that you pay your way and don't exploit their generosity. Even if they insist you stay in their home or share their meal, it doesn't mean that they can afford it. It may be OK to stay for a night, or for dinner, but don't take advantage of their hospitality unless you have some means of repaying the kindness.

'In Asia, people were particularly concerned about me being alone – it was one of the first things that came up in conversation. Because I was on my own, I was invited a lot to people's houses and asked to share with them in what they were doing. I found it extraordinary and touching that they were so willing to share everything, although most of them were very, very poor people. I tried to make sure I brought food with me, or repaid them in some way, 'cause I know they had very little to give.'

'An Indonesian woman I met on a ferry invited me to stay at her house, but when I got there, they didn't have enough beds. The woman, who had a problem with her back, said, "You sleep in the bed and I'll sleep on the floor." I said, "No, I can't take your bed", but she wouldn't hear of having it otherwise: she physically put me in the bed. So I shared the double bed with her daughter and she slept on the floor. The Indonesian people's generosity goes to such extremes that it's embarrassing. And they don't expect to be repaid. If you want to thank them, send them a letter or a postcard or take photos of them and send them prints. They're great letter-writers; they love correspondence.'

'In Japan, people tend to take you under their wing and treat you as a daughter, so it can be a struggle to plan an independent trip. People immediately want to take you into their family, and you can get stuck in a place for two or three weeks when you only intended to stay two or *three days. They insist that you stay on. It's common courtesy to give your hosts something in return. You don't have to, but it's polite to do so.'*

HANDLING POVERTY

In many parts of the world, people live in harsh conditions. Witnessing their poverty, illness, oppression and despair can be hard to take. As individuals, we feel we can do so little to help. And if you're not part of the solution, it's easy to feel like you're part of the problem. Along with compassion and outrage, travellers faced with extreme human suffering often experience feelings of guilt. We are affluent Westerners, and this is made so clear to us when we're travelling. What we spend on some trinket could often feed a local family for weeks.

'In Zaire, you could trade empty bottles for beautiful carvings, because they needed the money. It was sad.'

'As far as the Chinese people were concerned, I was very wealthy. Which I'm not by a long stretch. In their terms, I was – I earn in a day what they earn in a month. But your cost of living is higher. So we tended to side-step that issue a bit, and not talk money or hard figures, because you don't feel that you can achieve anything by it.'

'In the Philippines, you notice so much the difference between rich and poor – more than in Thailand or Malaysia or Indonesia. It was so glaringly obvious, this absolute division between the filthy rich and the filthy poor. I was shocked.'

'A Filipino girl I met in Manila kept insisting that I come home with her to the local village. I was hesitant – but she really did insist. So I went. When we got on the bus,

I started to realise that it wasn't just because she wanted to share with me: she also wanted me to pay her bus fare, and then pay for some things, and it turned out her father was in hospital and the family needed financial help. At that point, I realised that she had an ulterior motive. When we got there, the whole village was there to greet us. I was a real novelty. I stayed with the girl's family and was shown around and went to see the father in hospital. It was all a bit surreal – and difficult to deal with. So many people want help, and there's only so much you can do. You're passing through, and you're touching on these people's lives, but in the long run, you're not going to be there to do anything for them.'

'There's a huge class system in China. The poverty is terrible. It's something that you come to terms with but it's still very hard: there are the rich people and the peasants. And people everywhere – I've never been to such a densely populated country. How could I, one little person with not very much money, help so many? I just felt overwhelmed.'

You can help by allowing people their dignity. Regardless of a person's situation, treat them with respect and help out however you can. Be sensitive to people's material circumstances when accepting offers of food, help or hospitality, and even if people insist they don't want payment, reimburse them somehow.

'It's hard to give people money, but you have to try to buy them food or things like that. Just something to repay their kindness, because often, they'll still insist that you eat with them when they really can't afford it.'

'I took over some souvenir pens and postcards to China, and if anyone did anything for me, I'd give them a pen or a postcard, and they'd think it was fabulous. It was a small gesture, but it was something.'

Some travellers set aside a certain sum to give away to people in need each day. Others don't give anything to individuals, but choose instead to support an aid organisation or foster a child in need. Even if you have nothing material to offer, you can help by joining an aid project and doing some community work (see pages 307–8).

> 'When I'm travelling in poor, Third World countries, I don't give much to beggars on the streets, because it's so endless and what I could give would be like a drop in the ocean. But I do try to help in more formal ways. I support a foster child in Honduras, one of the poorest countries in the world. I give money to self-help overseas aid organisations like Community Aid Abroad. And I do volunteer work for Amnesty International. As a privileged Westerner, I feel obliged to help, even if it's only in a small way.'

BEING POLITICALLY SENSITIVE

In countries with very different political systems from our own, it can be rude – or even dangerous for you or for your hosts – to talk about politically sensitive topics. Avoid getting into trouble or causing offence by:

❏ reading up on the politics of the countries you'll be visiting, so you don't naively rush in and make inflammatory statements

❏ asking locals what is appropriate to discuss and what shouldn't be talked about

❏ only discussing sensitive issues if a local person introduces the topic, and even then, adopting a noncommittal or conservative line

❏ obeying official directives, even when these seem trivial

❏ not taking photographs of any activity or installation that could have a political purpose.

'In Israel, I made a big political decision – suddenly, while I was there, I realised that I was pro-Palestine. I actually had to reverse everything I'd thought about how wonderful Israel was, and how the kibbutz system was fabulous and so on. It took a lot – in the face of all these gorgeous people I was working on the kibbutz with, who so believed in the things they were doing in their country – to stop and think, This is really not OK. Israelis are very passionate about their politics, so when the people I met would go on about Israel, I'd either have to be silent, or state my point and then have to talk about what I believed in – which they didn't want to hear. It was really the end of me being on the kibbutz. If you can't go with the flow, it's not worth it.'

'I was careful of what I said in China. They can be very cagey about the politics over there, or the class system, or anything to do with the structure of their society. So I tended to steer clear of those topics in conversation. Because I didn't know who I was talking to, and I didn't want to put anybody's nose out of joint. So if they didn't bring it up, we didn't talk about it. We just talked about other things. I was also cautious about taking photographs in what could be considered politically sensitive areas. I always made sure to ask people if I could take photos before doing it. In Guangdong, in southern China, a very green, lush, beautiful place, surrounded by limestone peaks, and lots of mists, these guys were playing this card game which was really interesting and I wanted to take a photograph, so I asked them, and they said no. We found out later that the game was semi-illegal – you could play it, but you weren't really supposed to. That's why they'd said no.'

'In China, I tried to make sure I didn't overstep the line. In the smaller cities, you weren't so conscious about that sort of thing, but in the larger cities, because they have so many *more foreigners and are so densely populated, there is a bit of crime, and the People's Liberation Army don't tend to be as friendly as they are in the smaller centres. There was only one time I felt uncomfortable – in Beijing, two days after the anniversary of the massacre. At dusk, at Tiananmen Square, they fly kites: hundreds of the most colourful, beautiful kites you've ever seen, and I went down there to buy some. The whole square was blocked off and there were police everywhere. It was a really spooky feeling. It was like everything you did was being watched. You're watched doing everything anyway, under normal circumstances, but at that time, they were being exceptionally cautious about everyone – Westerners, males, anyone going onto the square. I felt like something could go off anytime.'*

AN OPEN-HEARTED ATTITUDE

Don't pre-judge or presume. The behaviours or beliefs of the people you meet may seem strange or even opposed to your own, but that doesn't mean that you're right and they're wrong. Many Western travellers, subconsciously or otherwise, assume a superior stance – they believe that they're more civilised or more sophisticated than people from cultures that are less 'developed' than their own. Let go of concepts of 'better' or 'worse', 'superior' or 'inferior', 'primitive' or 'civilised' – they're neither useful nor unifying.

Be human and humble. If you start off with an arrogant, superior attitude, you'll be forced, sooner or later, to change your views and swallow your pride. Travel has a tendency to broaden your perspective. Contact with very different cultures and belief systems will challenge your socialisation and undermine your assumptions, altering the way in which you see yourself and others. It will make you realise that there are many different definitions of success and happiness, and many ways to survive in the world.

'The girls in Manila were great – they all wanted to talk. They wanted to know what Western guys were like, and what it was like for me being a woman from the part of the world they were longing to go to, to escape from their poverty. It really made me think about my privileged position in the world – it broadened my perspective.'

'Seeing the way other people live, and the way you live, as a Westerner, makes you appreciate the value of what you have – and of what they have. Whenever I see something better on my travels, I think, "Is there a reason why I can't have that, or live like this?" It sends you looking for other things.'

'I learnt a lot about my weaknesses, travelling. Because, especially when there's a language barrier, people tend to be very blunt. Sometimes they tell you things you don't expect to hear! I also learnt to be a good listener, because if you don't listen properly, whether it be to directions or advice, you invariably look back and think, "Oh God, I should've really paid attention to what that old man was telling me".'

'What I like about travelling is that it brings you down to earth. You see that these people are so happy with what they've got – and they've got nothing, they're so poor. And you realise you don't need lots of material things to be happy: you just need family around you and good friends. The idea of happiness being people-centred, of how little you need for basic survival: you can put those concepts into your own life.'

MEETING PEOPLE

For many women, the most enjoyable part of travelling alone is the opportunities it gives you to meet and to get to know people with very different cultural backgrounds, beliefs and expectations.

'I would never in my wildest dreams have met the people I met had I been with another person, male or female. People told me, "We came up and spoke to you because you were on your own".'

'The contacts I've made around the world mean I can go most places and know people there that I met last time I travelled in India, or wherever. I have friends in just about every country.'

MEETING OTHER TRAVELLERS

Encounters with other travellers can lead to lasting friendships or memorable experiences.

'There's a sort of loyalty that travellers have to each other.
When people travel alone, they form close bonds very
rapidly. It's a special kind of friendship that builds up in a
very short period of time. You never find that if you're
forming friendships in your own country. The whole
framework of how you make friends is completely
different.'

'I met people all along the way, people who'd travelled for
so long and seen so much. I was so naive when I first
went, so I would just sit there listening to them and going
"Wow!" I learnt so much. I'd even make notes, and
annotate my guidebook with their tips on where to stay
and where to eat. I got loads of good information from
other travellers.'

'Once I was sitting in a taverna in Corfu, having a glass
of retsina, and some people at the next table started
chatting to me. Eventually they said, "We're going to
dinner, do you want to come?" They were English, and
they were going to a birthday party for Suzanne, the girl
out of the Leonard Cohen song. They said it'd be
spectacular. So I went, and Leonard Cohen was there.
Here was I sitting there, at a long table with about 45
people, a young thing who'd only been on my own for a
few days, thinking, "No-one's here to see this except me –
no-one's going to believe me." Sometimes when you're on
your own, you need a little camera or tape recorder, just
so you can record the experience and say, "I really did do
it." Those sorts of things would never, ever have happened
to me if I hadn't been on my own.'

Even if it's just temporary companions you're after, it can be fun to share a hotel room for a couple of days, or link up for a meal, a night out or a shopping expedition.

'I would meet people and go on little adventures for three or four days, usually from a base. We'd go off to a nearby city or go sightseeing. I found the best short-term companions were other girls. Put up a notice at hostels or tourist cafés, or ask around for companions – there'll usually be one or two people interested.'

'It wasn't a problem at all finding people to hook up with – you'd bump into someone, get chatting, realise that you got on fairly well and say, "Which way are you heading?" I'd tag along with different people while we were going the same way, then be by myself for a while. I'd sit back on a beach and relax, gather my energies again, and then go off somewhere on my own or meet somebody else to travel with.'

'I found it really easy to meet people in Australia, especially as I was going to a lot of backpacker-style pubs, where people tend to let go of their inhibitions and everyone lets their hair down. I also had more confidence, because I was travelling.'

Joining forces with other travellers can make your trip safer and more economical: you can share a double hotel room, the cost of hiring a guide, or your taxi fare home from a nightclub. You may even decide to travel together for part of your trip.

'In LA, I decided it'd be safer if I went out in company so I went into the common room of my hostel, where a bunch of travellers were watching TV, and said, "Does anyone want to come nightclubbing with me? I have a car, and I'm going soon." This little guy from Manchester who I'd never met pops his head up from the couch and goes, "Fantastic.

> I've been so bored, I'm waiting for me mate to arrive from
> London. I'll come with you." He became my clubbing
> partner for the next four days. We drove all over town
> looking for places to find good music and interesting people.
> I would have done it on my own, but it was reassuring to
> have a guy with me. Some of the clubs we went into –
> some of the best ones – were in pretty seedy locations, so I
> appreciated his presence, even just walking from the car to
> the club. And we had a lot of fun. He was just a friend and
> never hassled me for anything else. I appreciated that too.'

If you stick to the tourist trail and follow the advice given
in popular guidebooks, you're bound to cross paths with
other travellers, in hostels, Ys, railway carriages, beach
resorts – even in remote areas.

> 'I was on a two-day ferry trip travelling from Jakarta to
> Sulawesi. There were over 1000 people on board and I
> was the only Western woman. There were all these
> rumours going around: people were touching me and
> telling me that there was "another Westerner on the
> boat". We eventually met up – a day later, because it was
> such a big ferry.'

> 'I was scared when I landed in Thailand – I didn't know
> what I was in for in an Asian country. I was scared of
> being hassled, being on my own, being raped. I went
> there planning not to have a big rage, just to lie on the
> beach. But I met people straight away.'

> 'All the travellers in Australia seem to be doing the same
> route, so you keep meeting up with the same people all the
> way. You might stay with them for three days on Fraser
> Island, then you may not see them again till Cairns, then
> they'll turn up again in Darwin. It was really sociable. At
> the end of the day it was one big party, and then everyone
> went their separate ways.'

In most instances, overtures from travellers are genuine. But just because someone speaks English, carries a backpack or stays in the same hostel doesn't mean you should treat him or her like an old friend. Be cautious about committing yourself to joint arrangements. Before you make plans to cross the Atlas Mountains together, make sure you like and trust your new-found companion.

MEETING LOCALS

Locals can show you a side of life you'll never see if you just hang around the tourist traps with other travellers. Establishing common ground may take some fishing around initially, but it is possible to breach cultural barriers and forge deep and genuine friendships.

> 'I've got many dear friends who I met in Indonesia, and I don't think I'd have them if I hadn't been on my own. I wouldn't have spent as much time with them; I wouldn't have needed them as much; they wouldn't have needed me. I'm not very good at keeping in contact, but I go back and see them when I can.'

If you want to make contact with local people on your travels:

❏ Take the time to chat with the people you meet – hotel and restaurant staff, market stall owners, taxi drivers, tour guides, students, kids.

> 'I didn't meet many locals in transit. It was more when I was in the villages, walking around, with the time to talk to people.'

❏ Find local haunts and frequent them – you'll find yourself recognising faces and getting to know the staff and regulars.

> 'I was travelling alone, but I can't recall ever having to go into a restaurant and sit down to eat by myself. Because as soon as I was in a place, I'd meet people. I'd meet the other people who were staying in the same guesthouse or hostel, and I'd find my little local place to eat, and there are always going to be other people there. And in most parts of Asia, especially the Philippines, the local people hate to see you sit there by yourself, so you get invited along with them.'

❑ Go shopping. Local women often work in shops or behind market stalls, and in this relaxed, semi-private setting, they may be more inclined to strike up a conversation.

> 'I was walking down a laneway and happened to spy some stuff in a little corner shop. I went in looking, started talking, and next minute, I'm upstairs with the family having dinner. Two hours later, I've had dinner and someone else is there, and everyone's crowded around like I'm some sort of new toy. Those are the kinds of opportunities that happen to you when you're alone, but hardly ever do when you're with other travellers.'

> 'It's always good to leave out some things when you pack, because it keeps you shopping. I always have a shopping mission – usually a gift to bring home for someone. Once, I bought a fishing rod; another time, I bought special brushes for my mother, who likes to paint. Or something that I want to buy or repair that involves a deal of work, like getting new spectacles fitted, or fixing shoes. I have tasks to do that take me out on errands around the place, so I get to know the walks. Even if I'm just in a place for a few days, local people nearby will start to get to know me.'

❑ Try speaking the local language, using a phrasebook when you get stuck – it can be a good way to break the ice. Often, local people are as keen to practise their English as you are to learn a few phrases in the local tongue.

'In Turkey, I'd always take my phrasebook with me when I went out and I'd use it to try to communicate with the villagers, who spoke minimal English. The locals thought it was really funny – on one occasion I had about 20 kids and half a dozen women laughing at my pitiful Turkish – but it was a great way to get people to relax around me. They'd start off correcting my pronunciation and end up inviting me to stay for dinner.'

'In Italy, I'd often get out my phrasebook in cafés and try things out on the guy behind the bar. I'd ask things like "Where is a good disco?" and "Is this a safe area?" so I wasn't just practising my Italian, I was also finding out stuff I wanted to know. He'd correct my pronunciation and answer my questions, and I'd teach him a few phrases in English. It was fun.'

❑ Establish common ground: show people photos or postcards from home; ask them about their families, their work, their lives; play with their children; get them to explain things you don't understand about the culture or customs.

'In Indonesia, a lot of kids come up to you. Instead of saying, "Go away, you're annoying me", I'd always turn around and play with them, or sing a song, and they'd follow me down the street. They'd get such a kick out of it and it'd give me a real high, too. In Indonesia, it's so open. The whole community looks after the children. So you can pick up a two-year-old and walk around with it in your arms and the parents don't freak out – they love it. It's that sort of society.'

'I always carried photos of my husband, my family, my godson and nephew. People loved looking at them, and it was a good way to make them remember that you were a normal woman with a normal relationship and a family, not some brazen Western hussy out to snare a local man.'

'I found that asking people questions about their culture was a good way to start a conversation. It's better to talk about stuff that interests you than to make silly small talk. And you get the sort of information you can never pick up from guidebooks.'

❑ Don't just take photos – talk to the people you want to photograph. Not only will you get a better picture, you might make some new friends.

'If you go somewhere and you want to take a photo, always ask first, and always offer to send the person a copy of the photo. People just love it – they really respond to it – and it's a good icebreaker, too. If you send the photos, they'll probably even write back to you.'

❑ Get off the beaten track. You're more likely to meet locals and get invitations to community events and family homes if you stay in villages and beach resorts rather than cities, in family-run hotels or homestays rather than tourist hotels.

'I met a local girl who lived two doors down from my hosts in this village on Mykonos. Through her, I met a lot of other people, from that town and from a neighbouring town. We'd all go out on motorbikes, and I just kept meeting more people. I ended up staying there three weeks, and it wasn't long enough.'

'If you want to meet locals, get yourself a good guidebook with cultural information in it. And get out of the cities,

into the rural areas. Don't stay at expensive hotels or eat at expensive restaurants. In the down-market places, it's more communal. If you're by yourself there, you'll meet other travellers as well as locals. Having some knowledge of the language helps, but it's not crucial. It's in the small places off the tourist trail where you'll get opportunities to take part in local activities and be invited back to people's places.'

❑ Have an open, friendly attitude to the people you meet, and be enthusiastic in your responses – appreciation is always appreciated. Be positive and you'll get more invitations.

'All the locals I came in contact with, men included, really wanted me to like their country, their island, their town. It was obvious I loved being there, and in return for my enthusiasm, I got a lot of free drinks and free meals. You get so much more attention if you're a single girl. You get it so much easier.'

'People are so open to me when I'm on my own, and it's because I'm more open. When you travel, you give off a sense of "I'm as excited about being here as you are to have me in your lounge room." And people pick up on and respond to that.'

INTERACTING WITH LOCAL WOMEN

As a lone female, you'll have no trouble meeting men, but you may have to make special overtures if you want to get to know the local women. In conservative, patriarchal cultures, such as exist in many Islamic countries, men dominate public life and it can be difficult even to make contact with local women. A woman who's busy working, minding the kids or doing the family shopping, and who speaks no

English, isn't all that easy to make contact with. But this doesn't mean that she doesn't want to know you. It's just that her circumstances don't give her much of a chance to socialise with foreigners.

> 'It was harder to meet women in Greece – I met more men, and got a lot more help from men. Women were always inside, or working, and a lot of them didn't speak English.'

> 'In Pakistan, it was virtually impossible to meet local women. They just weren't out and about. If they were on the streets, they were all covered up and going about their business. They certainly weren't sitting around chatting with Westerners.'

> 'I met lots of local women travelling in Japan, but that was the exception. In most countries, you meet more men. Local women don't tend to get about on their own, without families or friends or security.'

Remember that most women, particularly in traditional and developing countries, are so burdened with work and family duties that they have few opportunities to meet travellers. Even when they do, the interaction may be limited by shyness, lack of a common language (local women are less likely than men to speak English), and by the fact that they'll almost certainly be busy – doing housework, cooking the meals, looking after children, or working to boost the family income.

> 'In Indonesia, the women are at the heart of the family and do everything: all the work, bringing the kids up, and keeping the economic situation at bay. They control the finances. The women are strong – men are the lazy ones. The men will go off and play chess and stuff. It's the same in a lot of developing countries.'

'China's a society that's not used to women, particularly Western women, travelling around. Women over there aren't really recognised as much as women in our society. So on my travels, I mainly met men and other foreigners. Very few women approached us to speak – it was all men who wanted to practise their English.'

'In Morocco women were around, but it was difficult to approach them. On the streets they don't look you in the eye and they always look like they're on a mission, or they're talking to other women or looking after kids, so it's hard to make contact. And most of the people you deal with in shops and markets and hotels are men. Maybe if you went to the more Westernised cities like Casablanca or Rabat and hung around the universities, you'd meet women that way, but you don't get much chance to meet them in the normal course of events.'

'In China, all the people who chatted to me or offered to help me were males. I was amazed that no females came up to me or wanted to talk – they just sat back in the background and did their own thing. They would serve me if I was buying something and do all those things they'd normally do but they wouldn't take the time out to actually come and talk to me, whereas with guys, there wasn't that reticence. At one restaurant in a very small town, the whole kitchen came out and sat around the table to watch me eat. But there were no women at all.'

Meeting local women may require special efforts on your part. Increase your chances of making meaningful contact by:
- going outside of large towns and tourist areas and into villages
- organising to spend time with local families
- seeking out local women in situations that give you a chance to interact: markets, family-run hotels, women-only train compartments, women's baths

> 'In Asia, I found it easiest to meet local women in shops, markets, hotels or restaurants – somewhere where you can get the chance to speak with them initially. If you get them in a situation where they have a bit of time to chat, they're usually really friendly.'

> 'I was on a boat going from one island to another in Indonesia. I was in a six-berth cabin and there were five other women in with me. When you're in that sort of situation, the women really, really look after you. I got invitations to go back to their places, offers to show me around. When we arrived, they did a lot of things for me. They took me out, we tried all of the local cuisine, they made me stay at their homes.'

❏ dressing and behaving modestly so as not to embarrass or offend: in traditional or strongly religious cultures, women (particularly older women) may be more conservative in their attitudes than men

> 'Western Turkey, around Istanbul, is very liberal, but further east, they're strongly Muslim peasant people and they really are covered up. The people's attitude changes a lot if you cover up too. You get respect from the women.'

❏ focusing on points of commonality: family photos are a good way to start a conversation
❏ using a phrasebook, gestures and smiles to get around the language barrier
❏ talking to younger women – they often speak some English and may be less shy about talking with travellers than older, more conservative women

> 'In Greece, it's still very old-fashioned in the villages. But the girls my age were really warm and friendly, and very similar to me in their ideals. They were a bit frustrated about living in the villages – that repressive small-town

thing where you have to watch everything you say and do. But they were very open-minded, and they all spoke three different languages and had all these aspirations. There are a lot of rules but they get around them. The village girls all had boyfriends on the side, but if, for instance, a girl's brother was at the same nightclub, we'd have to be much more conservative about our behaviour. There's a lot of hiding it from the family, basically. But the girls know how to have fun. They were great.'

'In Estonia, I was sitting in a pizza joint and a girl about my age came over and put a note on my table. It read, "The guy at my table wants to know what book you are reading." He wanted to chat but we had no common language. So I ended up talking with the girl. She spoke very good English and was so friendly. She said, "I'd love to show you around my country. I'll drive you here, I'll drive you there." She was talking about driving to the beach resorts, the mountains, everywhere. Unfortunately, I had to leave the next day, or I certainly would have taken up her offer. I had offers like that from women all over Europe – they really want to be hospitable.'

❑ remembering that women, especially in Third World countries, usually have lots of work to do. If you're staying in a family home or in a village, offer to help with daily chores or childminding.
❑ participating in the activity of a local community – working can be a great way to make friends with local women. If you can't get a paid job, sign up for a stint of voluntary work at a child-care or medical centre, English school or aid agency.

Once you've broken the ice, you'll find that women all over the world are welcoming and helpful, supportive and protective, and that there are common bonds between women that transcend cultural and language barriers.

> 'In the Third World, I found women very friendly. Particularly if you just sit by yourself – or squat, like they do, on the side of the road. They'd often come up and sit beside me out of curiosity, or I'd go and sit near them and chat to them. I don't remember a negative encounter of that nature, any time. Sometimes the conversation would be brief or they would be embarrassed, or, because of their caste system, they wouldn't be able to look you in the eye, but other times, it would be like you weren't there, or you were one of their mates, and off they'd go, la-la-la-la, chatting away about themselves, and what they were doing, and how many kids they had, and why wasn't I married, and why didn't I have any children. They were really interested in talking to someone from outside their culture, once you made the overtures.'

'Honorary male status'

Gender roles differ from culture to culture – in more traditional, patriarchal societies, a Western woman travelling alone doesn't fit the prescribed female role. In some cultures, local people may deal with this dilemma by treating you as an honorary male. You're expected to sit, eat and talk with the men, while the women and children of the household hover silently in the background, waiting on you and cooking your meals.

It can be difficult to sit back and allow yourself to get special treatment while other women do the work, but to insist on being treated similarly to local women could cause difficulties and might be perceived as a slight to your hosts.

If possible, find some way of spending time with the females of the family and helping out. If you're told that the women don't need any assistance, be persuasive. Express a desire to learn how to cook a particular dish, ask to be allowed to mind the kids or hold the baby, or accompany the women to the market.

'In the Golden Triangle, I stayed with the chief of an Akha village and his family. When I arrived, they sat me down in the main room with the men and then the women started preparing a meal around an open fire in the floor. I got to eat first, with all the men of the household and my male guide, then the women cooked a second meal and they and the children came in and ate afterwards. Then the women disappeared into the back room and I sat around and talked with the men. They came out later dressed in full traditional gear and asked me to take photos to send back to them. But that's really the only contact I had with them. The next day, I made a point of going along with a couple of the women of the family and helping them collect food and firewood. They were very friendly and funny; we got on really well and felt comfortable in each other's company, even though they didn't speak much English. They just don't get the chance to talk with travellers, normally, because they're always working while the men laze about.'

INTERACTING WITH LOCAL MEN

Women travelling without male companions may attract particular attention from local men. This can range from simple curiosity to genuine offers of protection, hospitality, guidance or friendship, to overt or covert sexual advances or harassment.

'You get no shortage of men approaching you when you travel. Just walking down the street, people will follow you. You have to learn to be relaxed about being the focus of attention.'

'As a female by yourself, guys hassle you, and too many of them want to help you. You have to be careful about the offers you accept. But you meet some good people, too.'

It can be difficult to maintain an open, friendly attitude in the face of persistent pestering, or where sexist attitudes and actions create uncomfortable or threatening situations.

Even when it seems like men are threatening rather than welcoming, try to keep your cool and maintain an open mind. Attempt to understand where people are coming from before you overreact. Most situations are harmless if you deal with them appropriately.

> 'Around the Mediterranean, a lot of the men were sleazy, but I just fobbed them off. You have to be strong and stand up to them. I got my bum pinched by some old guy: I turned around and gave him a dirty look, then just ignored it. I never felt really threatened.'

> 'European men don't hold back, they're very vocal and they'll pinch you on the bum. But I didn't have a problem with them. Some of them were a bit scary, a bit suspicious, but I just stayed away from those ones.'

You don't want to be so trusting and naive that you fail to recognise a potentially threatening scenario. But neither do you want to get so closed off and cynical that you refuse friendly offers and fob off genuinely nice guys.

> 'One night on Mykonos, two Greek guys spent the whole night trying to get me and the girl I was with back to their place. They were using all sorts of lines and we were just laughing and fobbing them off. In the end they gave up. But they were really nice about it. They said, "We'll walk you to the main square: it's pretty hard to get a taxi from here." They paid the taxi fare and everything. They were real gentlemen.'

> 'Normally, I tend to be more comfortable with women, because I don't feel threatened by them. But most of the

people I met who became very good friends were males.
They were non-physical relationships – most were fairly
intellectual.'

'I met a guy in LA who took me out to dinner a few
times. It wasn't a romantic thing, I just liked his
company. I didn't feel at all threatened, because I'd met
him in his workplace in front of some other people, and I
got an honest vibe from him. We became good friends.
Once I even stayed at his place for the night. There was
nothing sleazy about it: I slept on the couch and he made
me coffee in the morning, then took me around to buy
CDs and stuff. He drove me to the airport and even paid
my departure tax. So you definitely can meet nice guys in
big, bad cities.'

Sex and romance
Provided you practise safe sex (see pages 274–5), there's
nothing wrong with indulging in a holiday fling or two.
The exotic can be very appealing – but cultural differences
can complicate matters, too. It helps if you and your
friend share a common language and have some understanding of each other's society and attitudes, particularly
with respect to sex and relationships. Even in a casual
affair, cultural and language barriers can make for misunderstandings. Try to communicate your needs and intentions clearly *before* you get into bed.

'I got propositioned by local men who were so sweet and had
looks to die for, particularly in southern and eastern Europe,
but I just couldn't come at it. Conversation is too important
to me, and I only speak English, so I'd always say no.'

'I was in a club on Ibiza and this gorgeous man tried to
pick me up. If we had had a common language, I
probably would have chanced it. But he was from the

> Ivory Coast in Africa and spoke virtually no English, and
> I didn't want one of those "situations" to arise, especially
> since some guys don't like wearing condoms. So I decided
> to play it safe and go home alone.'

In some countries, men don't like to wear condoms – they
see it as a slight to their masculinity. You have to be
assertive, and the sooner you raise the issue, the better.

> 'Getting Asian men to wear condoms is like getting an
> Australian man to wear a skirt. It's much harder than in
> Australia. They take it as an affront to their male
> sexuality. They think you think they're not clean. You
> have to make it clear beforehand that you want them to
> wear a condom. Don't leave it till you're in bed with
> them – it could be quite dangerous.'

> 'Emphasising your desire not to get pregnant is not helpful
> in getting African men to wear condoms, because their
> male virility is bound up in getting a woman pregnant. A
> lot of African men think that if you have sex with them,
> you have to have a baby.'

> 'I had quite a few romances while I was in Europe and
> the States. I spent most of my time in London and New
> York, where men aren't all that different in their attitudes
> to women than they are at home. I never had any trouble
> getting guys to wear condoms – well, no more than I'd
> have at home.'

Women travelling alone often wind up having flings with
local men or fellow travellers. Have fun while it lasts but
make sure you don't abandon common sense. Just
because you're sharing a bed with someone doesn't mean
you should let down all your boundaries. You're away
from your usual support network, so you need to take special care of your physical and emotional self.

'I met a guy from Israel who was travelling the same way I was. We hooked up for a few weeks, had a fling, and it was great. He was a lovely guy but I made sure I kept my feet on the ground. I never expected it to be a serious thing. I'm glad I didn't, too, because I just would have had my heart broken. It turned out he had a girlfriend back home.'

'If you're having a one-night stand, you really just have to make sure you do it somewhere safe and he wears a condom. As long as you have those things sorted out, you can't come to much harm – unless you fall in love!'

Don't become careless with your valuables, either – it's unlikely, but women have been known to wake up the morning after to an empty bed and an empty money belt.

'It might seem paranoid, but even when I went to bed with someone, I'd still be on the alert, because I was in traveller mode. You can't let down your hair completely, even in a sexual situation, because you have all your important documents on you and you can't be 100 per cent sure of any person you don't know well. I always knew exactly where my passport and money were and made sure I could lay my hands on all my stuff, get dressed and get out of there in a heartbeat if I needed to. You have to look after yourself any time you sleep with a stranger, but it's especially important when you're travelling on your own.'

Don't ditch your travel plans to follow some guy you've fallen for, or tie yourself to travelling in tandem. Holiday romances are by their very nature transient: you don't want to be stuck somewhere godforsaken with a guy you hardly know once the romance fades.

'I met some gorgeous men in Europe but the only fling I had was with an American traveller. We were waiting to *catch the same ferry to the Greek Islands and we got talking – I felt like I'd known him for years. We ended up sharing a cabin, he offered me a massage, and you can guess what happened from there. All I'll say is yes, we did use condoms. We had a great time together for four days. Then he wanted me to come to Turkey with him, but I decided to stick to my original plan to go to Italy. I was tempted to go with him but the romance was already starting to wear a bit thin and I decided I'd rather be on my own again. We swapped addresses, though, and we keep in touch.'*

'I had a couple of short but sweet affairs with Spanish guys. I speak pretty minimal Spanish, but I never found communicating a problem in that situation. In a short fling, you don't have many deep and meaningful discussions. They were both nice guys. I kept in contact with one of them and have been back to visit him twice. He's not a lover any more but he's become a friend.'

It's naive to expect holiday romance to last – but you can't rule out the possibility of a strong and serious attraction. Many lasting relationships have resulted from chance encounters in exotic places.

'I met my husband on a trip to Bali. He was an artist in Ubud, and I was over there trying to set up a clothing import business. We got to know each other through mutual friends, and I found him so loving and good-humoured and such a genuinely nice guy that I just couldn't help falling for him. It took a few years for us to realise it was a serious thing – I kept going back to visit and we got more and more attached to one another. Eventually we decided to get married, he came to live in Australia with me and we opened an Indonesian restaurant. We're still together and now have a beautiful daughter. We go back to Bali for holidays.'

'My fiancé and I met on a bus tour of New Zealand. He's Australian and I'm British. We spent nine days together on the tour, and got on so well we ended up hiring a car with a couple of other people and spending another week together driving around the South Island. Then we went our separate ways and agreed to meet up in Australia. It was obvious that there was something serious going on. We ended up living together.'

Refusing offers

You'll undoubtedly have to turn down some men's offers – either because the situation seems unsafe or unsavoury, because you've made other plans or simply because you're not interested. There's no need to be rude when refusing an invitation. But do be direct: you don't want to mislead him.

'I have girlfriends who will just accept a guy's offer, make an arrangement and then stand him up. I don't like doing that. I think it gives people the wrong attitude about foreign women, that they're a pain in the arse and dishonest. I'd rather be direct.'

'In Paris, I met two young French guys in a park. We got talking and they seemed pretty nice. After a while, they said, "Come with us, we have a car and we'll show you all around Paris, then go out on the town later." It was a good offer but I refused, because I didn't know them well enough. I thought, "Once I'm in a car with two guys, there really isn't much I can do if they want to take me somewhere I don't want to go." I refused as politely as possible, but I think they were a bit offended 'cause they could tell I didn't trust them.'

'I met a French doctor about 65 years old who wanted to take me to a resort in Portugal for two weeks for free, and all I had to do was be company – I didn't have to do

anything sexually. I thought about it, and decided to say no. It was a bit suss.'

'Greek men can get really angry and can become quite violent if you reject them. You mightn't have been doing anything to encourage them in the first place, but the mere fact that you were there, drinking in a bar, and you're a Western woman, is enough for them to think of you as an easy conquest.'

'I arrived in Venice and spent about two hours walking around with my backpack on trying to find my pensione. A guy came up and said, "Can I help you?" I told him I was trying to find this place and he said he'd help me. Together, we found it. But of course, then it was, "So what are you doing tonight? Can I take you out to dinner? Can we go for a drink? Blah, blah, blah." I said, "Thank you very much for helping me, but no. I'm really tired and I don't know what I'm doing tonight." It's a case of being polite but firm. Even if they're really annoying you, it's not worth getting angry, because that can provoke a reaction from them and things can escalate.'

Setting limits

It can help to set a few 'personal safety limits' when you're socialising with strange men. If you know that you *never* put yourself in situation X, Y or Z, you're less likely to do something foolhardy in the heat of the moment – or after a few drinks.

Where you choose to set your limits will depend on how confident you feel about your ability to handle various situations and on the culture you're in. You may have to put more restrictions on your behaviour in a strict Muslim country than you would in Europe. If you have solid self-defence skills, you may feel comfortable in a wider range of situations.

'In Indonesia, it's hard to pick the genuine accommodation offers from the sleazy ones. If the invitation comes from a guy, you generally have to decline, because if you accept it, he thinks you're accepting him rather than a room in his house.'

'I know I've probably missed out on some fantastic dinners and opportunities by saying no to men when I was on my own. But I've weighed up the pros and cons and decided where my limits, my boundaries lie. My rule is that I won't go with men alone. I'm not confident enough to do that, and the one time I did, it was disastrous. But I'd go back to a woman's place for dinner.'

'I make a rule never to drink or take any drugs except caffeine when I go out with people I don't know. So I always have my wits about me. I know I'm not going to get drunk, forget where I am and end up in some dodgy club on the wrong side of town, or in bed with some strange guy in a strange country.'

'In my opinion, the only people you meet on your travels who you should be going out with are those you're introduced to by people you already know. People you meet through a business or personal contact, people you meet at the place you're staying, or people you meet on a plane or train journey. Never anyone you meet on the street. I might miss opportunities by following that rule, but I don't care.'

WHO DO YOU TRUST?

Often, women travellers are warned that you can't trust anyone you meet, that people don't help you unless they have an ulterior motive. It's smart to be wary of total strangers who promise over-the-top favours, but silly to be so paranoid that you pass up offers that could lead to exciting encounters.

> 'I've never had a distrustful attitude. I don't think it's a good idea to be too cautious – you have to take a few risks. If I get a good feeling about something or someone, I just go with it. If I get the slightest bad feeling about someone, I avoid the situation, 'cause it's not worth it.'

> 'You can tell whether someone's coming on too strong, or what they're really interested in. Genuine people will talk to you about their country, and ask why you're travelling and things. It's like at home, when you meet a guy in a pub – you quickly get an idea of where they're coming from.'

> 'The first time I travelled alone I was probably too adventurous on a number of occasions. I had a very positive outlook on people, and didn't calculate how other people might take certain situations. You learn pretty quickly when to trust and when to say no.'

Relying on your gut instincts may seem like a crude method for judging people and situations, but it can be a surprisingly sound way of separating sharks and shonky situations from good guys and genuine offers.

> 'You can tell whether someone can be trusted, unless they're an excellent con man. There's a special mentality you have when you're travelling: your instincts are finely honed.'

> 'Because you have all your money, your passport, your livelihood on your person, you get very conscious of someone who's acting strangely or edging a bit close. You feel it. I'd love to be able to have that mentality all the time, but you can't. At home, everything's familiar: you don't need to be sharp in the same way.'

Unless intuition tells you to steer clear, view offers of help and friendship as genuine and go with the flow. Most of the friends you make on your travels, and some of your most memorable and rewarding experiences, may come from taking a chance on a stranger.

'In India, my girlfriend and I stayed with the owner of a gem store for a couple of nights. She'd met him on a previous trip through a family contact. We were staying at his place in Jaipur, eating his food, going out to the Sheraton for lunch. At the end of it I found out he was married and had three kids: they were away on a holiday. But he never approached us sexually. He was quite genuine.'

'You have to be a bit careful, especially with guys – lots of them want to talk with you and chat you up. It's easy to get cynical and assume they're all after one thing. But I met some very nice men on my travels. And I made some close friendships with men where there was nothing sexual between us.'

'One time I ended up on the back of a motorbike with a bunch of uni students riding around a volcanic mountain. I guess it was a bit risky, but they seemed like a safe bunch of people, and I trusted them and they were fine. You have to do those out-there things occasionally – they're all the stories!'

'Travelling solo, I tend to go off the beaten track more, so I'm forced to make more overtures towards people. You get more invitations, too. I tended to hook up with local people who were in the know and have faith in them – you have to take those risks, sometimes. You need to be streetsmart to an extent, but for me, trusting people always paid off.'

Some people do have ulterior motives, but they're usually as innocent as wanting to practise their English, get a bit of extra cash or show off a Westerner to their friends.

'A lot of people wanted my address so they could write. I gave my address to one girl and did actually write to her a few times. But fairly early in our correspondence, things started to come up, like could I help her to come to my country so she could get better schooling? Stuff like that. And you think, yeah, I'd like to help you, but . . . There's a limited amount you can do.'

'Sometimes I had second thoughts after accepting a local's offer. You're stuck in someone's house drinking tea all afternoon while they parade you in front of their friends and introduce you to lots of people. It's a prestige thing – their "celebrity" status goes up if they're friends with a foreigner.'

You may get fleeced of a bit of cash, but provided you steer clear of dodgy offers, drug deals and dubious men, your encounters are unlikely to land you in serious trouble.

'You have to have your wits about you. In Bangkok, this Thai couple approached me wanting to show me the sights. I was so innocent I thought they were genuine, but before long, they'd started asking for money. I came to my senses and said, "No thank you, I'll do it by myself." As I walked off, another guy came up to me and said, "You're well rid of those two", so I guess my instincts were right. But you have to start off treating people as genuine, otherwise you never get to meet the locals or have exciting experiences.'

'I arrived in Sicily and was trying to get to a hotel on the far side of the island. The public transport system isn't great. I'd met an Irish guy on the plane and he came up *to me at customs and said, "I've met this English couple who are hiring a car and can give you a lift to the other side of the island." So the English couple, who'd never even met me, and were middle-aged and seemed OK, gave me a lift. We had lunch on the way and they took me all the way to my hotel and wouldn't let me pay for anything. So people do look out for you. Whenever I was thinking, "Oh God, I hate doing this stuff – I hate being on my own", someone would shine down on me and make it all so easy. You never forget the kindness of strangers.'*

PERSONAL SAFETY

There's a myth about solo female travellers: that they need to be especially tough to survive. But if you have a positive, streetwise attitude, prepare yourself physically, follow your intuition and use skills you already have, you're unlikely to wind up in trouble.

> 'You take the same precautions in any city as you would at home. You wouldn't go to a very seedy area. You wouldn't deliberately expose yourself to danger. That's the same all over the world. You apply what you know to new situations.'

> 'You can always have bad luck, but in general, the people I know who've had bad travel experiences tend to be people who did things they wouldn't normally do at home. They'd do things like wander down the streets alone not knowing where they were going at three or four in the

> *morning, and that's when they'd get attacked. Some people let their guard down when they go away and think that it's all OK and they don't have to worry about anything. But you are left to your own devices – there's no-one there to look after you – so it's important to be well prepared.'*

> *'I do overseas what I do in my home town. The rules I use walking around my own city at night are the ones I take travelling and apply when I'm on the street in a foreign country. I've honed these abilities to precision over years of travelling. My advice to other women is, if you feel OK about being somewhere on your own, then you can be there on your own. But you need a game plan, you need strategies.'*

Women of all ages, levels of physical fitness, skills and strength travel successfully. The ability to floor someone with a karate kick is a handy skill, but it's not essential to your enjoyment or your survival.

> *'People assume women travellers are more vulnerable and can be taken in more easily. It's silly, because women who travel alone are usually gutsier and more streetwise than men in the same position. They are stronger and wiser because they have to cope with more day to day.'*

Most women have a great facility for talking their way out of threatening situations.

> *'I had some terrifying times, times when I was scared for my life. But I got out of them, and I got out of them because I used my innate skills. I was able to talk the person out of a hostile situation because I was confident in myself that I'd be able to get out of it.'*

A great many women also report that relying on intuition

and following your gut instincts is the best way to steer clear of trouble. And travelling solo helps to hone these instincts.

> 'One of the stresses of travelling on your own is meeting the right people. By making contact with people, you're putting yourself into a vulnerable position. You become more ruthless when you've been travelling for a while. You start to be able to perceive whether or not a person is genuine.'

> 'You get to sum up people really quickly when you're travelling on your own. It's an instinctive thing that you develop. Just by looking at somebody, I knew whether or not I could trust them. You might judge people mistakenly in some cases, but as far as safety goes, it's necessary. Whenever I went against my gut instinct, things went wrong.'

Wherever you go, use your common sense to keep you safe. Be aware, informed and sensible. Read guidebooks and ask locals and fellow travellers about local scams, safe and unsafe districts, and problems with crime or violence towards women. Forewarned is forearmed.

But take advice from others, especially men, with a sensible dose of scepticism. What a guy thinks is a great hotel, a cool club or a wonderful place for an evening stroll may not appeal to a woman alone.

> 'Men don't see the added problems we have because we're female. They tell us to go to certain places and give us advice which is valid for them – but it's not the same for us. You can't rely on the advice male travellers give you. You have to ask other women or suss it out for yourself.'

Remember that risks, unsafe areas and unwise behaviours vary from place to place, situation to situation. What's fine in one country may be asking for trouble in another.

> 'I'd walk around in my own country at night. But in a
> strange place, if something did happen to you, you
> couldn't go running to mum. So you have to be more
> careful.'

SEXUAL HARASSMENT

No society legally condones rape or assault. Even in cultures
that are reputed to be difficult for Western females, very few
female travellers report incidents of physical or sexual
violence. Your biggest worry isn't fending off rapists – it's
coping with low-level harassment on a day-to-day level.

Media stereotypes of Western women, previous encounters or wishful thinking lead many men from non-Western
cultures to view unaccompanied female travellers as sexually easy prospects.

> 'All the guidebooks say Japan is so safe, and it lulls you
> into a false sense of security. After the men in Muslim
> countries, I found Japanese men the worst harassers. They
> had very strange ideas about Western women. They have
> these really explicit, horrible sexual cartoons, and guys sit
> and read them on the trains. In most of them, the women
> who participate in all these weird sex things are Western
> women, not Japanese ones. So they have some very
> strange ideas about what Western women do, and they try
> to live out their fantasies on you. My saving grace was
> that I'm tall: most of them only came up to my shoulder.
> So they didn't hassle me much, but they hassled other
> Western women I knew. I had a lot of weird experiences
> there, not threatening, but intruding on my privacy in
> various ways.'
>
> ' "Australians and Americans come to Italy for the men" –
> that's what this Italian guy told me, and that was his
> approach. He wasn't good-looking by any means. But he

> *thought because I was an Aussie girl, I'd fall for him anyway. It was partly my fault for agreeing to go out with him.'*

A macho, 'conquest' mentality compels some men to intimidate or sexually harass women to make themselves feel more masculine, and this sort of behaviour may be endorsed by the culture.

> *'The attitude Indian men have developed towards Western women is that we're just the pits. They rank Indian males at the top, then foreign males, then Indian females, and Western females are way down below. It was never physically threatening. It was more a psychological imposition. They made you feel like a loose Westerner without even touching you.'*

> *'I had men wanking in front of me in various places – Spain and Greece were two of the worst countries for things like that. They just have no shame.'*

> *'I was on a bus trip through Indonesia and I was sitting next to a young local guy. He got out an English book and asked if I'd help him, and we talked for hours. Then I fell asleep. I woke to find he'd put a sarong over us both. He had his pants down and a hard-on, and his hand on my tit! I went off my brain. An old woman told him he was a naughty boy but she could understand it because I was a Westerner. She was blaming me for leading him on.'*

> *'In Cairo, at a big five-star hotel, I woke up in the middle of the night to find a bellboy standing at the end of my bed. He'd let himself in with the house keys, and was just having a good look. I said, "What are you doing?" and he ran out. In the morning, I told the concierge what had happened and he looked at me as though I was stupid, like "You're a woman alone. What do you expect?" '*

In some countries, you'll have to make a special effort to avoid inappropriate male attention. It helps if you:

❑ know what to expect in the countries you plan to visit. Read up on cultural and religious customs, male and female roles, attitudes towards and treatment of women.

> 'In the Hasidic area of Jerusalem, there are signs everywhere saying that women should be covered up and that you shouldn't be riding bikes or driving cars on the Sabbath and so on. So you're pre-warned before you go into those areas.'

❑ adjust your expectations according to the places you're travelling through

> 'I was told by lots of people that I'd get harassed by men in India, so I was prepared for it. If I had just come in cold, I think I would have found it intimidating. But because I expected it to happen, it didn't really faze me.'

> 'Cairo's one of those cities I knew I'd love, despite the hassles, and I did. It's such a hell-hole. It's so hot, and it's the dirtiest city I've ever been to. As far as men go, it's a very hard city to travel in. But there's something really raw about it. It's like being in the jungle, like survival of the fittest. You have to be on your guard. Men chase you down the street and grab you, and you fight them off.'

> 'There are some things you just can't do in certain places. Like you'd be foolhardy to walk around with skimpy clothes on in the Middle East. You can bitch and complain all you like about sexism and heat, but that's the way it is. You just have to accommodate or you won't have a good time.'

> *'Once you hit the Muslim countries in Africa, you have to be careful because the customs are so different from ours. For example, southern Sudan is African and northern Sudan is Arab: as you go further north, you can see the women getting more covered up; you get more stares. And the men become more sleazy.'*

❑ talk with other women who've travelled to places you plan to visit and ask them for tips on what to expect, how to dress and behave, where to stay and eat

> *'Once I got to Nairobi, I met up with so many people, especially in the hostels, and exchanged stories and advice. They were all coming south and I was going north. The majority were couples – there weren't many women alone. But they all said, "Be careful, use your common sense and you shouldn't have any problems." I followed their tips and I had no trouble.'*

❑ dress appropriately for the culture. Clothes that are perfectly acceptable at home may bring you negative attention in more conservative parts of the world.

> *'In Pakistan, it was pretty sleazy. A constant sea of people, nearly all of them male. All the women are covered up. You only really have to be covered to go to mosques, and because it was so hot, I didn't want to cover my arms and legs much. I was wearing skirts or shorts, and T-shirts that weren't revealing, really. But I still got heaps of stares. As a Westerner, I was so obvious.'*

❑ cover your hair, or become a brunette. Blonde hair singles you out for extra male attention in some countries, such as Italy and India. Long hair also attracts attention and makes it more obvious that you're female.

'South American men can be a bit hot-blooded if you're fair. The woman I was with was beautiful, with dark hair and eyes, but she wasn't the sort they went for. They made a beeline for me because I was blonde and blue-eyed. If you're fair, that's it.'

'The place I got the most harassment of the "Hey chicky babe" variety was in India. Because you're a white female with blonde hair, the men are always at you. I got a lot of hassle in India. Men were always touching me – they thought it was a novelty to touch a white woman's skin.'

'The blonde girls I spoke to in Pakistan had had a terrible time. The men there hassled me – and I was a brunette. So I can imagine how awful it was for blonde women.'

❏ observe how men and women interact and note the boundaries of acceptable behaviour. Make sure you don't send the wrong signals to men – non-verbal cues can differ dramatically between cultures. In conservative countries, just looking directly at a man or engaging in a casual conversation may be misconstrued as a sexual advance.

'I avoided making eye contact with men in the Mediterranean countries and in Turkey. They construe it as a sexual come-on. It's like asking to be harassed.'

'In Marrakesh, a local man came up and started talking with me in a café. He was a healer from the Sahara who did massage and read palms. He was really interesting and it was the middle of the day, so I wasn't worried. He started touching my arm while he was talking, in quite a natural way, and 'cause I like to give people the benefit of the doubt, I just acted like it was a normal thing to do – as it would be in the West. But it isn't normal in

> Morocco. The guy was so excited that this Western woman was letting him touch her arm that a giant erection rose up like a cobra from his baggy pants. I decided it was time to say my goodbyes. After that incident, I was careful about asserting my boundaries – not 'cause I minded, but because I realised that touching meant something very different to Moroccan men than it did to me.'

❏ have an explanation for why you're alone. In parts of the world where it's rare for women to travel unaccompanied, you may be viewed as an oddity, or even an outcast or whore. Take steps to help local people understand your purpose for travelling and your reasons for being alone; to let them know that you come from a culture where it is normal for a respectable woman to travel independently.

> 'In Asia, it's hard for people to understand that in the West, it's considered quite normal for women to travel independently. Unless you go to great lengths to explain it to them, they assume there's something wrong with you – that you're an outcast from your own society, or a prostitute. I would always tell them that I was there to visit family friends and do some sightseeing before I rejoined my husband, who couldn't accompany me for this part of the journey 'cause he was working. They seemed to accept that.'

❏ say you're married with children. In situations where people are aghast that you have no protector or are making unwanted sexual overtures, talking about a real or fictitious husband and children can be helpful. Carrying photos of your 'partner' and 'kids' and wearing a wedding ring makes your story more plausible. In more traditional, family-based

societies, women tend to treat you with less caution
and men with more respect if they think you're a
married mother.

> 'I have never been hassled by a man on a trip, not even
> in a nightclub. Normally, they assume that because I'm a
> certain age, I must be married, and I make sure I wear
> my wedding ring. I also dress conservatively and wear
> long sleeves.'

> 'In Malaysia and Indonesia, men hassle you all the time.
> They'll want to come up and say hello and talk to you,
> and they want a girlfriend. The best advice is to say that
> you're married, or you have a boyfriend and you're
> engaged. Then their interest becomes just curiosity. But
> it's not a violent thing. Because I knew where I was going
> and spoke the language, I never had any problems.'

❏ know your limits and plan your trip accordingly:
you may feel completely comfortable touring
Scandinavia or Eastern and Northern Europe
alone, but decide to take a companion when
travelling through Africa, South America or the
Middle East.

> 'I hooked up with a German girl I met on a bus to go to
> Morocco. I'd heard it could be a hassle for a woman
> alone, and I thought I'd be more comfortable doing it in
> company. She felt the same way.'

❏ don't automatically assume that all male attention
is sexual harassment – sometimes it's genuine
friendliness or innocent curiosity.

> 'There were a lot of drunken locals in the north of
> Australia, whites and Aboriginals. But they were harmless
> – you could push most of them over with a feather. I had

❏   keep an open mind. Even if you've had 999 dodgy
      offers, that doesn't mean all men are bastards. If the
      thousandth one seems genuine and you feel
      confident, accept.

Recognising hustlers and harassers

If you can spot them, you can outsmart them or avoid
them. Here are a few 'types' to be wary of when travelling.

Lotharios

There's the guy who begins with an innocent series of
standard questions: 'What's your name? Where are you
from? Where are you going?' and moves on to more intimate topics: 'Where is your boyfriend? Would you like to
go out with me? Have you ever had a Latin/Moroccan/
African/Balinese lover?' The best way of dealing with these
guys is to completely ignore the questions. If that doesn't
deter them, make a few personal enquiries yourself, such
as 'Where is your wife? Don't you have a family to go to?'
or 'Why are you harassing me?'

*'Getting off the ferry from Corfu to Patras, there was a
guy in a suit waiting for his car to come off the ferry. He
started asking me questions about myself, and after a
minute or two he asked me where I was going. I said,
"Athens", and he said he was driving there, too, and I
could come with him if I wanted. It was a much faster
way than going by train or bus. Then he said, "Are you
alone?" When I told him I was with a male friend, he
immediately stopped being helpful and the offer wasn't
mentioned again. It was probably a dubious offer.'*

Hound-dogs

Then there are the guys who follow you. Some trail you silently at a distance; others give a running commentary as they walk along behind or beside you, trying to start a conversation. Being followed is almost always harmless and is actually a sign of appreciation in some cultures. But it can be annoying and disturbing for the woman being trailed.

Ignoring the talkative follower usually does the trick: within a few blocks, most will give up if you refuse to be drawn into a conversation. To shake off a persistent trailer, walk towards a busier area. Turn and confront him if there are others around. Or find a public place to use as temporary refuge: a hotel, restaurant, shop or police station. Wait a few minutes, then continue walking once he's disappeared, or hail a taxi from there.

> 'In Italy, you sit in a café and you're never alone for more than about five seconds – you get surrounded. Often I'd get up and move on, but they'd follow me. Sometimes I couldn't get rid of them until I got back to my hotel.'

> 'On the Greek Islands and in the towns, I'd get young men – well, men of all ages – following me around at night. They'd latch on to me, flattering me and trying to get me to go back to their places for the night. But I didn't find it hard to get rid of them. You could just string them along, then tell them to go away.'

'Amateur' guides

Young men will often approach women on their own, claiming to be students wanting to practise their English. They may offer their services as guides in return for conversation. Many of these guys truly do want to better their language skills (as do most local people hoping to profit from the tourist trade). They may also be hoping to make a bit of extra cash from the 'transaction'.

'Student' guides can be informative and entertaining companions, and have the added benefit of stopping other men from harassing you. To ensure he doesn't get the wrong idea, make sure you:

❑   meet in public places, during the day
❑   don't accompany him to his home, car, private office or to remote places
❑   avoid being in any way provocative in your behaviour, dress or conversation
❑   make it clear that your affections are otherwise engaged. 'I'm married. My husband is a strong man. He does karate' are three sentences which are usually effective in deterring amorous advances. If he persists in turning the conversation to intimate subjects or is making you feel uncomfortable, tell him you don't want to talk to him any more.
❑   make it clear from the start, and at regular intervals, that you don't intend to pay him for his companionship or guidance, in cash or through sexual favours, so he doesn't get the wrong idea.

> 'In Morocco, you get continually approached by men wanting to act as your guide. They'd usually claim to be students wanting to practise their English, no strings attached, but it always turned out that they wanted money or sex. I used to tell them that I was married and had no money, then they'd leave me alone.'

Toyboys and gigolos

In some tourist areas, particularly beach resorts frequented by lone travellers (such as the Greek Islands, Bali, some parts of Africa and the Caribbean), local men keen to boost their incomes may act as temporary 'boyfriends' to foreign female visitors. These gigolos dream of snaring a rich Western girlfriend and using her to get a free ticket to the West. They're on the lookout for women on their own – and older, Western women are prime targets.

Some of these guys offer a pretty attractive package: holiday romance, sex and companionship – for a price. If you have some extra cash and feel like a fling, taking up with one of these enterprising local boys could be fun. If you do decide to indulge, go into it with open eyes, a good supply of condoms and a firm grip on your credit card; keep your wits about you, and don't make promises you can't or don't want to keep.

> 'There were lots of Nepalese guides in Pokhara who'd tell you they used to have an English girlfriend and they'd love to go to England, and wanted to get in your back pocket and get you to take them home to meet your mum and dad. You'd go into a café, and because Nepalese people are so friendly, they'd come up and talk with you and play backgammon. I met loads of those guys.'

Touts and hustlers
These guys are out to make money, and are unlikely to harass you sexually. They can be persistent and annoying, nevertheless. Fierce competition usually keeps hotel touts reasonably honest, and if you're stuck for a hotel room, the tout's offer of a free transfer to the accommodation he's selling can be an attractive option, especially if it's late at night and you're in a strange place. It's unlikely to be a scam or a rip-off. If in doubt, go with a tout who already has other travellers in tow.

> 'In Budapest, they have these rival gangs of hostel touts who get on the trains coming from Prague and try to get travellers to agree to go to their hostel chain on arrival. They come into the compartment and give you the whole spiel, with books of photos and discount vouchers and free transfers and everything. If you change your mind like I did, the other lot get really pissed off. It's cut-throat competition. But the hostels are really cheap.'

> 'In Fiji, hotel touts hang around the airport exit with little cards and books of photos. If you decide to go to their hotel, you jump in a minibus or jeep and off you go. It's really simple, and you don't pay any extra. The rates they quote are the same as the rates in the guidebooks.'

Hustlers frequent stations, markets and tourist sights with the aim of making money out of first-time tourists – by selling you goods at high prices, or by showing you around and encouraging you to buy things for which the hustler then receives a commission. If you're firm and don't let yourself be steamrolled into doing or buying things you don't want, the relationship can be mutually beneficial – but if the hustler thinks you're a sucker, he may try to take you for a ride. If you don't want a hustler's 'help', you'll have to get rid of him. And once he's latched on to you, getting rid of him politely can be difficult.

> 'Tangier is notorious for its hustlers, and even though I'd been warned, I still got sucked in. I had to spend a day there before catching the train to Marrakesh, so I put my bags in the station baggage room and was asking the station guy where the nearest bank was so I could change money. A man in his forties came up and said he'd show me. He said he was from the station and the guy behind the counter nodded so I thought, "Oh OK, just to the bank." But he latched on to me and insisted on showing me the medina, and going down all these tiny narrow winding laneways so I couldn't have found my way out without his guidance. He spoke very good English and was interesting, and he wasn't sleazy, sexually – he had a wife and kids – but it was obvious after a short while that he just wanted money. I didn't mind too much because I thought I was probably safer with him than wandering around on my own, and I'm pretty good at resisting pressure to buy stuff. But by the end of the day, I'd managed to spend about 10 times what I would normally

> *have spent. It was an interesting experience and I found
> the company entertaining, but I definitely got hustled.
> I felt like I'd been taken for a fool.'*

To deter touts or hustlers, be courteous but firm. Tell them you know where you're going and don't need their help. Then ignore further overtures. Don't vacillate or get into conversation – it only encourages them. It helps if you walk purposefully and look as though you know which way you're going.

> *'In Egypt and Morocco, you get guys coming up to you all
> the time offering to show you around or help you out. If
> you don't want a guide, you just say "No" really firmly
> in their language, and if that doesn't work and they
> continue to follow you, you tell them you have no money
> and don't want to buy anything. Then just keep on
> walking and if they talk to you, ignore them. Eventually
> they give up and go find another victim.'*

> *'The men in Kuta drove me mad trying to sell me
> perfume and watches. It's funny, because after you've been
> there a few days, they recognise you and stop hassling you
> and move on to the new people. I always had my
> valuables tied round my waist, and at first I always
> assumed people were out to steal my money, but after
> a while, I realised that a lot of the local people who
> approach you are just friendly, normal people. You have
> to be wary, but don't write anybody off.'*

Dealing with pesterers

Even if you try to blend in and downplay your feminine attributes, men may still harass you. In some countries, the mere fact that you're female means you have to deal with a stream of curious and attentive male 'admirers', and they can be incredibly persistent.

'Japanese men tend to get drunk, and in their culture
when you're drunk, you can do anything you like and be
forgiven the next day. But they don't have to be drunk to
hassle you. A friend from Sweden came and stayed with
me in Japan, and she's very big-chested. We were in a
café and there was a guy sitting at the table next to us,
with a newspaper over the table. It was a very narrow
space so he was quite close. My friend, who was facing in
his direction, said, "What's that guy doing? Why is that
newspaper jumping up and down?" He was sitting there
pulling himself. I suspect he was having a good view of
her chest and found it all terribly exciting. I walked up to
him, pulled the newspaper away and said, "What do you
think you're doing? Behave yourself! You're in a public
place." At which point you'd think he'd get up and leave.
Instead, he went to the toilet, and I don't know what he
did in there, but he came back afterwards and sat down
next to us again. He just wouldn't go away.'

Sometimes, you can just ignore it, laugh it off or enjoy the
game.

'In Italy, I didn't get approached or harassed, but I got
stared at and followed. I treated it as a bit of a game –
why stress out about it? One time in Rome, near the
roundabout with the huge columns, this guy was following
me, so I started hiding behind the columns. Then I did a
quick turn and went one way while he was going off the
other way. I saw him looking around trying to find me,
but he couldn't. I lost him!'

'I didn't find the men in Indonesia to be very aggressive –
the worst harassment is people coming up to you every five
minutes to say hello. It can be frustrating: you can get really
annoyed by little things like that. But you just have to treat
it as a game and say, "OK, how many times can a girl say
hello in a day? Five hundred?" It makes it a lot easier.'

At other times, it gets too much to handle. When a man's persistence proves problematic, try one of these techniques:

❏ Assert yourself: just say NO. Say it firmly, without denial or apology in your body language or tone of voice.

❏ Repeat your refusal several times, and if you can say NO in the local language, do so.

❏ Don't be embarrassed to raise your voice – or yell if you feel it's necessary – to attract outside attention or shame your harasser into leaving you alone.

> 'Women think they're so vulnerable, but I think we underestimate the power of turning around and saying, "Fuck off!" and shouting at people and running away.'

❏ Learn local ways to refuse invitations and to shame men who overstep the mark. Local women may be able to give you tips on the most effective ways to get rid of pestering men.

> 'In Italy, the men know how to hassle women travelling by themselves. They do everything – they hiss at you as if you're a dog, pinch your bum, follow you . . . But Italian men really appreciate spirited women. If I got hassled and said I was a feminist, the men would immediately back off. I thought that was a real joke – the first time, I only said it to see how it'd go, but it always worked.'

> ' "Get fucked!" is universal. It works everywhere. They know what you're saying. But you have to size up the situation before you say it. You wouldn't want to respond like that in a Muslim country.'

❏ Know what to say. Get a native speaker to translate useful phrases in the local language, such as 'Stop touching me', 'Go away', 'Stop bothering me', 'I'll

call the police', 'Help!', 'Rape!' or 'Shame on you!'
Write them phonetically in your phrasebook and
practise them as you walk around.
❑   Have a few self-defence skills up your sleeve.
Knowing how to defend yourself increases your
confidence and means if you're ever physically
threatened, you can fight back effectively.

> 'I was on a crowded Paris metro and I could feel this man
> bumping me from behind. I went Bang! with my elbow
> and he stopped doing it. I had to do something, because
> no-one else was going to help me out. No-one on the
> whole metro wanted to know.'

❑   Don't view men as the enemy. Even in places where
male attention is a constant annoyance, try not to
let it make you cynical, aggressive or defensive. Such
behaviour rarely deters harassers (in fact, it can
encourage a certain type of man) and it makes you
feel stressed and negative. Be polite but firm in your
refusals and most men will back off without a fuss.

> 'I got hassled by men on the French Riviera, but I didn't
> let it get to me. It was easy to get rid of them. They'd
> come up and say, "Hey, I've seen you round" and I'd be
> like, "Oh really? Bye!"'

> 'In Todja Gorge, on the edge of the Sahara, the men were
> sleazy. I was on a tour and we went to this hotel and had
> a big "Rocky Horror Show" party, where we all dressed
> up in sexy gear. Not surprisingly, we women got harassed
> by the local men. But we didn't make a big deal of it or
> get aggressive; we'd just politely say "Leave me alone"
> and the men would back off. They were OK, really – they
> just saw these sexy foreign girls and couldn't help trying
> it on.'

❑   Don't be embarrassed to ask for help: if someone's
     hassling you and there are others around, enlist
     their aid.

DEFENDING YOURSELF

Men are more likely to get attacked than women in most
parts of the world – particularly in cities. If you avoid isolated or seedy areas after dark, you should be just as safe
walking around as any male. You might get stared at or
hissed at, followed, chatted up or propositioned, but
such attentions are harmless in the vast majority of
instances.

When threatening situations do occur, most women
manage to extract themselves successfully, either by
talking their way out of it, running away or fighting
back.

Even though you'll probably never need to get physically aggressive, doing martial arts training or a course in
self-defence is good preparation for any independent journey. Self-defence skills help you to:

❑   project a more confident, less vulnerable persona
❑   recognise potential threats and remove yourself
     from situations before they become dangerous
❑   fight back effectively, if necessary.

'I'm sure self-defence training helps. I've done three and a
half years of aikido and that gives me a certain street
poise – an antenna for feeling things, too. I think you
tend to stay out of trouble better. You can recognise moves
that lead to aggressive moves – certain stances. And you're
quicker at reacting to sudden movements. Because that's
when you can lose your poise in a strange city – if
someone suddenly runs at you. Being centred in a
situation like that is an advantage.'

> 'I did six months of Indonesian karate. I didn't use it, but I felt heaps better for doing the course. I felt more confident in myself. It's being sensible – I'd recommend it for anybody going overseas.'

Self-defence courses

There are many self-defence training options available – some are geared specifically towards women; others offer broader training in fighting techniques and 'warrior' attitudes. Whatever course you choose, you'll need to make a regular class commitment and set aside time to practise skills. Regular, ongoing practice helps keep your body flexible and ensures the correct movements and techniques remain fresh in your mind.

Martial arts such as jujitsu, Thai kickboxing, wing-chung and tae kwon do focus on legwork, ground-fighting and speed or strategy over strength, and are thus well-suited to women. Training helps develop strength, fitness, flexibility and fighting skills; it sharpens reflexes and improves your focus. However, most martial arts take years to master.

Self-defence expert Penny Gulliver recommends that women take a specialised self-defence course before starting any martial arts training – that way, she argues, 'you develop a very practical context in which to apply martial arts principles'.

Specialist women's self-defence programs are probably the speediest, most user-friendly way to learn how to defend yourself. The best of them include commonsense strategies and simple, practical fighting techniques, along with the chance to engage in full-contact, full-force fighting with a heavily padded 'assailant'.

If you have the opportunity, sign up for a two-day Streetwyze training seminar, an intensive self-defence program based on the internationally acclaimed 'Model Mugging' program developed in the United States. The Streetwyze course is grounded in hard-hitting statistics, positive thinking and simple but devastating fight-back sequences, and is one of the most effective and empowering seminars of its kind. It's easy to learn and has an extraordinary success rate (of the 125 graduates in Australia who've subsequently been attacked, 123 escaped unscathed and over 50 knocked the assailants unconscious). Courses take place in most capital cities in Australia (ph 1-800-802 368 (toll free) or (07) 3367 3368 or fax (07) 3369 2768 for details), as well as in the United States, Japan, Germany, Switzerland, Mexico, Canada and South Africa. Streetwyze runs beginners and graduate self-defence seminars, as well as one-day TravelWYZE workshops, featuring techniques for outsmarting scammers and avoiding dangers while you're travelling. The Streetwyze hotline doubles as an advice line for travellers in trouble and crime victims.

The Australian Women's Martial Arts Federation holds annual training camps for women, at which you can try out a variety of styles and find the one that suits you best. The Australian Women's Self-Defence Academy runs women's self-protection courses anywhere in Australia, and can also refer you to self-defence and martial arts schools in your area. Contact them by phoning (02) 9130 8064 or faxing (02) 9365 6253. Information on self-defence training courses can also be obtained through your state's Department of Youth, Sport and Recreation, through Rape Crisis and community centres, YMCAs and women's information centres, or by asking at your local school or gym.

Self-help books

If you don't have time to do a course, at least read up on self-defence for women. There are a number of helpful books containing practical information, exercises and safety tips:

❑ *Penny Gulliver's Self-defence Handbook for Women* by Penny Gulliver (Hale & Iremonger, 1994)

❏ *Not an Easy Target: Paxton Quigley's Self-protection for Women* by Paxton Quigley (Simon & Schuster, 1995)
❏ *Defending Ourselves: A Guide to Prevention, Self-defence and Recovery from Rape* by Rosalind Wiseman (The Noonday Press, 1994)
❏ *Attitude: Commonsense Defence for Women* by Lisa Sliwa (Sidgwick & Jackson, 1987)
❏ *Stand Your Ground: A Woman's Guide to Self-preservation* by Kaleghl Quinn (Optima, 1983).

Attitude

Attitude is crucial to your ability to deter a potential aggressor or successfully fend off an attack. A confident, assertive stance generally works better than a passive, fearful or hysterical one. Don't be afraid – be angry. If someone is violating your personal space, you have a right to be! Then channel that anger into positive action.

'I've found myself in situations where I was shocked that something was being tried on me, and that shock and anger brought out assertiveness, which gave them an excuse to back off. If you're hesitant or too calm, it doesn't work. Having a show of outrage, but not aggression, is what's worked for me.'

'Not being afraid: I think that's really important. I didn't use any physical defence at any time but I was pretty confident. Just having that air of knowing what you're doing, even if you don't. Sometimes I'd meet women who were travelling who were really tense, uptight, and they seemed to attract trouble.'

If you are threatened, don't freak out. Take deep breaths, then draw on the self-defence skills that have been drilled into your psyche to fend off physical advances and hit your attacker where it hurts.

'You remember the kind of advice your mum gave you when you were a little girl: don't talk to strangers, don't accept gifts. My parents told me, "If you're ever in danger, go for the eyes and the balls – the two most vulnerable parts on a man's body." I've never had to do it, but I think those things get ingrained in your thinking.'

'There's nothing worse than feeling that sense of physical vulnerability, that fear of being threatened. If you're walking around after dark, you start worrying before you have to, before there's any danger. But if you know you have certain self-defence skills, it really enhances your confidence. It's a matter of confronting somebody before they confront you. You can reverse their whole script if you have the confidence to do so.'

STREETSMARTS

Each destination brings its own challenges and requires different responses, but if you follow a few ground rules, you're unlikely to run into trouble. You may not be prepared to stroll through the back streets of Naples late at night, or brave Cairo's bazaar unguided, but that's not being a wimp: that's being smart.

❏   Find out about local scams and unsafe spots, and heed locals' cautions. If you hear from a number of sources that a particular district should be avoided by lone females, give it a miss – or visit it in a group.

'If you're travelling through America on your own, especially in cities, you really need to do your homework. I was working in Chicago, which is similar to New York in the way that you can be in one neighbourhood, which *is quite yuppie, safe as houses, and you walk two blocks west and you're in snipersville. It can be dangerous. I did it by mistake one time – as soon as I realised, I wandered straight back again! You have to be really streetsmart about bad areas. As soon as you get into town, you need to find out from local people which are the places to avoid. Avoid those areas at night – it's pretty risky.'*

'The only places I've really had problems being a woman alone were in Malaysia, and a little bit in Indonesia, mainly in the Muslim areas. I was on my own a bit but I tried to stick with other people when I was going through those areas.'

'In Barcelona, the guidebooks warn you about unsafe districts, and they're right. If you find yourself wandering around alone in those areas, which I did one time when I was making my way back from the Miró museum on Montjuïc, you really notice the difference. There's more poverty, and people are hanging around on street corners and empty allotments, staring at you. You feel the risk. They're not pleasant areas to walk through. I walked fast and looked like I knew where I was going. It was OK because it was still daylight, so I used my sense of direction and the sun to guide me through – I didn't let it fluster me. But I did hang on to my bag.'

❑   Be vigilant in transit and when you first arrive in a new place.

'I always make sure I'm on the ball when I first arrive in a country. I check my guidebook just before I get to the station or the airport – they usually have an orientation section that tells you how to negotiate the various arrivals terminals. So as soon as I step out into that new place, I look like I know what I'm doing. That way, I'm not an easy target.'

❏   Get oriented as soon as possible.

> *'Always look as if you know where you're going. By taking out a map in public, you're making yourself open to a crime and announcing yourself as a foreigner.'*

❏   If you feel tired or under the weather, don't push yourself – lie low and chill out.

> *'If you've been up early and you've been walking around all day and you've had a lot of new experiences, it's not a good time to be going out, because you're much more susceptible to poor judgement, losing things, getting ripped off, getting lost, all those sorts of things, when you're tired.'*

❏   When out and about, stay alert to your surroundings and keep a firm grip on your valuables.

> *'Be careful walking around, especially at night. If you have to walk down a deserted street, walk in the middle of it, not down the sidewalk next to the doorways. And if you have keys, put them between your fingers.'*

> *'It's important to act confident and have your act together. Not to be flustered. And the obvious things, like not having your bag open when you're walking around. I'm very careful with my important documents. I wear a money belt.'*

❏   On the street, stick to areas where there are other people – there's safety in numbers.

> *'In Asia, everywhere you go there are people. So the fact that you can't communicate with them is a problem, but the fact that there's always somebody there makes it safe.'*

'In London, you can get away with walking around the centre of town until quite late. If there are plenty of people on the streets and you're feeling streetwise and confident, then it's OK.'

'It's amazing what you notice when you are walking alone. I'm always looking out for other people who are also walking alone, and if they're heading to the same place, and I'll often speed up so that I'm walking alongside them and start chatting.'

❑ When on the street, walk purposefully with a confident air, and look like you know where you're going.

'It's good to be alert, and being fit is important, because you walk such a lot. It's the best way to get around and I think one of the safest ways, if you can do it purposefully.'

'Even if you're walking down a street, lost, turn into the entrance of a house if you're followed, and make sure that person thinks you know where you are and what you're doing. Don't show you're scared of anyone. If you've got reason to be scared, act!'

❑ Trust your instincts about an area – if it feels unsafe, chances are it is.

'You can usually tell by the feeling whether a place is safe. Beware if there are no women on the streets. Rome is like that. It gets really sleazy after 10 p.m. All the women go indoors and it's just guys on the streets. You're constantly accosted. There's no point being out walking after that time. It's not safe. And you pick up on that really quickly.'

❑ At night, catch taxis and avoid walking in isolated or unsafe areas, such as red-light or slum districts, parks or beaches.

'When I was living in London, I used to get off the bus at what the locals referred to as the "dangerous" stop. It was dangerous, apparently, because you had to walk past three pubs to get to my street if you got off at that stop, whereas you didn't have to walk past any pubs if you got off at the "safer" stop. What they failed to recognise was that there was a whopping great park with no lights on the so-called safe route, where you'd have to walk almost three blocks of nothing. I felt a hell of a lot safer walking past those pubs than I did walking past the park. Sometimes you have to use your own instincts.'

'Paris is fairly safe if you stick to the popular areas, because there are so many tourists around. There are a lot of sleazy areas, though. You wouldn't want to walk in the Moroccan area – around the red-light district near the Moulin Rouge – at night. Men keep following you.'

❏ Check to see that you're not being followed when leaving places alone at night. If you think you are being trailed, turn and confront your shadow, walk (or drive) purposefully towards an open shop, a police station or a well-frequented area, or jump into a cab.

'I was in Barcelona with a friend. We were sitting by the harbour having a bottle of champagne and the whole time, I was aware that there was a guy watching us. We eventually got up and went wandering through the back streets to find a little tapas bar. I knew this guy was following us, whereas she had no idea. I was totally aware he was there; that when we'd got up, he'd got up. So I said, "Let's stop", and we stopped quite calmly and looked at him. He was much more uncomfortable than either of us, and obviously thought, "Well, I'll go now." That "other eye" you have watching out for you is something you develop by travelling alone.'

❑   Take care when walking down dark or lonely streets at night, particularly in cities.

> 'In Dar es Salaam, two girls who were staying at the same campground as me came back one night from town and said they'd been threatened by a guy with a machete who wanted money. They'd been told not to walk down a particular alley but they went down it anyway. They didn't give the guy their money, they just bolted. But they shouldn't have been in the situation in the first place. When locals tell you things like "Don't go here after dark", take notice, because they're usually right. You can always get a taxi from one end of the bad area to the other and it's worth it.'

❑   After dark, keep to busy areas, take taxis or team up with others.

> 'If I'm walking in a city at night, I stick to busy streets, preferably ones where there are cafés or clubs or shops and lots of people walking around. If I have to take a longer route to avoid going down a dark alley or through a dodgy area, I always do it. If someone looks like an unsavoury type, I'll go into a café or hotel, or turn around and walk in the opposite direction to avoid them. I don't take risks when I'm on the street, and I'm sure that's part of the reason I've never had any trouble.'

> 'In Western cities, I catch taxis or stick to well-frequented areas at night but I'm usually not at all worried about being out on my own after dark. In developing countries and places which have a reputation for crime, it's a bit harder. I'm more wary of going off on my own at night, so I usually try to team up with other travellers.'

> 'A city is a city is a city – they're all potentially dangerous, and you use similar strategies for staying safe whatever

> *city you're in. Don't walk down deserted streets or dark alleys, through parks or red-light districts, at night. If you see someone who looks sleazy, avoid them. If it feels unsafe, catch a cab. And wear sensible shoes so you can run if you need to. They're my rules.'*

❑ In more remote areas, carry a torch and know where you're going.

> *'If you're in a village at night, there's not a lot of street lighting and it gets really dark, so it's good to have a torch with you. I always wear a money belt for security. And I carry my Swiss army knife.'*

❑ Let someone at your accommodation know your movements and when you expect to be back, so if you don't turn up within a reasonable time, they can send someone out to look for you.

> *'You have to make people accountable – say something in front of witnesses. Get the taxi driver to come to the hotel reception and say, in front of the hotel staff, where you're going. That way the hotel people know where you're going, and the driver knows they know.'*

> *'In South America, the most hazardous thing for anyone travelling alone is that you could easily disappear. There were plenty of times when there would have been no trace of me if I had gone missing. If you're not on an organised tour, you should keep someone posted on where you're going, when you can.'*

❑ Don't get intoxicated unless you're in trusted company and in a safe environment.

> *'I never drink and I never take drugs while I'm travelling. Because I think being alert is so important. When you get*

into those states where you're not as aware as you normally would be, things happen. Your judgement's out. Relax when it's appropriate, in situations where you know it's going to be safe.'

'Drugs are one of the biggest problems when you're travelling. They're not worth it. You get stoned and you lose your whereabouts. And you don't know the rules. People can take advantage of you too easily. It's just stupid.'

❏ Be cautious about accepting food, drink or smokes from strangers.

'We were on a safari to Ngorogoro crater, and we got a night bus down to Dar es Salaam. There was a scam going on: people on the buses injecting oranges with tranquillising drugs and giving them to tourists, then robbing them while they slept. A lot of people offered me food but I always said "No thanks" because I'd heard about this scam. I didn't want to wake up in Dar es Salaam with no luggage, no travellers' cheques, nothing.'

❏ Avoid situations in which you're the only female, and when you're on your own, don't accompany men to isolated places, on picnics, in cars or into private homes.

'I feel reticent about accepting offers from a guy. I'd go to a restaurant with a man but not to a private home. I tend to not get into cars with men and not go to men's places unless there's at least one woman in the party. And if the woman leaves, I leave with her.'

❏ Once you feel confident and have a handle on the new environment, don't cower in your hotel room – get out there and experience it.

'I got more gutsy when I travelled: I adopted the "I'm in control of this" attitude. When other people were nervous, it reinforced my feelings of strength. If they said, "Oh, don't you think it's risky to go out here?", I'd be like, "Come on, don't be a wimp, we're going out." I met a lot of women who wouldn't go out at night in cities in Europe. I thought that was being too cautious. You can always find someone to go out with.'

'You rise to the occasion – your survival skills kick in and you just do it, the same as any man would. Now I've become stronger as a person, I travel differently. I don't rely on other people now, I'm quite happy to travel on my own. And I accept more offers. Because I know I can get out of any situation I put myself into.'

AVOIDING PETTY CRIME

As a traveller, you're a potential target for pickpockets, thieves and scammers. The contents of your backpack represent a small fortune to the average person in a developing country. Unless you want to spend your entire trip worrying about being ripped off,

❏ keep valuables to a minimum. Try not to travel with anything that's irreplaceable (your heirloom Rolex, your genuine '60s biker jacket) or you'll spend your entire trip worrying.
❏ carry documents, credit cards, travellers' cheques and extra cash in a secure inside pocket or money pouch; and sling your daypack diagonally across your body, gripping it in front of you
❏ make sure you're adequately insured for loss or theft.

Avoiding thieves and rip-offs

Where robbery is the motive, people don't care what sex you are. The key to not being targeted is to heed advice, take precautions and stay alert.

To minimise your likelihood of being a crime victim:

❏ Time arrivals for daylight hours, especially if you haven't pre-booked accommodation. Take a taxi to your lodgings or to the tourist district rather than negotiating public transport with all your baggage.

> 'I would often travel early in the morning. I'd get up at 5 a.m. to catch the first train, if it was a longer journey, so that I travelled in the daylight hours and arrived before nightfall. And I think that saved me a lot of anguish. There were only one or two times I arrived anywhere late at night.'

❏ Know where you're going and what you're doing. Look assured on arrival and you're less likely to be targeted by hustlers who prey on disoriented tourists.

> 'I don't like getting to a place and having no idea of what I'm doing, so I always have a guidebook of some sort. I just don't feel comfortable travelling without advice on where to go and stay. When I arrive, I like to have at least some inkling of where I'm heading, so I don't look all lost and vulnerable.'

❏ Don't burden yourself with baggage. If you can easily handle all your gear and keep a hand free, you don't have to depend on others for help and are less of a target for thieves and touts.

> 'The time you're most susceptible is when you're in a situation where you have to rely on someone else, and therefore you don't have the choice of using your instinct.'

*That could be not knowing where you're going, or not
having much money, or carrying too much luggage –
anything that you need help with. Make sure you don't
have to be reliant on someone you don't know.'*

❏   Don't stand out as a wealthy Westerner by wearing
     expensive watches, accessories or running shoes.
     Keep documents, travellers' cheques, credit cards
     and cash under your clothing in an unobtrusive,
     safe spot.

*'In South America, you have to be prepared to stash your
valuables very well, and have a bit of money out to give to
anyone who tries to rob you.'*

*'In New York, I never wore jewellery or a good watch –
I wore an old plastic scuba diving watch. And dressed
down, like the locals. Leather jackets and street gear are
fine around Manhattan. You're better off not carrying a
bag – if you do, wear the strap across your body and keep
it in front of you. Walk purposefully, and don't look up at
all the buildings and gaze around like a tourist. Then all
the locals will think you're one of them.'*

❏   Become a daytime person.

*'I became an early-to-bed, early-rising person, and I
found that helped me avoid any problems. I got up at
some ungodly hour of the morning – five, six – I'd never
do this at home – and hit the streets of Florence and just
wandered around, and it was the most spectacular time.
I was completely by myself, it was so quiet, there was all
this history and amazing stuff. It was very emotional,
very heart-wrenching for me. It was great to realise,
"I'm having a fantastic time – I'm by myself and I
love it".'*

'For travelling, the morning can be one of the best times of the day. It's really great to get up early, before things get going. You get to see the city coming alive. You've got a different reason for being there. It's good to go out at night, too, but that usually will create itself. If you don't push it, you'll meet someone or you'll be introduced to someone. And because you've waited for the natural time, the right opportunity to go out in the evening, you often have a fabulous time.'

❏ Heed tips on how to spot con men, thieves and scammers. Locals and fellow travellers can advise you on what to watch out for.

'On a bus trip in Greece, I met a Cypriot girl on holiday. We got by with the bit of Greek we both knew. She was forever saying, "Honey, you have to watch out for this or that." She seemed to know all the tricks. Every time the bus stopped, for instance, she'd go down and watch the luggage so no-one disembarking would pretend it was theirs and steal it. She told me about all the local scams – I don't know how real a threat they actually were, but I was glad to have her there.'

'You have to be cautious. People I met worded me up on the scams, so I was lucky. I was careful with my luggage, not leaving it with people. Even in supermarkets, people will occasionally try to rip you off 'cause you're a foreigner: at one place they tried to short-change me $10. Because you're not familiar with the currency they think you're not going to notice the difference. I always check my change.'

❏ Be vigilant in transit, particularly at busy bus and train terminals and on crowded transport.

'I was walking into a station at night with my backpack on, and these guys rushed at me. They pushed me against

> *a wall and I couldn't move to take my pack off. I was in
> the process of getting my pack undone and they just
> slashed at me and I fell backwards. It's like upsetting a
> tortoise, and putting it on its back. Once they've done
> that, there's nothing you can do. Luckily someone came
> past and they ran off. But it made me realise that a pack
> can make you vulnerable.'*

❑   Don't get so paranoid about being ripped off that
     you're scared to move. If you've packed sensibly and
     take reasonable precautions, the worst you're likely
     to lose is books, clothes, toiletries, your camera or
     your Walkman – none of which are irreplaceable.

> *'Everybody who goes overseas is going to get something
> ripped off once or twice, especially if they're travelling for
> a long time. It goes on every single day. I had stuff stolen
> from me. But I also had great kindness done to me at
> other times.'*

> *'I only ever got ripped off once in the whole time I was
> travelling, and that was having my washing stolen off a
> clothes line. I think it was partly having an attitude that
> it wouldn't happen to me.'*

TROUBLE SPOTS AND SAFE HAVENS

Some places are notorious for crime. If you're travelling
through poverty-stricken areas, war zones or in countries
where law enforcement is erratic or corrupt, you'll have to
take special care to guard your belongings and your person. Take heed of guidebooks' and locals' warnings about
unsafe areas and scams – they're usually right.

> *'South America is notorious for scams, especially theft.
> There are lots of things that people who've been there*

*before teach you to do: like trying not to be on the streets
on your own – have a buddy system so you can look out
for one another. And when you're taking a photo, get
someone to watch you, 'cause you're particularly
vulnerable at that time.'*

*'I heard a lot of stories about Mexico being unsafe and
I don't speak Spanish, so I did my first two weeks there on
a camping tour, then spent three weeks on my own. I
found it so easy, I was surprised. I think a lot of the scare
stories must be about Mexico City and I didn't go
anywhere near it.'*

*'A friend and I went to Rio, and you know that if you
have anything valuable with you it's just going to go, so
you make sure you don't carry anything. We never got
into an uncomfortable situation because we took the right
precautions.'*

*'I was in Nairobi walking along the street, wearing a gold
chain – a really thin one, but it was gold – and I had my
hair up in a ponytail. A guy came up, grabbed the back of
my neck and ran off, and I realised he'd stolen my chain.
A few days later I was walking along with my purse,
gripping on to it, and a guy ran past and whipped it out
of my hand. A few locals did try to nab him, 'cause when
I yelled, they saw I was a white female and realised what
had happened. But I said, "Don't worry about it." There
were only about three US dollars in the purse – my
valuables were round my waist. Those two incidents shook
me. But Nairobi's that sort of place – they nickname it
Nairobbery. It was a place where I should have been more
aware and not gone around by myself.'*

*'I had trouble in Italy. Italian men probably don't mean
harm, but they scare you – they grab you and grope you,
and they whizz by on those bikes. I always feel like my*

handbag's going to get stolen. I spent three days on my own in Rome and hardly went out. I just thought, "Nup, I'm not having fun here", so I moved on, up to Florence and Perugia, and that was fine.'

'The worst place for crime was in the Central African Republic. I was on a tour, and people would literally try to get the water tanks off the back of the truck we were riding in. The tour manager stupidly left all the money lying in the front of the truck one time, and they just smashed the window and stole it.'

'I don't know that I'd travel through South America by myself, because I'm not strong enough, physically, to fight off the tackles – and you need to be able to defend yourself 'cause they'll tackle you, any time, anyhow. If you've got money, they'll try to get it off you.'

'LA's a pretty scary city for anyone, and it's even more so if you're alone there. I only spent a couple of days there and on one of them I spent the day at Universal Studios, which was great – and safe. But LA just has this feeling, this ambience of "Keep your wits about you, you're in a tough place".'

'I travelled through Sumatra with another person, and I'm glad I did, because I think it would have been tough going for a woman by herself. Tourists weren't all that common and there were some pretty strict Muslim areas. It was OK when you got somewhere and stopped, because there'd usually be more tourists around, but it wasn't easy when you were in transit.'

'In South America security is so bad, even travelling in a group. You constantly see people getting their bags slashed and stolen, people getting pickpocketed right in front of you. I had a fantastic time, but I was continually aware of the danger.'

Other places have such a reputation for being safe that it's easy to become complacent. While it's great to be able to relax, it's still a good idea to observe normal precautions.

> 'New Zealand's an easy place for a woman on her own. Its society is very similar to Australia's, and not much different to travelling in Australia. But I still wore a money belt and watched my stuff.'

> 'In China, everyone who said they would help me didn't rip me off and was really, really good. The only thing I had to watch out for was hanging on to my bag getting on to a packed bus, but you'd do that anyway, anywhere.'

> 'In Scandinavia, I never felt endangered or sexually threatened, even for a moment. Everyone was so civilised, even the kids seemed well behaved. I heard stories of people who left bags by mistake in public places, came back and found them still sitting there. You could never do that in most countries.'

And some countries yield mixed reports: one woman will have no trouble at all travelling through them; another will find them threatening and uncomfortable.

> 'In Thailand, I felt completely comfortable – I never felt threatened or in danger. I thought it was a really safe place for women to travel – then I heard the horror stories.'

> 'I was working as a tour leader in north Thailand and got held up at gunpoint by a bunch of guys. It was really out there. I think they were waiting for the Thai guy I was walking with – he may have owed them some money. They came around the corner with guns, and he ran off and left me. I didn't understand the language well enough to know what was going on. I hid in the bushes

for about half an hour until they went away. I remember being able to hear and smell everything; I was so alert. I have no idea how far a gun can shoot, but as soon as I decided they were out of range, I ran. I held it together for three days, then went back to the company in Bangkok and said, "I'm not going back there." I have my limits.'

'I felt very safe on my own in the Philippines – I went island-hopping to some very out of the way places there. In Thailand, I stuck more to the beaten track.'

'I would suggest being very cautious with your valuables in the Philippines. I got ripped off three times, and I wasn't a novice: I'd travelled quite a bit before I went there.'

'I went to Amsterdam and didn't see any sleaze or get offered drugs on the street, but my girlfriend went and said she got harassed on every street corner and found it a really scary place. I guess it's different for everyone. I didn't find it threatening at all. I'd walk along those quaint cobbled streets and look at those bridges and think, "How can you feel unsafe here?" '

DEALING WITH AUTHORITIES

In some countries, you may have to deal with a frustrating amount of red tape and 'officialdom' in order to get where you want to go. This especially applies if you're travelling through politically sensitive areas, war zones or countries governed by dictatorships of one sort or another. It can also be the case dealing with the police in developing countries.

'In Indonesia, I tend to avoid the military – they're probably the most aggressive people in the country, because they have power. They can look at you, decide

they don't like you, and make life hell for you. That never happened to me, but there were a couple of times that were a bit scary. Once I saw a whole bunch of soldiers. I had a camera and wanted to take a photo. They came over and told me not to. Their tone of voice was so different to that of the local people's. I was glad I'd only done something minor.'

'I've heard of some people having a hard time in China and getting hassled by the police. I think it depends very much on your state of mind, on your attitude.'

Be polite, and look as presentable and conservative as possible when crossing borders and dealing with officials. Have the appropriate documents on you and ready to present. If you don't speak the language, carry a phrasebook.

'I dressed fairly neatly going through the borders in Central America. If you look all right when you go through the border formalities, they don't hassle you at all.'

Take visa, health certificate and currency requirements seriously, and don't assume you'll be able to charm or pay your way through a border without the appropriate documentation.

'I got thrown off a train once at three o'clock in the morning, because I didn't have a Slovakian visa. I was travelling on a night train between Prague and Budapest and hadn't realised that the train cut through a corner of Slovakia to get to Hungary. The border police checked my passport, shook their heads and said, "No Slovakian visa, no go." I had no Slovakian money and only about 10 US dollars, not enough to buy an on-the-spot transit visa, even if they had let me, which they didn't. They told me I had three minutes to get dressed and disembark. I couldn't believe it – I was asleep in my pyjamas. But I

> had no choice. Two Romanians and I were bundled off
> under police escort and had to wait in the police hut next
> to the station till a train came through for Vienna. One
> of the Romanians was bawling: her handbag looked like it
> had been gutted, so I guessed she'd been robbed on the
> train. The border police sat in their office drinking coffee
> and watching TV while we shivered outside in the
> hallway. At first I was upset but after a while I realised it
> wasn't so bad. The situation was frustrating but it wasn't
> dangerous. So I chilled out, ate my supplies and wrote
> about it all in my journal to pass the time. Three hours
> later, the police "escorted" me onto the train and sat with
> me as far as the Slovakia–Austria border. I spent the day
> in Vienna and took the night train to Budapest. Luckily
> I had a rail pass so all it cost me was a few hours' sleep.'

If you have hassles of any kind, try to enlist the support of
someone who speaks a common language and can act as
an interpreter. It can be useful to have local currency plus
some US dollars on you, in case you need to buy a visa or
repay a favour from an official.

> 'I got to the Tanzanian border and they weren't going to
> let me through because I'd had my purse stolen and lost
> all my vaccination forms. They refused to let me enter the
> country. It was basically because they wanted a bit of
> kickback, some American dollars, and I had to pay my
> way. It was only 20 US dollars, but still, it was the
> principle of the thing. Then again, you wouldn't want to
> have to get a vaccine shot, not in Africa.'

> 'If you're dealing with the Indonesian militia and you've
> done something they think is wrong, it's best to give them
> a bit of money – 10,000 rupiah – and say "I'm really
> sorry, I hope this will help solve it." It's part of their
> income – like tips to a waiter. They get a lot of their
> salary from bribe money.'

Try not to get aggressive when dealing with officials in foreign countries, even if you feel you're in the right. Police officers, soldiers, customs and immigration officials and border guards have more power than you in the situation (regardless of your legal rights) and some of them may not be as responsible about using that power as you would expect.

'I was hassled more than once by officials in South America. In Colombia, I was in my hostel room one night and the police came with some excuse about needing to check my visa details. They wouldn't accept that I was OK – they kept asking me questions. Eventually I asked them to leave and then they got heavy. They wanted to take me to the police station. Luckily, I'd made friends with some guys at the hostel, so I yelled out to them and told them what was happening and they managed to get me out of jail after one night. Basically, the police wanted to have sex with me and when I refused they got nasty and put me in jail. We bribed them and they let me out.'

'In Brazil, I once tried to report some stuff I'd had stolen to the police. It was afternoon, and they said they were too busy and I'd have to come back that night. When I went back there, I walked in and one of them was already waiting for me in the corridor, in his underpants. I just ran out.'

'Never, ever be in a situation where you don't have cash or you're going to run out of money, especially on borders. You get offers left, right and centre from border guards to pay them with sex. Taxi drivers too. Anyone who you're forced to rely on can use you sexually.'

GETTING HELP

As a woman, you're more likely to attract sympathy and offers of help if you're in trouble. Don't be afraid to ask for assistance – other travellers, hotel staff, even strangers, are usually willing to come to your aid if they see you're in genuine need.

> 'I feel confident that if I'm on my own on the street and get into strife, I'll go to the nearest person and say, "I am in trouble" or "Someone's following me." Or go straight into a pub and loudly say, "I'm being followed – can someone help me?" I know that someone will react, despite the stories about how no-one comes unless you yell fire. I know I can handle myself in those situations.'

You're more likely to get help if you:

❑ ask women or fellow travellers. Because they've experienced harassment themselves, they're likely to be sympathetic to your plight. Other travellers, male or female, will usually rush to the aid of a fellow Westerner.

❑ don't appeal to everyone: in a crowd, you're more likely to be helped if you single out one person in particular

❑ call for help in the local language. If you don't know how, gesture for help by pointing at yourself, then your harasser, with the appropriate expressions.

❑ learn to identify police and familiarise yourself with the locations of police stations, booths or beats, so you can go directly to them if you need assistance

❑ call for the conductor or seek support from a local woman, family or fellow traveller on public transport

❑ make a fuss – if people are made aware of your plight, they're more likely to take notice, and this may shame your harasser into desisting

> 'In Asia, arguing's generally not a good thing to do. Nor is getting upset or angry. Don't raise your voice if you can

> *possibly avoid it, because it just tends to draw a crowd.
> But if you find yourself in big trouble, start screaming –
> you'll get a crowd of a hundred people in five minutes.'*

❑ don't assume that people will come to your aid.
Even if they're sympathetic, they may not wish to
get involved.

> *'Sometimes, local women have assumptions about white
> women travelling. Like that you're a prostitute. If you're
> in trouble, they may not be inclined to help you. Their
> attitude to me when a Thai soldier was dragging me off
> a bus against my will was, "Sorry – this is the situation
> you're in and there's nothing we can do about it. We're
> not taking your side because regardless of how Thai men
> treat Western women, they're our husbands; our men".'*

> *'In South America, locals are really nice to you if they
> think they're not going to get into any trouble. In crowded
> local trains, they'll give you their seat. But if you have
> your bags stolen – and it happens to most people – no-one
> in the street will help you.'*

COPING WITH CRISES

Unfortunately, traumatic experiences do occasionally happen, even to seasoned travellers. The good news is that your chance of surviving even the most threatening situation is extremely high.

> *'I had a horrible situation in Germany – your classic
> "meet someone in a railway station" scenario. I was in a
> station and this couple sat down and started chatting to
> me, and ended up inviting me to dinner. They were
> gorgeous so I went to their house, and another guy came
> to dinner who was equally gorgeous. They were all*

students in Frankfurt and they had a little tiny house out in the middle of nowhere. I was going to go back to my hostel but they said, "Why don't you stay and we'll drive you back tomorrow?" But they didn't have any room, so the other guy, who lived on his own, said, "Come and stay with me."

'So I went back to his place, which was a university room nearby. When we got there, he started drinking and threatening me. He had recently split up with his fiancée and I guess he wanted a woman to take it out on. He was terrifying, but I managed to talk him round by talking about how sad he must have felt about the loss of his relationship. I was running on pure instinct, but I managed to soften him enough to say, "I need to go to the bathroom really badly" and he let me out.

'Luckily I had remembered where the other couple lived, so I went around and woke them up and said, "Your friend has gone absolutely berko." They were mortified – so embarrassed. For a few days I was really shaky about being on my own again. I was pretty blown away by it. But then I thought, "That incident could have happened in Melbourne – it's not any different." For me, travelling is about basic survival on an everyday level. Maybe I should never have got myself in that situation but I did, and I was able to get out of it. I look back now and think, "I did it. I survived".'

'In Greece, a girlfriend and I were sitting at the Acropolis, and of course we looked like tourists, and these Greek guys came up and started chatting. They were very friendly and it was early in the afternoon and stinking hot. They said they were going to a great café nearby, and that lots of good people hung out there, and why didn't we come? We could have walked there but they had bikes, so they took us on the bikes to the café, and we sat around and talked there for ages. Then it was like, "What are you doing tonight?"

'We decided to go out to dinner with them, and it was all fine till the end of the night, when one of the guys got very violent. He had had a couple of drinks, but I don't think it was the drinks, it was his attitude, too. He wanted sex. Through the day, we were all talking about all different things and nothing like that ever came up in the conversation – there were no offers to come and stay or anything, nothing sexual. I think they thought, this particular guy especially, that they'd shown us around and wasted their time, when they could have met somebody else and got something more at the end of the night.

'It was a situation that snowballed really quickly. When it started it took us girls by surprise. It was very ugly. Because I was with other people, I let it go too far. In the end, even the other guys were trying to calm him down, but he was going over the top. So I grabbed the other girl's hand and we just ran. He chased us for a bit and then gave up.

'Situations like that make you smarter, and stronger. It gives you some experience, so that if you ever get into a similar situation and it's building to that point, you'll know to walk away and you'll get out of it sooner. You just never know – in different cultures, guys have a different idea about women. You don't know how the local men think. A lot of English girls go to Greece looking for the holiday romance, so maybe the guys think we're all there looking for the same thing.'

Even when you manage to defuse or escape them, such experiences are unnerving. And the fact that you're in an unfamiliar environment, far from your usual sources of support, can make crises more difficult to weather.

❑   If you've been robbed, injured or assaulted, you'll need to report the crime and get medical treatment and doctor's and police reports as soon as is practical. This is especially important if you intend to prosecute or make an insurance claim.

❑ Most cities and tourist centres throughout the West have crisis hotlines and sexual assault centres – most good guidebooks list emergency numbers. In rural areas and in most developing countries, you'll probably have to rely on the police.
❑ If there's a legal problem, contact your embassy.
❑ You may have to alter your travel arrangements till your replacement documents or travellers' cheques arrive, or until you've recovered from your experience.

If you've had an unpleasant experience, it's natural to feel insecure and fearful in the aftermath. As well as dealing with the event itself, you may have had to spend tedious hours reporting to police, organising replacement documents or obtaining medical treatment. Take time out after any trauma to relax, regroup, and think about ways to make the rest of your trip positive and hassle-free.

'When it looks like you're in an unfortunate situation, you just have to realise that shit happens, and you've got to have a sense of humour. Remind yourself that you'll look back and laugh about this one day for sure. It's part of the travelling experience.'

If you feel in need of support or a sympathetic ear, call a crisis line or phone home. If that's not possible, make contact with sympathetic locals or other travellers: hostels and tourist resorts are likely places for finding temporary companions. You may feel more comfortable if you link up with someone for a while following a traumatic experience. Once you regain your confidence, you can continue on alone.

Pat yourself on the back for surviving, then think about what you can learn from the experience. Many women report that situations and encounters that traumatised them at the time turned out to be memorable lessons in successful survival.

'So many travel experiences are such incredible hassles you wonder why you do it. But in retrospect, it's often the worst parts that become the highlights. It's as if this perverse part of your personality rationalises those "bad" experiences as character-building exercises. So some of the worst things that happen to you become your reference points, the lynchpins of the whole experience. They strengthen you. In a way, you actually go out and seek it. You have wonderful times and it's really good, but travelling alone is also an opportunity to take risks so that you learn to look after yourself. And that's really important – to be able to look after yourself and to do it in different situations. You learn that by travelling alone, and you won't necessarily learn it travelling with someone else.'

'I haven't had a bum trip. There are experiences that are wild or adventurous, but you can't ever call them all bad. The first time I went to America, I broke my jaw. It was radical, healthwise, but it turned out to be one of the best things that happened to me, 'cause I ended up staying there on my own, meeting other people and having a great time. If you're open to taking things as they come, and don't have too many rigid expectations, it can't be a bum trip.'

'I've racked my brain to think of awful things that have happened to me as a result of being female and on my own. But they're really few and far between. Even the hassles were learning experiences. And obviously, I survived them, 'cause I'm here, I'm happy, and I'm in one piece.'

STAYING HEALTHY

When you're travelling, it's important to pay attention to your general health. Changes in climate, time zones, food and sanitation put added stress on bodily functions. At home, your body builds up resistance to common ailments, but you may have no resistance to the unfamiliar bugs you'll encounter in foreign countries. Unless you monitor your health, it's easy to get run down and become susceptible to illness.

If you take a few sensible precautions, however, you should be able to stay healthy wherever you go.

❑   Have general medical, gynaecological, optical and dental checks and treatment, along with any vaccinations and medicines you might need, before you go (see pages 51–2).

'The medical services in China can be pretty scary. The dental surgeries we went past had the 1940s foot-pedal

*drills, and hygiene isn't a consideration. It's not a place
I'd suggest getting really sick in. That's why I had a good
medical check-up before going. Get your teeth checked
too, particularly if you're going to be there a long time or
you're travelling to remote areas. We took our own
syringes, too – we didn't use them but it's better to be
safe. In the bigger cities, though, they have all the modern
facilities and there are far more doctors who speak
English.'*

❑ Get fit, to ensure you leave in optimum physical
condition.

*'Before I went trekking, I did six months' uphill walking
and stepping at the gym and went on weekend bushwalks
to try to get my fitness levels and stamina up. I also
stopped smoking, 'cause I knew at the high altitudes I'd
be struggling to get enough air as it was.'*

*'I took a course of mega vitamins before I went to Europe.
'Cause I knew the long journey and the change of climate
from summer to winter would make me stressed and
susceptible to flu. And I tried to get fit and healthy.'*

❑ When constructing your itinerary, keep health
considerations in mind: plan rest periods; allow
yourself time to adjust to different time zones,
climates and conditions before engaging in
strenuous or stressful activities; and space long
journeys so that you give yourself time between
them to recover.
❑ Watch your food intake. When travelling, it's easy to
neglect your dietary needs or even forget to eat. It
can be hard to maintain a balanced, healthy diet in
places where food may be limited or very different
from what you're used to eating. Try to include
grains, fruits, vegetables, some form of protein

(eggs, meat, soy products, seeds or nuts) and useful fats (cold-pressed oil, fish oils) in your daily food intake.

> 'If I'm unsure of the food, I eat vegetarian. You can always get cooked vegetables, and some sort of grain – rice, or pasta – and bread.'
>
> 'Wherever I could, I ate at vegetarian and health-food restaurants. They're easy to find in the big cities, and they're always pleasant places to eat. It's good to have a really healthy meal at least once every few days, 'cause it's easy to fall into the bread, cheese and tomato trap, especially in Europe. The other thing I used to do was carry muesli with me – it makes a great snack on its own or you can buy yoghurt or fresh fruit to eat it with. Carry a plastic spoon and a takeaway container, and you have instant healthy breakfasts.'

❑ Drink plenty of water. It flushes toxins from the system and stops you from getting dehydrated, and keeps your skin healthy and well moisturised. Always make sure the water you drink is safe: see page 284 for more information.

> 'If I was going on a long walk or sightseeing, I always took a bottle of water with me. Two litres of water is heavy to lug around, so you feel encouraged to drink it and that keeps you hydrated. Otherwise, I'd buy bottled drinks or fruit on the street.'

❑ Avoiding drinking too much alcohol or coffee – they stress your system, dehydrate you and lower your immune response.
❑ Carry vitamin and mineral supplements (especially vitamins A, B, C and E, and minerals zinc and magnesium) to compensate for an unbalanced or

restricted local diet. Use C to stave off viral complaints and keep your immune system healthy, B to boost energy levels and combat stress, E to speed healing, and A, magnesium and zinc to fight pollution and toxins, maintain healthy tissues and promote clear skin.

> *'I'm a great believer in carrying vitamin supplements with you when you travel. They are such a good way to prevent you from getting run down or ill. I just work out exactly what I'm going to need and put them all in one big container together – I know what's what. I've never had a hassle with it at customs.'*

HEALTH IN TRANSIT

Being on the road a lot can lower your resistance to infection, and on long, crowded journeys, you'll inevitably come in contact with other people's germs. When you factor in missed sleep and poor-quality food, it's not surprising so many travellers end up getting sick after long or back-to-back journeys. To minimise the physical stress of being on the road:

❑   Bring your own food supplies (fresh or dried fruit, hard-boiled eggs, bread, cheese, tomatoes, carrots and nuts are healthy options).

❑   Carry plenty of water or other fluids – travel can be dehydrating and you can't necessarily trust the drinks you buy from roadside or station vendors.

❑   Get as much rest as possible en route. Carry a blow-up neck pillow and a sarong or sleeping bag to keep you covered and comfortable. If taking a mild sedative or donning an eye mask and earplugs helps you sleep, do it. Make sure your valuables are secure before you doze off.

❑   If possible, avoid sitting next to, touching hands or

sharing food or drink with people who are sniffling, coughing or otherwise ill – it's a sure-fire way to pick up an infection.

ACCLIMATISING

When you arrive in a new country after a long journey, your body needs time to adjust. The best cure for jet lag is rest. After a day or two, your sleep patterns and energy levels will probably be back to normal. It can take more time to adjust to differences in climate or altitude, especially if you've come from a place where conditions are very different.

Heat

Intense heat and high humidity can make you feel weak, lethargic and uncomfortable. Minimise the debilitating effects of tropical heat by:

❑ wearing loose clothes made from natural fibres (cotton, silk) – they keep you cool by allowing air to circulate and your skin to 'breathe' and sweat freely (synthetic fabrics trap the heat and don't absorb sweat)

❑ choosing clothes and hats in light colours that reflect rather than absorb heat

❑ where possible, travelling in light-coloured vehicles with airconditioning or open windows

❑ wearing a hat with a shady brim

❑ drinking lots of fluids (water, fruit juices) but going easy on the alcohol and tea/coffee

❑ increasing your salt intake to replace salt lost in sweat

❑ avoiding unnecessary exposure to sun – at least till you've acclimatised

❑ wearing a 15+SPF sunscreen and sunglasses to minimise UV damage to skin and eyes – even when the sky's cloudy

❑   maintaining a balanced diet – it helps your body
     cope with extreme temperatures.

Cold

Travelling from a tropical or temperate country to somewhere very cold can stress your system and bring on all
sorts of ailments. To stay healthy, make sure you:

❑   dress appropriately for the weather. Wear layers:
     they insulate you better than one heavy jumper or
     coat, and you can add or remove clothes to
     compensate for differences in temperature
     (remember that in cold countries, indoor areas are
     often heated).
❑   avoid going suddenly from a heated environment
     into an outdoor one, and don't sit around in wet
     clothing – it ups your chances of catching a chill
❑   when outdoors, wear a hat, gloves and thick socks –
     you lose a lot of heat through exposed extremities
❑   drink plenty of hot fluids – herbal tea, tea, soup –
     and eat regularly so your body gets the energy it
     needs to stay warm

Altitude

High altitudes can have a strong effect on the system, especially for women who are on the Pill or at the pre-
menstrual stage of their cycles. Most fit, healthy people
take two to three weeks to adjust to the effects of altitude;
six weeks to feel comfortable. Take your time, and you
should have few problems adjusting to the effects of
altitude.

The most important thing to remember is to go at your
own pace and descend immediately if you start to show
symptoms of altitude sickness. In mild form, symptoms
include headaches, weakness, nausea and insomnia.
Treatment is to stop and rest for a few days. More severe

symptoms are a persistent headache, bluish lips, drowsiness and confusion, breathlessness even when resting, a phlegmy cough and infrequent urination. If you develop these symptoms, return immediately to a lower altitude and rest.

Travel and trekking guides and travellers' health books list signs and symptoms: learn to identify them if you plan to travel at high altitudes, especially if you'll be doing it independently.

Initially, ascend slowly (especially if you're more than 3000 metres above sea level) – don't climb too high, too fast. How far you ascend per day depends on how you feel, but don't try to match your companions' or guides' pace. Plan rest days and assist the acclimatisation process by climbing to a high point, then descending to a lower level to spend the night. Above 3000 metres, ascend no more than 300 metres a day, or 600 metres one day, followed by a rest day. As you climb higher, you may have to halve this.

When travelling at high altitudes, stay healthy by ensuring you:

❑   drink more fluids: your body needs them to cope with dry air and increased respiration. And watch your alcohol consumption: at 3000 metres, one standard drink has three times the effect that the same drink would have at sea level.

❑   travel light. If carrying your baggage is overtaxing you, don't be embarrassed about hiring a local carrier to help you out.

❑   start off as healthy as possible and expect to lose some weight en route. Try, if possible, to eat plenty of carbohydrates and proteins and less salt.

❑   rest and let your body adjust, especially if you've just arrived in a high-altitude town such as Johannesburg or Lhasa. Expect to feel unwell for the first few days.

COMMON TRAVELLERS' AILMENTS

Diarrhoea

Most travellers expect to get at least one bout of 'Delhi belly' or its equivalent, but you can avoid catching the bugs that cause diarrhoea. Pay attention to what you eat, drink and touch, and you'll spend less time on your trip running for the toilet.

Most attacks come from food or water contamination and are usually mild, clearing up within three days. To treat diarrhoea:

❑   eat nothing for 24 hours; instead, drink lots of fluid – water, clear soup, herbal tea, rice water or green coconut milk are all good. Sip rather than gulp and you're more likely to keep it down.

❑   up your salt intake with Oral Rehydration Solution or a mix of water, sugar and salt

❑   after a day, try eating bland foods such as rice, yoghurt, bread, crackers or bananas, but avoid fatty foods until your stomach has settled.

If diarrhoea persists for more than three days, you find blood or mucus in your faeces, or you get cramps in the lower abdomen, see a doctor immediately – you could have a serious infection.

Constipation

Unfamiliar diets, excessive sweating or insufficient exercise (sitting for days on trains and buses) can make even the most 'regular' women constipated. Avoid the problem by drinking more water and eating fibre-rich foods such as fruit, vegetables and whole grains. Use gentle laxatives only if you must.

Motion sickness

Car, sea or air sickness are all forms of the same thing –
motion sickness. There are a number of ways to minimise
its effects:

❑ Take motion-sickness tablets (antihistamines), or
  wear a motion-sickness behind-ear patch or armband.
❑ Sit in the most stable position. On buses, choose
  seats in the front half or middle section rather than
  the rear, and sit on the lower decks of double-
  decker vehicles. In cars, sit in the front rather than
  the back.
❑ If you're feeling queasy, look out the window –
  don't read.
❑ Focus on a fixed point in the landscape, rather than
  letting your eyes scan things briefly in passing. Once
  you pass your chosen fixed point, choose another.
❑ On boats, go up on deck if you're feeling nauseous:
  the fresh air helps, you can steady your insides by
  focusing on the horizon, and if you need to be sick,
  it's easy.
❑ You may find you travel better on an empty
  stomach. Especially avoid fatty foods.

Prickly heat

In hot, humid climates and sweaty conditions, you may
develop a red rash from blocked sweat gland ducts, especially around the groin, at the waist and under bra straps.
The usual cause is too-tight, chafing, non-breathable
clothing that prevents sweat from evaporating. The best
prevention is to wear loose, cotton clothing and cotton
underwear (pants and bras) and to forgo skirts and pants
with elasticised waists in favour of wraparound skirts or
sarongs. To cure it, avoid sweating – get somewhere cool,
preferably airconditioned, and chill out. Wash the affected
areas in cold water, without soap, and dry gently, dusting
with talc. Calamine lotion will help soothe the itch.

Minor burns

Immerse the burnt area in clean, cold water for as long as it takes to stop hurting (at least 10 minutes); then apply a sterile gauze dressing but no creams or ointments.

Conjunctivitis

Contact lens wearers may be particularly prone to common eye infections, such as conjunctivitis, especially in tropical climates. Eyes irritated by dust and smoke, and infections passed from eye to hand or spread via shared towels are the usual causes. Treat with antibiotic eye drops or ointment (such as Brolene) and avoid touching or rubbing your eyes.

Foot problems

The best way to prevent aches, pains and blisters is to wear comfortable, well-worn-in footwear made from breathable, flexible materials such as leather or canvas. To toughen your feet before you go, apply surgical spirit to heels and toes two to three times a day.

Moleskin applied to chafing or tender spots will help prevent blisters, and blister pads are great if you suffer from them. If you don't have a blister pad, apply antiseptic and a Band-aid.

When sharing showers, the smart thing to do is wear thongs or plastic sandals. If you do get a dose of tinea (athlete's foot) – which is easy to pick up in tropical areas – wash and dry your feet thoroughly and apply medicated talc and/or Canesten cream (the same anti-fungal treatment you can use to treat thrush).

It's usually not a good idea to go barefoot when travelling. There are many hazards: glass or syringes on beaches, sharp coral or rocks, biting, stinging creepy-crawlies (scorpions, snakes, spiders or bull ants) and parasites that burrow into the feet (such as hookworms).

Cuts and scrapes

Under normal circumstances, minor abrasions aren't a problem, but you must take special care to treat them if you're travelling in tropical climes. Unless they're kept sterile, minor cuts, scrapes and even mosquito bites can turn into nasty infected sores, or tropical ulcers. These are painful, take ages to heal and can leave ugly scars.

To prevent infection of minor cuts and scrapes, immediately wash them in clean water and soap or antiseptic solution, paint with antiseptic solution (not cream, because you need to dry it out) and cover with a Band-aid or sterile gauze.

Treat deeper wounds by cleaning thoroughly, applying antiseptic solution, then holding the edges of the wound together with a butterfly clip (or, if necessary, stitches – although this, of course, will require medical attention). Get a tetanus booster shot for deep cuts and puncture wounds that may have been contaminated, unless you're sure you're up to date. If you do develop an ulcer, sea water helps, and local treatments may prove effective.

'It's often things you don't expect that cause you problems. In Africa, I developed the worst sore on the back of my leg. It started off as a little mossie bite, but because of the climate and the humidity, it didn't heal and it just went mad. It became a tropical ulcer – an amazing big pus-filled thing at the back of my knee. Because I was always having to walk, it could never heal over, and it kept getting bigger and grosser. I ended up going to a local pharmacist who gave me some antibiotic powder to put on it and said, "When you get to Mombasa, go in some sea water." I followed his directions and it cleared up just like that.'

COMMON AILMENTS OF WOMEN TRAVELLERS

Every traveller occasionally suffers from diarrhoea, flu or some sort of health problem. But men don't have to worry about – or put up with – unusually heavy periods, itchy vaginal discharges, pregnancy or coping with PMS. Minimise your worries by anticipating any likely problems, taking appropriate precautions and knowing effective treatments.

Thrush

Thrush (*Candida albicans*), with its annoying itch and discharge, can make travelling uncomfortable. It's more likely to flare up in hot, humid conditions in which it's hard to keep clean or to eat a balanced diet. Stress, excess sugar, caffeine or alcohol, dehydration, chafing and sweaty clothes all help provide the conditions that *candida* thrives on. Take these steps to minimise the chances of thrush occurring, or to get rid of it once it does:

- ❑ Eat a balanced diet: go easy on the sugar and acidic foods and eat lots of natural yoghurt.
- ❑ Cut down on coffee, sugary soft drinks and alcohol.
- ❑ Avoid antibiotics, as they kill off the natural bacteria that keep candida yeast levels in the vagina under control. If you must take antibiotics, supplement your diet with natural yoghurt and/or acidophilus tablets to help restore the correct internal balance.
- ❑ Avoid wearing tight jeans or pants that chafe around the crotch.
- ❑ Wear cotton underwear, and change it regularly.
- ❑ Observe hygienic toilet habits – wipe from front to back after urinating, rinse the genital area well with clean water, and dry it.

If you have thrush:

❏   don't use soap to wash your vulval area. Instead, rinse with water and clean the area with olive oil on cotton wool.

❏   use yoghurt externally to soothe the vaginal area, or soak a tampon in yoghurt and insert it

❏   bathe in a solution of water and vinegar, bicarbonate of soda, or salt, to help restore the vagina's acid–alkaline balance

❏   carry a reliable remedy for thrush. Herbal candida-cure tablets are simple and effective. You can also use a one-dose Nystatin pessary, insert Canesten cream or paint the affected area with gentian violet, but if you adopt one of these messier methods, you may need to use sanitary pads while you're treating yourself.

Cystitis

This urinary tract infection can be debilitating and uncomfortable, especially when you're travelling. It usually occurs when bacteria from the bowel find their way into the urinary tract. The most common symptoms are a burning sensation when taking a pee, the feeling that you need to urinate frequently, even after you've just been; and in more severe cases, lower abdominal pain and strongly coloured urine.

Take these steps to avoid it:

❏   Maintain scrupulous hygiene: wipe from front to back, or rinse well with clean water after using the toilet.

❏   Wear cotton underwear and loose cotton skirts rather than pants.

❏   Drink plenty of fluids (water, non-acidic fruit juice and herbal tea) to keep your system well flushed and avoid dehydration – concentrated urine is an ideal breeding ground for bacteria.

- Cut back on acidic foods and drinks. Especially avoid alcohol and coffee, which are also dehydrating.
- Take vitamin C regularly to fight off bacteria.
- Urinate directly before and after sex, and make sure you wash well as soon as possible after sex.

To get rid of cystitis once you're affected:

- act promptly – as soon as you notice that burning feeling, start drinking lots of liquids (water, cranberry juice or weak herbal tea)
- take a cystitis remedy (sodium citrate – available in sachet form as Ural – or potassium citrate), or make your own: a teaspoonful of bicarbonate of soda, in water, as soon as possible, then once every hour, should do the trick
- every time you urinate, however little, rinse the area well in water
- keep warm, and if you can find one, place a hot water bottle on your lower back or between your legs to reduce pain
- if the condition persists, you may need to take antibiotics (a suitable one is Cotrimoxazole) to stop the cystitis from developing into a kidney infection.

'If you're prone to attacks of cystitis, especially in places where the water supply varies, you should take cystitis remedies with you. There are many parts of the world where getting those sorts of things is difficult.'

Vaginal discharge

It's worth keeping an eye on any unusual vaginal discharge, as it can indicate a pelvic infection or an STD that, if left untreated, could lead to infertility. Especially look out for discharge that is smelly, is yellow and frothy, looks like thick, creamy pus or is accompanied by pain on urination. If you have pain in the lower abdomen and/or fever, these could be symptoms that the infection has spread to your Fallopian tubes. Seek medical advice.

MENSTRUATION

Travelling can disrupt your normal menstrual cycle. Many women miss periods, menstruate erratically, or notice differences in the duration or intensity of their menstrual flow when they're moving around a lot. The greater the changes in climate, time zone or stress or activity levels, the more likely you are to find your cycle affected.

Don't panic about infrequent periods – consider yourself lucky that you don't have to change tampons as often, and remember that the less you menstruate, the easier personal hygiene becomes. Do make sure you're adequately protected against pregnancy, however – it can be hard to tell you're pregnant when your menstrual cycle is erratic.

Heavier or frequent bleeding can be a hassle – going on the Pill may help to normalise your menstrual flow. If you're losing more blood than normal, up your intake of green leafy vegetables (for iron). Use a pad for extra protection, especially on long bus journeys, treks or sightseeing expeditions.

It's possible to avoid menstruating altogether while travelling by taking the Pill continuously to prevent your periods. This may be suitable if you're planning a short trip. See your doctor for advice.

Tampons, sponges and pads
You're best off taking your own supply of tampons. Outside of the West, they can be difficult to come by, expensive and of poor quality. Sanitary pads are available

virtually everywhere: in developing countries, try shops in larger towns.

> 'Take lots and lots of tampons, because not only are they hard to get, they're really expensive in Asia. You can get Tampax everywhere – but sometimes they're really old ones that have come from other countries. And take your own contraception, definitely.'
>
> 'I took tampons with me to China – I could have bought them in a few places, but they weren't around a lot. Local women use pads, or strips of material.'
>
> 'Before I left Europe for the Middle East, I stocked up on medicines and tampons. Israel's very civilised, but elsewhere they don't have a lot of tampons, they've just got sanitary napkins. When you're travelling around, pads are hard to get rid of. You can always get rid of tampons.'

Make sure you deposit pads and tampons in the appropriate receptacles. Septic toilet systems, which include virtually all toilets outside of the West, don't take kindly to tampons.

Reusable sea sponges (inserted like tampons) are extremely light and compact. They can be useful in a tight spot, and are handy if you're staying at a beach resort where you can wash them out in salt water. They are impractical, however, if you're travelling in areas where sanitation is poor: you need fresh, clean water to rinse them out in and a sterile place to store them between periods.

PMS and cramps

Bring any remedies you normally use to combat PMS or menstrual cramps, along with doctors' notes or prescriptions. Plan your itinerary and daily activities to take account of your menstrual cycle – you may not want to climb a volcano on the first day of your period; you might plan more relaxing activities during the PMS phase.

CONTRACEPTION

Most common forms of contraception are widely available but it's still sensible to take your own supplies. You may find it difficult to find a chemist who stocks your brand of the Pill or favourite condom. In developing countries, high temperatures and poor storage methods can render condoms, cervical caps and diaphragms unreliable.

If your contraceptives get stolen along with your baggage, you decide to extend your trip and need to renew a prescription, or you have a problem with the method you're using, local hospitals, family planning clinics or doctors should be able to help you out. Obtain a list of family planning centres worldwide by contacting the International Planned Parenthood Federation, Inner Circle, Regent's Park, London NW1 4NS, UK (ph 44-171-487 7900), or call your local family planning clinic and ask for information. Thanks to population planning programs, you can often find family planning clinics even in remote parts of the developing world.

Condoms, caps and spermicides

Tropical climates can play havoc with condoms and diaphragms – they can deteriorate rapidly in the heat, becoming thin, sticky and unreliable. It's important to try and keep them cool, clean and dry: store them in a closed container in a cool spot.

It's best to have your own condom supply, as condoms outside of the West may not conform to the same standards. Besides, poor storage, heat and humidity mean they may have deteriorated by the time you buy them. When buying condoms, especially in developing countries or remote districts, check expiry dates carefully and don't buy from stockists who keep the wares in the heat or display them in direct sunlight. Carry your condoms in a cool, safe spot and check them before using. Know how to use condoms correctly, and dispose of them thoughtfully.

Spermicides, especially those in solid pessary form, are affected by heat and direct sunlight. Better (and less likely to melt) are spermicidal creams and jellies, but you'll still have to keep them cool. Ideally, condoms, caps and spermicides should be kept in a refrigerator or an airconditioned environment. Carry adequate supplies of contraceptive jelly, as it can be difficult to buy outside of cities and Western countries.

If you have to get a new diaphragm, go to a reliable doctor or family planning clinic to have it fitted.

The Pill

Many women find the Pill the most convenient method of contraception while travelling. If you do use it, take a good supply. You can buy the Pill over the counter in most countries, but brand names, ingredients and dosage levels may be very different from what's available at home.

Carry a prescription (giving both brand and generic names), or the empty packet or manufacturer's notes from the Pill you've been using, so you won't have trouble finding a compatible brand if your normal make isn't available. If you move from a higher to a lower dose pill, use additional contraception for the first fortnight.

Remember that you have to take the Pill regularly once a day, and in the case of progestogen-only Pills, within a specific three-hour period each day, if it is to be effective. When you're travelling, and especially when you're crossing time zones, it can be hard to keep track. One solution is to keep a clock running on 'home time'. If it becomes inconvenient to take a Pill at the 'old' time (for example, if before dinner has become 4 a.m.), move the time back slightly each day rather than forward, so you won't be underprotected.

It's important to have a fallback option – given that the Pill offers no protection against STDs or HIV, smart women also carry condoms. If you're vomiting, or have diarrhoea, even for a day, the Pill may not be absorbed efficiently in your system.

If you vomit less than three or four hours after taking your Pill, take a second Pill and see if you can keep it down for the next 12 hours – if so, you're covered. (Note that this is not possible if you're taking a progestogen-only Pill.) If you can't keep the second Pill down, and/or if diarrhoea sets in less than 12 hours after taking a Pill, assume that you're no longer protected. Use alternative contraception for a fortnight after you recover, but continue to take the Pill.

If you've been taking the Pill regularly and miss one in the middle of your period, you probably don't have to worry, but if it occurs any other time in your cycle, a missed or malabsorbed Pill is risky: use other forms of contraception for the next 14 days, as well as continuing to take the Pill.

Some antibiotics interfere with the action of the combined Pill, although they don't disrupt the effectiveness of the progestogen-only Pill. Keep this in mind when taking antibiotics, and if the antibiotic you're on is known to reduce the Pill's effectiveness, consider yourself unprotected for that cycle. Other drugs, such as Cotrimoxazole and Metronidazole, can enhance the effects of the Pill.

Remember that taking oral contraceptives can increase your chances of altitude sickness at high elevations. If you catch hepatitis, you should stop taking the Pill, as it puts extra strain on the liver.

IUD

This is a convenient, hassle-free way to protect yourself against pregnancy when travelling, but only if you're comfortable with the method. If you're going to switch to an IUD, have it fitted at least a couple of months before you go. Most problems with pain, bleeding or expulsion occur, if they're going to, within the first month of having an IUD fitted, so if you don't have any initial problems, it'll probably be fine.

The drawback to an IUD is that if you do get a vaginal infection, it can travel up the string of your IUD and become a pelvic infection, so you have to be especially careful with hygiene. Remember, too, that IUDs provide no protection against STDs or HIV transmission.

Morning-after pill

If you've had unprotected sex or fear your Pill hasn't been properly absorbed, you may decide to use the morning-after method of post-coital contraception. It involves taking two pills containing 250 mg of levonorgestrel and 50 mg of ethinyloestradiol less than 72 hours after having unprotected sex, and is usually effective in preventing pregnancy – you should have a normal period within three weeks. This is neither a foolproof nor a sensible method of regular contraception. The high hormone doses in morning-after pills can disrupt your normal body cycle, so only use them in an emergency. Consult your family planning clinic for advice.

'I would never travel alone without being on the Pill because of the possibility of being raped. It's not enough to think, If I want to have sex it's OK, because I've got condoms or a diaphragm, because unfortunately it's not always your choice. Although, obviously, condoms are necessary for avoiding STDs. I wouldn't dream of travelling without them. I also take lubricant, which came in handy after I'd been raped and I was really sore. It helped soothe the swelling and the cuts.'

'I actually had to reject a good offer once, because I didn't have any condoms with me! So if you're going to take them, you have to carry them in your daybag all the time. It's no good just having them in your backpack and leaving them in the hotel room. Because inevitably, when you're travelling, the time it happens is that one time when you didn't expect to meet anybody.'

'They had the Pill in India. You took it for a week and you were safe for a year. But we weren't game to try that – there were a lot of kids running around with mothers who'd been on that Pill.'

STDs

Sexually transmitted diseases (STDs) are on the increase worldwide, and travellers are not immune. In fact, they can be part of the problem.

In many parts of the developing world, especially certain regions of Africa and Asia, HIV infection rates are high and growing. The commonest means of HIV transmission, globally, is through unsafe heterosexual sex. The spread of HIV and AIDS by tourists and independent travellers is a serious concern to local health authorities.

To help solve the problem and minimise your chances of contracting an STD, including HIV, make sure all your sexual encounters, with locals or travellers, males or females, are safe. The only foolproof option for avoiding STDs is abstinence. But if you don't want to abstain, it's smart to be prepared.

❑ Make the use of condoms or dental dams a condition of any sexual encounter. If a partner refuses to wear condoms, don't have sex. To avoid hassles, establish this before you let yourself get into a compromising position.

❑ Use spermicidal jelly or condoms with Nonoxynol

9 as additional protection against HIV (and pregnancy).

❑ Wash in clean water before and directly after sexual intercourse to minimise your chances of picking up minor STDs and getting cystitis.

❑ Keep an eye out for STD symptoms if you've had a sexual encounter, even if you believe it was safe. Look for any suspicious sores or unusual vaginal discharge, or even a sore throat, especially in the first fortnight after the encounter. If anything seems amiss, go for a medical check-up.

'The best place in Asia to treat an STD or have an abortion would probably be Bangkok. It's not so much of a stigma there, since the Vietnam war – they're aware of it. There are heaps of STD clinics and condoms are widely available.'

'There are STD clinics in Indonesia. But the local men are ignorant and irresponsible – they think they're "cured" of syphilis one hour after an injection of antibiotics. Their attitude to STDs is really dangerous.'

HIV and needles

HIV can also be passed on through contaminated blood products or poorly sterilised medical equipment. In developing countries, needles may not be sterilised before medical or dental treatments, so get a dental check-up before you go, and if you're worried, take disposable syringes in your medical kit.

Don't have a blood transfusion, unless absolutely necessary, unless you know the blood has been screened (your consulate may be able to advise you). In countries where you're not sure that needles are sterilised, avoid having acupuncture, tattoos or piercings.

PREGNANCY

It's fine to travel during pregnancy, as long as you monitor your health carefully. Carry a letter from your obstetrician that details your medical history and all relevant details of your pregnancy. Make sure you continue to have regular pre-natal checks while you're overseas, and visit a doctor if you have any illness or problem that's more than a cold or a mild attack of diarrhoea. Avoid contact with animals, and don't eat fermented or unpasteurised cheeses when pregnant, as you may contract a disease that is harmful to your baby.

You should notify your airline of the fact you're pregnant – some airlines require a doctor's certificate saying you're fit to travel if you're more than 28 weeks pregnant, and you may not be allowed on international flights after the 35th week. Note that your insurance may not cover you for problems if you haven't notified the airline of your condition in advance.

For general information on travelling when pregnant, see pages 340–2.

Medicines and treatments to avoid

Some vaccines and medications can harm a developing foetus, especially if taken in the first 14 weeks of pregnancy. 'Live' vaccinations are best avoided during pregnancy. Consult your doctor to see what's safe, and, if necessary, get a letter from your doctor saying that a particular vaccination (such as that for yellow fever) is contraindicated, for use at border controls.

Many antibiotics aren't safe for pregnant women – tetracycline, Streptomycin, or any antibiotic in the sulfonamide group, which includes cotrimoxazole (Septrin). Avoid threadworm treatments that contain pyrantel pamoate or mebendazole. Use mild laxatives containing senna rather than preparations that include phenolphthalein. It is safe to use paracetamol throughout pregnancy but you shouldn't take aspirin in the final weeks.

It is best to avoid travel in malarial zones when pregnant as you and your unborn child are both at risk. Mosquito avoidance should be a priority when in these areas. Anti-malarials that are safe to use in pregnancy include chloroquine and proguanil; Maloprim can be used as a substitute in areas in which there's resistance to these drugs, but you shouldn't take it in the last two weeks of pregnancy or the first six weeks of breastfeeding. Fansidar, generally not prescribed these days in any case, should not be used during the first three months or after the 28th week of pregnancy until six weeks after birth.

Swelling – when it's a worry

It's common for pregnant women to experience slight swelling of the feet, ankles and even hands, especially when in transit. It's not a problem, and can usually be alleviated by rest. Put your feet up! If swelling becomes severe and your face starts to bloat, or you get puffy around the eyes, get a doctor or hospital to check your urine for protein, as you could have eclamptic toxaemia, which requires proper rest. If you don't treat the condition it can lead to blurred vision or flashes of light, headaches and, in the last stages, fits. It can be fatal to you and the foetus, so it's important that you continue to have regular urine tests while travelling.

Bleeding

If you bleed, don't ignore it – call a doctor and stay put. If the bleeding's slight, rest in bed. If it's accompanied by lower abdominal pain it's a sign of miscarriage and you should stay in bed, resting, till three days after bleeding stops. If it's severe, seek medical help immediately, as it could mean you've suffered an incomplete abortion and will need an operation.

ABORTION

If you need a pregnancy termination in a foreign country, find out how the local authorities feel about abortion before you attempt to get one. In places where religious beliefs or traditional customs outlaw abortion, it may be difficult, expensive, dangerous or illegal to have one. In many Western countries, and in developing regions where abortion is encouraged as a method of population control, such as China, getting an abortion may be a cheap and simple matter.

> *'If you had a medical crisis, it would be quite easy in France, because they have excellent centres for rape and abortion. However they may not speak English.'*
>
> *'I wouldn't get an abortion in India. If I got pregnant there, I'd take the first plane home.'*

If possible, go to a Western doctor or an international hospital, rather than a mission or religious hospital, where staff may hold more traditional views about abortion. A community family planning clinic is another option, although in strongly Catholic cultures even these clinics may refuse to provide terminations or their staff may try to dissuade you from having one.

If you feel it would be dangerous, medically, or if it's illegal to have an abortion in the country you're in, your best alternative is to travel to some place where you'll be able to get a safe abortion. This may not mean you have to fly home – it could just mean crossing a couple of borders.

Carry a list of family planning clinics worldwide (see page 270) on your travels.

BREAST SELF-EXAMS

Just because you're travelling doesn't mean you should skip doing your monthly breast self-check. If you're not sure how to do it, see a family planning clinic doctor before you leave. If you find an unusual lump, don't wait till you get home before doing something about it – seek medical advice.

HAZARDS

Swimming
Before jumping into unfamiliar waters, check for hazards. Ask local people, consult authorities, observe other bathers and use your common sense. Potential dangers include:

❑ rips and currents: these can make conditions dangerous on many of the world's best surfing and swimming beaches

> 'The lifeguards are always hauling travellers out of the surf at Bondi Beach. They all come there 'cause it's a tourist attraction, and they don't realise that it has strong rip currents. The locals all know about them and are strong swimmers but people from places where they don't surf much – like the UK and Europe or Japan – don't have a clue and they just get washed out to sea.'

❑ dangerous sea critters – sharks, stingrays, poisonous fish, sea snakes and sea urchins – can create problems for unwary swimmers, snorkellers, divers and people exploring tidal rockpools
❑ coral cuts – common on and around reefs

> 'I went to Lombok and the Gili Islands, where I snorkelled for the first time, and got coral cuts 'cause I didn't realise you couldn't snorkel at low tide.'

- diving into unknown waters – always a risky activity. Many paraplegics got that way by diving into shallow waters or hitting a submerged rock, sandbank or piece of trash.
- sewage and industrial waste – in overdeveloped tourist resorts and on beaches near urban centres, this can make waters unpleasant to swim in and hazardous to your health
- the disease schistosomiasis (bilharzia) – in many parts of the Third World, this makes fresh water dangerous for bathers. Even if the locals swim or wash there, this doesn't mean the water's safe for you. Consult local authorities before taking the plunge.

Mosquitoes

Mosquito bites aren't simply itchy – they can infect you with a variety of nasty fevers and carry all sorts of diseases. Malaria is spread by the bites of infected female mosquitoes, usually most active between dusk and dawn in malaria-prone areas (most of which are in tropical Third World regions).

If you're travelling through a malaria zone, it's wise to take appropriate prophylactics (see your doctor for advice before you leave). Anti-malarial tablets usually need to be started some time before entering the malarial zone and continued for at last two weeks after leaving it. Consult with your doctor.

Dengue fever, found in all tropical areas, and even, at times, in Australia, is a debilitating illness for which there's neither a treatment nor a vaccine. The best prevention is to avoid being bitten. Yellow fever is a mosquito-carried disease most prevalent in South America and Africa. Vaccines against it give 100 per cent immunity and are required.

Ticks

These carry many diseases and are found in rural areas worldwide. Ask locals whether ticks are a problem. If travelling through a tick-prone area, check your hair, scalp and body (especially armpits, groin and backs of knees) every night. Ticks burrow into the skin, and the longer they go without detection, the sicker they make their hosts. If you find one, it should be removed immediately, as if they're left to burrow in they can cause fevers or even paralysis. Embedded ticks are best removed by applying kerosene or turpentine to kill them, then removing them gently with tweezers, trying not to squeeze the insect's body (this can release more venom into the wound). If a tick has burrowed into your ear, use oil to flush it out.

Worms

Schistosomiasis, or bilharzia in Africa, (see page 280) is caught by contact with infected fresh water. The disease, carried by microscopic worms, affects waters in over 70 countries, but it's most prevalent in parts of Africa, China and Central America. Area health authorities are your best source of information on whether water is hazardous – don't follow local people's lead (they may have no choice but to use the water and take the consequences). Avoid bathing, wading or washing your face or hands in affected waters.

Hookworm is a parasite that burrows into your feet. Avoid hookworm by not walking barefoot in areas known to be affected (for example, parts of Africa).

Threadworms are harmless but irritating. You catch them by coming into contact with their eggs, so wash your hands thoroughly after using toilets.

One of the best all-round worm treatments, suitable for treatment of threadworms, roundworms and hookworms, is Pyrantel embonate, which you can buy in Australia under the brand name Combantrin.

Tse-tse flies

These can carry African sleeping sickness but fortunately they're only found in tropical Africa. If planning to travel through affected areas, consult your travellers' health guide. To avoid being bitten, use repellent and cover up – remembering that tse-tse flies can bite through thin fabrics.

Dogs, monkeys, cats, rats . . .

Rabies is a problem in many parts of the world, including Europe, the USA and much of the Third World. Rabid dogs are the worst offenders, but you could also get infected from the bite of a monkey, squirrel, mongoose, skunk or even bat. Avoid such animals, and if bitten, seek medical attention within 24 hours and let the doctor know that you may have been infected.

> 'In Asia, stray dogs can be a hassle. If they bite you, there's a chance they'll be rabid and will infect you with rabies. They skulk around the back streets but they generally don't attack. If they come towards you, pick up a stone and throw it at them, or pretend to. They'll usually run off.'

Protection against bites and stings

Your best protection is knowing what hazards are out there and taking the appropriate precautions. Read your guidebook before you leave, and ask local authorities for information once you arrive.

To minimise your chances of being bitten by flies and mosquitoes:

❑   wear long sleeves and pants, shoes and socks
❑   use repellents, especially in mosquito-prone areas. For the best protection, apply repellent to your clothes as well as your skin.
❑   wear light colours: they repel mosquitoes

- increase your dose of vitamin B: mossies hate the smell of it on the skin
- don't wear perfume: mosquitoes are attracted to it
- sleep, where possible, in rooms equipped with mosquito nets and window screens (check for holes)
- light mosquito coils before going out for dinner and swat any mosquitoes you see before you go to sleep.

To deter other critters, you'll need to take further measures:
- Have a mixture of salt and petroleum jelly on hand when walking through leech-ridden areas (hiking in tropical areas, bushwalks). If you find a leech on your body, apply the mixture to it directly.
- Check bedding, clothes and shoes for spiders and scorpions in areas where they're prevalent (especially if you're camping).
- Wear shoes to avoid cuts, insect bites and burrowing parasites such as hookworm.
- On beaches and around rockpools, wear plastic sandals to avoid coral cuts and marine stings and injuries from broken glass or syringes.
- Take a torch when walking around at night: scorpions and snakes are easy to step on in the dark, and spiders often lurk around outdoor loos.

HYGIENE

Food and water

Most ailments suffered by travellers occur as a result of eating or drinking contaminated food. So it's important to be careful about what you eat and drink and to observe strict standards of hygiene, especially in countries where sanitation standards are poor or unpredictable.

> 'In Indonesia, I never got sick and that's probably because
> I was always careful about hygiene. I'd always eat hot,
> cooked food – I didn't eat anything that was cold. And I
> always drank bottled water – never water out of a tap. I
> found that in Jakarta, the locals always boil their water.'

❑ Drink only purified water, undiluted fruit juices,
   bottled soft drinks, or tea or coffee that's been made
   using boiled water.

❑ Always carry purified water or some means of
   sterilising it. If you're not sure local water is safe to
   drink, sterilise it using iodine solution (five drops
   per litre, or 10 if the water's cloudy) or chlorine
   tablets. Wait 30 minutes before drinking it, and add
   lemon juice or cordial to kill the taste. If you're
   boiling water to sterilise it, remember that it has to
   boil for five minutes before it's safe.

❑ Don't use unpurified water to clean your teeth or
   gargle with, and don't assume that cold water
   provided in hotel rooms has been sterilised. Avoid
   ice in drinks where possible.

❑ Drink milk that's been boiled or pasteurised, and
   eat yoghurt and cheese – they're all safe. Yoghurt
   can also be used to soothe an upset stomach (and
   to treat thrush).

❑ Choose restaurants and food outlets that have a
   high turnover of customers and hygienic food
   preparation conditions.

> 'In China, the food was cheap and great. I'd go to
> restaurants that were really busy, 'cause I knew they'd have
> a high turnover of food, and that it would be well cooked.'

❑ Eat freshly cooked food rather than lukewarm or
   re-warmed dishes. If you can see the dish being
   prepared in front of you, so much the better. Order
   dishes that have to be cooked on the spot, such as

omelettes, to be safe. Food from markets and street stalls can be fine, as long as it's freshly prepared; food that's been sitting around in the heat, uncovered, is risky, even if it comes from an up-market restaurant.

> 'I don't usually eat at street stalls or markets much. I tend to play it by ear – if I see flies all over everything, which is often the situation in India, I avoid eating at the place.'
>
> 'I think it's a bit of a myth that you can get better-quality food by going to expensive restaurants – check out what's happening out the back of the restaurant first. Sometimes eating off the street can be a healthier option. I always look at the person who's selling the food – if they look healthy, I'm more inclined to eat their food.'

❏ Don't eat raw, unpeeled fruits or vegetables – they may have been rinsed in unpurified water. If you must eat salads, drench them in vinegar or lemon juice, which have antiseptic properties.

❏ Wash your hands thoroughly after using the toilet and before touching food. If you can't find washing facilities, at least wipe your hands, and avoid touching the food with your hands while eating.

❏ If you're worried about eating from dirty utensils, bring your own (carry chopsticks), or wipe the ones provided with a refresher towel.

❏ Adapt your eating patterns to what's around you – what you eat in France will be different to what you eat in Turkey or Thailand, and your tastes and appetite may change depending on the climate and your activity levels.

❏ If you're not sure about the food, or the menu's written in local script, use the 'ask and point' method – check out what others are eating and if you like the look of it, ask the waiter to bring you the same.

> 'Choosing a meal in China was a bit different, but it was fun. There were three ways to do it: you could either just hand over some cash and say, "Bring me a meal" – which is a very dicey option because most of the time you'd get really undercooked or raw food, and I just wouldn't eat anything that was raw. Or there was trying to find a restaurant with an English menu, which wasn't an easy task. Or you could just go into a normal restaurant and stand up and walk around all the other tables, and pick meals by what others were eating. Everybody thought that was hilarious. And then you'd point and say "I want that, that, that and that, cooked up with this." And they'd do it.'

TOILETS

Few travel guides mention the problem of finding toilets in a foreign country. Yet being desperate to relieve yourself with nowhere to go is a common frustration for travellers. Lack of appropriate toilet facilities presents particular problems for women, who can't just unzip and pee by the roadside, and who may need to change pads or tampons.

Hotels geared for Western tourists usually have Western-style flush toilets or clean squat toilets, and generally provide toilet paper. Flush toilet systems are also the most common variety in North and South America, and in most parts of Europe, although you're unlikely to find paper in South America or Greece.

> 'When I'm travelling, I always carry a loo roll, because toilets are unreliable in so many countries.'

In developing countries, toilet facilities may be very different from what you're used to. Even finding a loo can be difficult. If you're out and about and need a toilet, try department stores, larger hotels and restaurants, or public buildings (colleges, libraries, museums, town halls, cinemas). As a rule, toilets in places with limited public access are cleaner. Petrol stations and markets may have public toilet facilities, but they're often pretty basic.

In some countries, you'll find it difficult to get the privacy you're used to. In China, women crowd around and watch you as you pee; in some countries, men have been known to look under the toilet door.

'I had days and days travelling along where even going to the toilet, there would be people everywhere. And Asian toilets aren't very private at the best of times. At times in Sumatra, I had people hanging over the top of the stall, and if there was a gap between the door and the floor, there'd be men actually lying on the floor trying to watch me go to the toilet. That was pretty intense.'

'When I was at the Great Wall, I needed to use the bathroom. You can smell a Chinese toilet from several kilometres away. Most of them consist of two holes in the ground. It's a totally open bathroom – you all sit around and squat. The women were checking me out thoroughly to see if I was any different to them, which was quite humiliating. They were looking right up my skirt. You have to hold up a towel if you want any privacy.'

On bus journeys through remote areas, you may find yourself having to relieve yourself on the roadside. Wearing a long, loose, full skirt is the best solution – you can use it as 'cover' if you have to go outdoors or in places where facilities provide no privacy.

BATHING

In many parts of Asia and Africa, water is a scarce resource. Hot and cold running water, showers and baths are a luxury that few can afford. Throughout most of the developing world, people save water by soaping their bodies first, then rinsing with the water provided. You may get a hand-held shower, or a tub of water and a bucket or scoop. Don't make the mistake of climbing into the tub: you're meant to scoop out fresh water and pour it over you, not get in and dirty everyone's supply.

Bathing facilities in a number of countries, such as Indonesia, Korea, Japan, Turkey, Hungary and Scandinavia, are traditionally communal. Communal bathhouses are often segregated and are great places to socialise or relax: you can soak in thermal pools, get a massage or rubdown, sit in the steam room, bathe, and generally chill out while you get super-clean. At first, the prospect of going to communal bathhouses may seem daunting, but they're actually friendly and relaxed places, and provide great opportunities for meeting other women.

Most hostels and budget hotels have communal bathing facilities. Bring your own towel and soap, leave the place clean, and don't spend hours in there washing your clothes or conditioning your hair, especially if there are lots of you sharing. In communal showers and washrooms, wear thongs or plastic sandals to avoid catching tinea (athlete's foot).

MEDICAL SUPPLIES

What you include in your travel medical kit depends on your destination, whether you intend touring remote areas or engaging in hazardous activities, and your personal health requirements. Here is a list of basics you may want to include. Don't adopt the 'better safe than sorry' attitude and bring everything on the list: select items appropriate to the length and nature of your journey and the destinations to which you'll be travelling.

❑ Any medication you take on a regular basis and treatment for ailments you are prone to, along with spare prescriptions with the generic and brand names of the medications written clearly or typed.

- ❏ Contraceptives, including condoms.
- ❏ Treatments for thrush and cystitis.
- ❏ Paracetamol or aspirin for relief of pain and fever.
- ❏ Diarrhoea tablets, such as Lomotil or Imodium.
- ❏ An antiseptic such as Betadine, which is best carried as an iodine solution and has multiple uses. Dettol can also be useful for treating cuts and scrapes, as well as for disinfecting unsanitary bathrooms.
- ❏ Antibiotic cream or ointment, including eye ointment, and a broad-spectrum antibiotic (discuss with your doctor).
- ❏ Oil of cloves – a good temporary toothache remedy.
- ❏ Sunscreen, preferably one with a high SPF factor.
- ❏ Caladryl – a cream similar to calamine lotion, which can be used to treat sunburn, itches and minor burns.
- ❏ Lip balm, especially if you plan to travel in cold, dry climates.
- ❏ Anti-malaria tablets (check the best brand with your doctor), if you're travelling to malaria-prone areas.
- ❏ Insect repellent.
- ❏ Eardrops (such as Aquaear), if you plan to swim in public pools or scuba dive.
- ❏ Water purifier (iodine or purifying tablets).
- ❏ Petroleum jelly and salt, if you'll be bushwalking in areas prone to leeches.
- ❏ Oil and kerosene (or turpentine), to aid the removal of ticks in areas where they are prevalent.
- ❏ An all-round worm treatment such as Combantrin.
- ❏ Motion sickness tablets, if you tend to get carsick or seasick.
- ❏ Tiger balm or some sort of mentholated medication (such as Vicks VapoRub).
- ❏ Throat lozenges.
- ❏ Antacid, to treat stomach aches and indigestion.

- ❑ Tinidazole (the brand name is Fasigyn), to treat amoebic dysentery and giardia, if you're travelling to the Third World (discuss with your doctor).
- ❑ Rehydration mix, to replace fluids lost by vomiting or diarrhoea, heat exhaustion or fever. This is usually easy to obtain in the Third World; in Australia you can buy it under the brand name Gastrolyte.
- ❑ Multivitamins, if keeping a balanced diet is likely to be difficult.
- ❑ Band-aids or Elastoplast, a sterilised gauze bandage, cotton wool and scissors.
- ❑ Tweezers.
- ❑ Thermometer.
- ❑ Contact lens cleaner and saline solution, spare lenses (consider disposables) or a spare pair of glasses, and your prescription.

'When I went on a safari tour in Africa, I took all the medical stuff, including malaria tablets and syringes, just in case. I ended up using my syringes to inject Malibu into pineapples on the tour truck. We had needles, we even had tubes for blood. Some people had the most amazing kits: they had tablets for this, tablets for that, stuff for if you get malaria, calamine lotion for bites and burns, gentian violet for mosquito bites, the works.'

'I take everything – Savlon, Gastrolyte, antibiotics, bandages. It doesn't take up much room in your bag.'

'If I'm going to travel in Asia, I get all the right injections and take medicines with me, but in Europe you're safe as you can easily buy most things.'

If you plan to travel in disease-prone areas, or off the beaten track, take a good traveller's medical guide (or the relevant pages, photocopied). Some references you may want to check out include:

- *Travel Well: A Health Guide for Travellers* by Jennifer Grimwade (APC, 1988)
- *The Pocket Doctor: Your Ticket to Good Health While Traveling* by Stephen Bezruchka, M.D. (The Mountaineers, 1992)
- *Staying Healthy in Asia, Africa and Latin America* by Dirk Schroeder (Moon Publications, 1995)
- *Travellers' Health* by Richard Dawood (Oxford University Press, 1995)
- *The Traveller's Guide to Homeopathy* by Phyllis Speight (Atrium Publications, 1990)
- *The Pill* by John Guillebaud (Oxford University Press, 1996)
- *International Travel and Health*, WHO Publications Center, 49 Sheridan Avenue, Albany, New York, NY 12210, USA (ph 1-518-436 9686; fax 1-518-436 7433)
- *The Diabetic Traveler* (published quarterly): write to PO Box 8223, Stamford, CT 06905, USA, or phone 1-203-327 5832.

WHAT TO DO IF YOU GET ILL

Doctors, hospitals and medical hotlines

The range and quality of health care varies enormously from country to country and between cities and rural areas. In Western countries, standards of medical care are usually high – but costs can be crippling. Make sure your insurance policy covers you for possible expenses, including doctors', dentists', ambulance and hospital bills, especially in places like the USA, where medical fees can be astronomical. If you have a choice between public or private care, check out both options – as a visitor, you'll probably have to pay, regardless, so if private health care services are better, use them.

Developing countries don't necessarily have substandard

health care – many have excellent modern facilities and highly competent staff. Most guidebooks list addresses of Western hospitals, family planning clinics and English-speaking doctors, or you could enquire through a large hotel or an English-speaking embassy. In places where medical standards are dubious, try mission hospitals or large teaching hospitals – they may have more English-speaking doctors and better facilities.

Some insurance companies offer policy-holders access to global medical advice and referral services. You can call your medical hotline from anywhere in the world to get referrals to the nearest doctor or hospital.

If you need medical advice, go to the out-patients department of the nearest hospital or find a reputable doctor (get recommendations from hotel staff, tourist information services, fellow travellers or expats; call a medical hotline or consult your guidebook). If you're somewhere remote and become seriously ill, you may be best off travelling to a large city for treatment.

'In India, I went to the cleanest hospital I've ever been in. I never got ill there, I just got constipated. But a girlfriend passed out on me and I thought, "I've got to get her to a hospital." We got into a tuk-tuk and he took us to a hospital which was just so Western, so modern. They gave her a couple of pills and fixed her up. And they checked me out for the constipation too. I wouldn't worry much about hospitals in India, as long as you're in a big town or city.'

'I got upset tummies and mosquito bites and coral cuts in Thailand and Indonesia, and I got tonsilitis in Cairns, but there was nothing major. I went to the doctor for the tonsilitis, which cost about $30, but just self-treated everything else. I didn't have insurance, which was naughty, so I'm lucky there was only that.'

It's usually possible to see a female doctor anywhere you go, including in Muslim countries and throughout the developing world. If you need a gynaecological examination, go to a family planning clinic or hospital rather than to a private male doctor. If you're nervous about being seen by a man, take someone along for support or request that a nurse be present for the examination.

For matters related to contraception, pregnancy, abortion or STDs, your best bet is a women's health or family planning clinic or a large Western hospital. Avoid going to hospitals or clinics run by religious orders as they may frown on abortion or sexual activity outside of marriage. The International Planned Parenthood Foundation can provide a list of family planning clinics in various countries: contact them at Inner Circle, Regent's Park, London NW1 4NS, UK (ph 44-171-487 7900). In Australia, call your local family planning centre and ask for information.

Information on travellers' health can be obtained from a number of sources, including specialist books, consulates or embassies, your doctor, and travellers' health centres, services and hotlines. In Australia, contact the Travellers Medical and Vaccination Centre in your state, or call their national Information Line on 1902-261 560. In the UK, phone the Medical Advisory Service for Travellers Abroad on 44-171-631 4408. Or try the Travel Clinic Health Line (part of the Hospital for Tropical Diseases), which runs a 24-hour helpline giving the latest specialist advice on diseases commonly afflicting travellers to 'exotic' destinations, on 44-1839-337 729. In the USA, access the International Travelers' Hotline at the Centers for Disease Control in Atlanta on 1-404-332 4559, or call Overseas Access EurAide on 1-630-420 2343.

A copy of the World Health Organisation's *International Health and Travel* can be obtained by contacting Boyd Publications in the USA (ph 1-518-436 9686 or fax 1-518-436 7433) or, in Australia, by phoning the WHO's distribution outlet on (03) 9417 5361.

Diabetics planning to travel may wish to subscribe to the quarterly American periodical *The Diabetic Traveler*: to do so, phone 1-203-327 5832 or write to PO Box 8223, Stamford, CT 067905, USA (back issues can also be obtained on request).

Local and alternative remedies

Local people often have considerable experience in treating local ailments, and their remedies often work as well as or better than Western treatments. If your ailment is minor, specific to the region, or something that doesn't require urgent medical attention, you may as well give it a shot: local treatments are often cheaper and simpler to procure than Western-style medical aid. If the remedy doesn't appear to be working, go to a doctor.

> 'I got my shots before I went to China and took every medical supply I could possibly have wanted – except constipation tablets, which I actually needed. I had to go to a Chinese doctor for them. I was in a very small town, and she had a big sign out the front saying "English-speaking doctor". She had only very basic English so I got out my phrasebook and pointed to the appropriate word. She nodded, and showed me some tablets and some tea. I asked her via the phrasebook which was the quickest method and she said the tablets, so I got those. Then it was a matter of working out the dose when the label was written in Chinese.'

'Alternative' remedies such as herbal preparations, acupuncture, acupressure, massage and hands-on healing are now being recognised as effective prophylactics or treatments for many conditions. If you have used such methods with success in the past, there's no reason not to go on doing so when you're abroad.

In most Western cities, you can find a health food shop

without much trouble. If you ask around, someone's sure to know of a good masseur, Chinese doctor, herbalist or healer. Be cautious about visiting male masseurs, and avoid having acupuncture if you can't be sure the needles have been adequately sterilised.

When to seek help

Sometimes, all you need to get better is a day or two in bed with a bottle of water and a book.

> 'If I feel sick and I'm by myself, I usually just take whatever remedy I have, drink lots of water and lie in bed till I feel OK.'

Other times, you may be too ill to fend for yourself. Don't be embarrassed about asking for assistance – ask a fellow traveller or hotel staff member to check on you from time to time, bring you supplies of water, fruit or medicine, or phone for a doctor if you need one. Most people will sympathise with your plight and be happy to help you out. It's polite to offer payment if a local person comes to your aid.

> 'One of my best friends got malaria when we were in the middle of Zaire. It was hideous, you wouldn't want to go to the doctor there. She couldn't move for three days and we had to nurse her. We'd pick her up and give her a warm shower, and put her back to bed, and then she'd get hot and cold sweats again. We had to slap her around the face, shouting, "Come on, wake up, Liz!" and put her back in the shower. I felt so sorry for the girl, but it's one of those things. I always carry a malaria kit and take tablets.'

> 'My girlfriend caught a chest infection in Sydney and collapsed on the pavement one day on Oxford Street. A complete stranger picked her up, put her in a cab, took

*her to the hospital and waited till she saw a doctor, which
was nice.'*

*'I was lucky when I got ill: I was staying in a hostel with
some really great people. That kindness, even among
transient travellers, happens all the time. If you've only
known someone for three days and they get sick, you don't
just dump them. You take them in and look after them.
There's that code of ethics. People look after each other.'*

If your condition seems to be worsening, don't wait – ask
someone to phone for a doctor, or haul yourself out of
bed and catch a taxi to the nearest hospital. A good traveller's medical guide can alert you to danger signs and
symptoms for likely illnesses in the regions you'll be travelling through. If your guidebook advises you to seek
medical attention – or if you feel you need to – don't play
the heroine. Get professional advice. If you require treatment, do whatever's necessary to ensure you're well cared
for.

*'It's not worth risking your long-term health or your life
by economising on medical care – blow the budget, keep
all your receipts, and then claim it back on insurance.
It's better than saying, "I'll be all right" and ending up
really sick.'*

PSYCHOLOGICAL WELL-BEING

Dealing with down times
No matter how exciting or enjoyable your journey, there
will be times when you feel lonely, flat or depressed.
When you're far away from your usual sources of support
and comfort, it can be helpful to have some resources of
your own to fall back on.

'When you travel with other people, it's very easy not to have those "negative", introspective emotions, because you can just go and socialise and block it out. People do get very lonely travelling in groups, and with partners, because there are times when it just isn't working. But you don't feel it as much as you do when you're on your own.'

'No-one else is there to save you. I was away for four months, and no matter what happened to me, my family weren't there to reach out and help. You have to look after yourself and you know it. You learn to be very self-reliant and resourceful.'

One of the benefits of travelling alone is the confidence that comes from realising that you can support yourself, comfort yourself and keep yourself company. You won't fall to pieces. In fact, you may even learn to love your solitude. Then you never have to fear being alone again.

'I got used to doing things on my own, and I grew to enjoy my own company. It was so peaceful – there was no talking. I found I really enjoyed those solitary things, like reading books and writing in my journal, or just staring out the window, dreaming. Far from feeling lonely, I felt privileged. It was actually quite difficult to break that pattern and go out and be gregarious. I can see why people end up doing monastic retreats.'

'At times, it was scary, and really lonely, and all of those things – but it was just me, and I was experiencing all of those raw emotions on my own. It allowed me to be more passionate than I was, or probably am, travelling with other people, and it allowed me to feel softer. So I didn't mind feeling what some people might call "down" once in a while.'

Constant change can be unsettling, so it's important to do things that make you feel comfortable. When arriving in a new place, even if it's only for a night or two, make yourself at home: use your sarong as a bedspread, prop photos of loved ones on the dresser, buy a bunch of flowers, burn incense or aromatherapy oil, put on a favourite tape, read a book and chill out.

'I take silly little things for security. I have this little wooden Navaho carving, this colourful painted figure with a tuft of blue hair. She's called "Hero Woman" and I got her in Arizona. She weighs nothing and she's become my travel mascot. I Blu-tack her to the bedhead wherever I stay; she's a constant.'

'I always take photos, in one of those concertina files, to remind me of the people I love and to show people I meet. And I take one of my pillow slips, 'cause they always smell of home – of me. If I'm staying in grotty hostels, I can put up with it, but I like the pillow to smell of me, not the person who's been there the night before.'

'When I first started travelling, I felt I had to be out there, "experiencing", all the time. Then one day I thought, "Hang on – I can do whatever I like, and what's more, nobody's going to know if I just lie in bed for three hours this morning and read a book".'

Gather a surrogate support network by staying in family-run hotels or hostels and seeking out local haunts where you can become a 'regular'. After a few days in a village, small town or beach resort, you'll find yourself on speaking terms with all sorts of people – fellow guests, hotel staff and their families, restaurant proprietors, shop owners. Frequent places where the atmosphere is sociable and you feel welcomed. Being treated like a friend and greeted by name helps you to feel at home.

> *'In Madrid, I'd often go to the same vegetarian restaurant for dinner. The staff got to know me, and I got to eat healthy food. I know people say you should go off and try different things every day, but I'm a creature of habit, and I'm fussy about what I eat, so once I found a friendly place with good food, I stuck to it.'*

Keeping centred

Habits can bring consistency and balance into an otherwise unstructured, unpredictable existence. Rituals help you to feel centred. So it's important when you're travelling to establish a few routines:

- Eat breakfast at the same local café each morning.
- Swim regular laps of the local pool.
- Do yoga or tai chi on rising.
- Go to a local bathhouse once every few days for a scrubdown, sauna and massage.
- Every evening, tot up the day's expenses or plan tomorrow's activities.
- Before bed, wind down by listening to music, meditating or writing the day's events in your journal.

Maintaining a positive attitude

If you feel a little down at times, don't panic – it's often a temporary state brought on by tiredness, stress, a low-level virus, a particularly frustrating day or PMS. If you relax and think calmly and logically about the situation, you'll usually find that things don't look so bad.

> *'I was in Scandinavia and I was premenstrual. I didn't realise it at the time, but when I look back on my diary notes, they were all negative during the days leading up to my period. The weather was too cold, everyone was boring, I wasn't enjoying it, I missed my boyfriend, I hadn't brought the right clothes. At the time, it seemed as*

though everything was a problem, but once I got my period three days later, it suddenly all looked fine. It had been a hormonally induced state of mind.'

'When you're travelling, you get tired out, physically and mentally. I'd just kick back, or sit by the pool, or go to bed early. You have to rejuvenate yourself – you can't be on the go seven days a week, all year. You can do it for a certain amount of time – if you're going for six weeks, it's OK to be on the go all the time, but if you're travelling indefinitely, there are going to be times when you need to chill for quite a few days.'

You can help yourself to deal with loneliness, depression, anxiety and anger by remembering the good things about the situation you're in and affirming your own strengths. Often, something this simple is enough to get you back into a positive frame of mind.

'I try to spend time before I leave home affirming to myself that I'm going to be really alert, and in the right place at the right time. I try to instil confidence in myself. And then I try not to worry too much, and have active faith – being sensible but not planning for disaster.'

'I think women have more tolerance for trying to work through things – we do it more easily than men. Also, our pain tolerance is greater than men's. We have stamina.'

Sometimes it takes a conscious effort or some constructive action – like changing your travel plans, treating yourself to a luxury hotel, a massage or a meal at a nice restaurant.

'If I felt down, I'd usually shout myself a treat as a way of coping with it. When you're on a tight budget you don't tend to do much of that. I'd buy something new or do something special, out of the ordinary.'

'In India, when I first arrived and felt like I was the only white person there, I went to a big hotel and had a banquet lunch. It wasn't too expensive, and knowing that I'd be surrounded by other Westerners made me feel more comfortable. When you first arrive in some places, such as parts of Asia, you need to settle in. That sort of thing helps you ease into it more gently than if you wander into the local restaurant where they offer you chicken feet for lunch.'

'If I got a bit lonely, I'd treat myself to some nicer accommodation for a night – something a bit more luxurious. That always made me feel better.'

Sometimes the best cure for a case of the blues is writing a postcard to a loved one, pouring your emotions out into your journal or phoning home.

'Once I had all my mail redirected and it got sent to the wrong island. I was so dying to hear some news, I got really depressed about it – I even started bawling. I got over it, though – I just made a phone call home.'

'I usually get on the phone to my family if I feel down or upset or lonely. I sometimes write in my diary. Or I read.'

'Sometimes things can get a bit magnified when you're on your own. Even silly things like missing a bus. When I got lonely or upset, I'd ring up my mum and have a bit of a cry, and that'd make me feel better.'

Remember that negative moods come and go, wherever you are, and you can't expect to be happy every moment of your trip. Feeling better may simply be a matter of chilling out and waiting. Your spirits are almost certain to revive after a day or two.

'I didn't get down very often, but if I did feel a bit depressed, I'd take some quiet time out for myself and go somewhere where I could just sit and think about what it was that was getting me down. Was it a language thing? A company thing? And then I'd decide from there what I needed to do about it – go and meet some people, or whatever the solution might be.'

'I think it's a mistake to expect you're going to have a fantastic time, all the time – that you're going to enjoy every minute of it. I mean, do you enjoy every minute of any six months of your life? Naturally, there are ups and downs. It's an experience rather than an enjoyment process. It's through hardship that you find out what you're capable of doing. As a result of my trip, I learned that nothing was impossible, provided I wanted to do it strongly enough. The fact that it wasn't constantly fun wasn't the important thing.'

'A positive attitude's essential. When I got into a terrible situation, I'd always think, "It'll pass soon." As long as you think positively, positive things come your way.'

WORK, STUDY AND DOING BUSINESS

One of the most rewarding ways to get to know another culture is by becoming actively involved in it. Working and studying overseas not only broaden your mind and deepen your understanding – they can also bring you new skills, new friends and extra cash.

You may set off with the intention of pursuing your profession, expanding your experience or just picking up a few extra bucks along the way. You may want to study at a particular overseas institution or take a short intensive course in language, cuisine or culture.

'I'd studied Spanish at school and university and decided to do a graduate course in Spanish language and culture in Granada. It was fantastic – a great group of students and a beautiful place to live. Every break, I'd pick up my backpack and take a trip to somewhere in Europe or down to Morocco or to the coast of Turkey. I had a fantastic

You may have no intention of working initially but end up taking a job to eke out your travel funds. Or perhaps you'll be offered a work opportunity that's too good to refuse.

WORK

Local unemployment, nationalistic policies and trading blocs, slow economies and the desire for staff with local knowledge all add up to the fact that overseas work isn't easy to come by. These days, getting a job abroad involves planning carefully, thinking realistically, selling your own skills, being prepared to work hard for low wages, and being in the right place at the right time.

Job opportunities differ from place to place, with type of work, pay, conditions and legal restrictions on foreign employees varying widely. Obtaining an official permit to work in many countries can be difficult, and usually involves lining up a job and a work permit or special visa well before your departure date. But if you're determined, you can usually find work.

> 'When you travel alone, you're more open to making decisions and being more assertive than you normally would be. This is why I got such wonderful work experience during my travels. I had that adventurous spirit, and I was a lot more confident about getting what I wanted. I searched for the jobs. I was game enough to ask the right people and persist.'

Working Holiday Visas

If you're an Australian citizen in your teens or twenties, obtaining a Working Holiday Visa (WHV) is the easiest way to make sure you can work legally while you're overseas. Reciprocal work agreements exist between Australia and a number of countries to allow young people to use their skills abroad. Currently, the Australian government has reciprocal agreements with the UK, Canada, Japan, Ireland and the Netherlands, allowing Australian citizens to work for six to 12 months in the participating country, provided they meet age, financial and skill requirements, and provided that the primary purpose of their trip is recreational. The amount of work you can take on is restricted under a WHV – you are expected to work for short periods only.

Dual citizenship

If you or your husband hold a foreign passport, or if your parents or grandparents were born overseas, you may be eligible for unrestricted work in that country, or in countries belonging to that bloc. Check with the Passport Office at the Department of Foreign Affairs for details.

Employer sponsorship

If you're not eligible for a WHV or dual citizenship, you'll usually have to obtain the sponsorship of an employer in the country you wish to work in before you can get an official work permit. Special rules may apply for people with particular skills (for example, doctors, dentists, journalists, artists and ministers of the church). The general rule is that your prospective employer must show that locals cannot provide the skills you have. Employer sponsorship must be set up in advance, and it can take weeks or even months to get approval and organise the proper documents, so you'll have to plan ahead.

> 'I'm a freelance journalist, which means I can work from wherever I am in the world. But you still need to get permits. I got an "I" visa for the United States: it cost me $160 and took two days to get a five-year working visa. It means I can write articles for the Australian publications that sponsored me while I travel around America.'

In-demand jobs

If you have professional skills, you may be able to arrange work in overseas countries by writing – well in advance – to the organisations for which you're interested in working. If you're already employed by a company with overseas branches, ask about transfers. Generally in demand are medical, nursing and agricultural skills (especially in developing countries), civil engineering, accounting, computing (hardware and software), domestic work and secretarial work (especially for those who have word-processing and computer skills).

Teaching English as a second language remains a firm favourite, and it definitely helps to have teaching qualifications (while many people who teach English and other languages have no formal training, a teaching degree or TESL diploma can help you get a well-paid job in this area, or secure a position in places where competition is stiff). In Australia, you can get more information on teaching positions abroad by writing to the Graduate Careers Council of Australia, PO Box 28, Parkville VIC 3052.

> 'When I was looking for work in Jakarta, I got a copy of the local English-speaking newspaper, the Jakarta Post, which has a section of ads for travellers. I looked through the ads, found an English college and got a job there as a teacher. Mostly I taught reps working in government offices, doing orientation English. You don't need any Indonesian: you just pick a topic, sit down with the group and talk about it. They're quite happy with that – that's all they want.'

Voluntary work

If you're prepared to work for love alone, you have a good chance of landing an overseas job. In many Third World countries, governments encourage foreigners to contribute their skills and services by means of special programs, many of which are voluntary. Voluntary work schemes exist in a number of developing countries in Africa, Asia and the Pacific, with most positions being for reasonably long periods (about two years is common). Especially in demand are teachers, doctors, nurses and medical aides, engineers, accountants, vets, farm labourers and carpenters. You may be paid a living allowance and/or part of your travel expenses, but don't expect an income. The rewards you'll get are 'hands-on' experience of the culture, contact with local people and the good feeling you get from helping.

In Australia, find out about such schemes through the Overseas Service Bureau, which runs the Australian Volunteers Abroad Program, the organisation responsible for placing most Australian voluntary development workers in positions overseas. Other organisations that deal with volunteers are the United Nations, Community Aid Abroad (CAA), the Australian Executive Services Overseas Program (AESOP), the Resource and Action Committee for Latin America (RACLA) and the Australia-Cuba Friendly Society (ACFS).

AESOP sends volunteers at short notice to provide short-term technical assistance in developing countries. RACLA and ACFS send work teams to Nicaragua and Cuba for periods of a month to a year. CAA sometimes recruits volunteers with specific skills from their register for 12 to 18-month postings on their overseas aid projects (some wages and expenses paid). You could also try the Red Cross, or ask at your local church.

'Experience' exchanges

Many organisations provide travel opportunities for people wishing to participate in cultural exchange programs. The range of programs is wide, catering for teenagers and adults, students and workers, and encompassing various types of 'experience', from teaching English in China or India, to organic farm work, business and computing placements, language courses and youth counselling. Most of the schemes require you to pay your own airfare plus a set fee, but certain programs provide you with full board, and a living allowance or wage.

'A girlfriend and I decided to stay on a kibbutz on the border of Jordan. We just walked in and said we wanted to volunteer, and they said, "Fine." We ended up with six other volunteers. I really enjoyed it – I got opportunities to do things you'd never do in normal life, like milking cows. I started off in the dining room and kitchen, then I thought I'd dabble in a bit of farm work, to learn some new skills. I did everything I possibly could while I was there. When you get to a kibbutz, you can actually get an adopted family, and that helps you to get a bit of a background on the kibbutz life. Whereas a lot of travellers just go in and stay on a kibbutz for a bludge, cheap grog and free cigarettes.'

SWAP program

If you're a student, you may be able to join an organised overseas work program such as SWAP (Student Work Abroad Program). SWAP offers students access to a variety of jobs, most of them unskilled, in participating countries – Australia, the USA, Canada, Japan and Britain. Applications are usually made in July or August for departure at the end of the year. Ask for details at your university or TAFE.

> 'Working at the resorts in Canada was fantastic. I made lots of friends, so after the season finished, I drove with two guys across Canada, where we stayed with a girl who'd worked with us on the mountain. It gave me a good start to my travels.'

Under-the-counter work

Many travellers work 'under the counter' (illegally) and this is still an accepted and relatively safe practice in many places. With any form of under-the-counter work, however, there are drawbacks: you're in no position to complain about pay or conditions, you cannot claim compensation for illness or injury, and if you're caught, you may face fines or deportation.

> 'I worked in a food factory in Germany and the workers were all Turkish women. It was extremely underpaid and the conditions were appalling. We weren't allowed to speak for eight hours at a time. There was water up to our knees, and we used to have to carry 40-kilogram boxes on our own. If we helped each other, we'd get into trouble. Women would just collapse at the end of the day, crying because they were so tired. They had unions, but none of the women would come forward because they were afraid of losing their jobs. I was always in trouble. They sacked me in the end. I was creating too many waves.'

> *'I met lots of girls who were working under the counter in the States, in Europe and in the UK. They all complained about the fact that wages and conditions were really bad, but they couldn't do anything about it, because they were illegal workers. It was a case of put up and shut up.'*

Resources

If you're after more information about the job market abroad, consult one of these useful guides:

❏ *Jobs Abroad: The Australian Travellers Guide to Working Overseas* (3rd edition) by Kevin Casey (Kimberley Publications, 1996)

❏ *Workaway Guide* by Karen Halliday (Workaway, 1996)

❏ *Live, Work and Play in London and the UK for Young Australians* by Sharyn McCullum (Kangaroo Press, 1995).

Country by country
Britain

If you're an Australian citizen aged between 17 and 27 and have sufficient funds, you can work for up to two years in Britain under the Working Holiday Makers' Scheme. (Reciprocal agreements allow young British citizens to work while holidaying in Australia.) A variety of skilled and unskilled work is available – secretarial, bar work, catering, nannying, waitressing, accounting and media jobs are all open to Australians.

Once you arrive, join at least one job-finding agency (they're listed in tourist publications) – either general, or dealing specifically with your field of interest; also read local papers, check hostel and university notice boards, and ask around. Pay and conditions for unskilled work are often substandard but there are compensations.

> *'I worked at silver-service waitressing and that was really easy, 'cause there are a lot of agencies in London. They don't have casual work vacancies like we do in Australia – if places need more staff, they call an employment agency. You register with the agencies and then call them and they'll tell you what work there is. Sometimes you can get a week's work at one place, or you can hang out each afternoon and see if there's a job for you that night. There's catering, there's work for nannies, and there's secretarial. The pay's not great. But I enjoyed it because you get to meet a lot of people and you get paid for it.'*

Europe

If you are eligible for an EC passport, you can work in most EC member countries (check before leaving Australia, however: some EC countries don't allow dual citizenship, and you don't want to sacrifice your Australian passport for the sake of six months' work). For Australians, the only other legal work options in countries apart from Britain and the Netherlands for holders of Holiday Makers' visas are jobs with British-based continental tour companies (for example, Contiki) as guides, drivers, cooks or cleaners; nanny work originating in Britain; jobs arranged through the SWAP scheme; or voluntary work team jobs.

> *'I was offered a job with a tour company in Europe and Africa, which I took. Then that tour company went bust so I worked with Contiki as a mobile cook – I couldn't boil an egg when I left home. I kind of fell into that job because I wanted to be a tour manager and they'd already taken their intake for the year, so they suggested I sign on as chef.'*

> *'I wanted to go to Sicily but I was told it wasn't safe to travel alone there. And I knew the only jobs I'd be able to do there would be teaching English or au pair work – they*

United States

It's difficult to find work anywhere in the USA without a 'Green Card' (work permit), which you can't get unless you're an American citizen, or you have a job officially lined up and the appropriate visa. Laws designed to protect locals' jobs mean an employer can be fined heavily for giving a job to a non-permit holder, so, naturally, employers are wary of hiring foreigners.

Short-term opportunities are available to Australians wanting to work at summer camps as counsellors or maintenance staff. For information, phone Camp America on (02) 9264 2477 or (03) 9899 5424.

Students from participating countries (including Australia) may apply to work in the USA under the SWAP scheme, which provides jobs for up to 10 months in a variety of unskilled and semi-skilled positions, such as bar work, waitressing and ski resort work. Apply around six months in advance (see page 309).

There are plenty of openings for Australians wishing to study in the USA, either as exchange students (for example, with the International Student Exchange Program), as scholarship holders or as fee-paying students. Enquire about opportunities through the Australian–American Educational Foundation, Australian National University (ANU), Canberra (ph (06) 249 5111); the US Information Service at the US Consulate (offices in Melbourne, Sydney and Perth); or the Fulbright Exchange Program (ph (06) 247 9331/2).

for the Hyatt hotel chain. I didn't line anything up in advance – I just picked up the work once I got there. I think for an Australian woman, the American response is a very positive one. They tend to be very positive, "yes" people overall, and especially in a work context. Quick to train you, quick to promote you.'

Canada

Unless you're eligible for a Working Holiday Visa (phone the Canadian High Commission for details), Australians wishing to work in Canada have to get sponsorship from a Canadian employer, or apply for work under the SWAP scheme (see page 309). Most work is at ski resorts and in summer holiday resorts, many of which are in remote locations.

'My first working holiday was fairly organised. I'd written away to a number of people I had names of at ski resorts in Canada and had lined up a job so I knew I'd have an income. Share accommodation in a condo came with the job, so I knew I'd meet people. It was an easy transition to travelling. I spent a week in Vancouver on my own, then caught the train to Banff. Someone came and picked me up from the station and took me to the resort. I worked there for the ski season, made lots of friends and a bit of money, then set out on my own.'

Japan

Any Australian aged between 18 and 27 can work in Japan for up to six months (renewable for another six) under the Working Holiday Makers' Scheme, provided you have a return ticket and sufficient funds. Tokyo's Working Holiday Centre gives local employment information, or check English-language newspapers.

The most common jobs for female foreigners are teaching English and cocktail bar hostessing. If you want to teach, look for ads in tourist publications or phone private English-language schools. When phoning for jobs, remember that British or US-sounding accents are preferred to broad 'Ocker' ones. You'll be more likely to get work if you have formal teaching qualifications. Or apply well in advance to the Japan Exchange and Teaching (JET) program, which offers 12-month placements in Japanese schools to successful applicants (details from Japanese consulates).

> 'In Japan, they're getting fussier about qualifications for teaching English – they often require some sort of certificate to say you have a degree or you've done an ESL course. You can still do home tutoring. The trick is to know someone who's been there. We have friends who, because they knew somebody, got fantastic English teaching jobs, earning over $100 an hour.'

Hostessing jobs are advertised in tourist papers, or go to the nightclub district and ask. Hostessing work can be boring and an insult to your intelligence, but it's generally safe, provided you make your personal limits clear and keep your wits about you. Money, generally, is great – but Japan is expensive, so you probably won't save.

> 'I couldn't get a job teaching English in Japan so I ended up hostessing. It was boring at times, but it wasn't dangerous. I didn't have any hair-raising experiences.'

WOMEN WHO DID IT

Kate
Office temping, bar work – Britain
'On my second trip to Europe, I decided to work in London. I was familiar with the place and, because they speak English, there's greater flexibility in the work available to

you. My grandmother's British, so I didn't need a special visa: I could work as much as I wanted to.

'I started by door-knocking and got lots of work in bars and restaurants that way. Pay and conditions weren't great – you have to be prepared for a drop in your standard of living – but it isn't hard to find jobs. In London, they think Australians are good workers so they're likely to hire you. I also looked through the local papers: I never thought I'd get a job that way, but I saw an ad in *Time Out* magazine, applied and was lucky enough to be hired by a media research and monitoring company, doing office assistance and some production work. They even trained me to type.

'I took a CV, references, work samples and "interview" clothes with me. They definitely helped – if you come prepared, it shows you're serious, not a fly-by-night like so many tourists. As well as doing my own hunting, I joined a couple of agencies: there are hundreds in London. They didn't charge fees and the procedure was simple – the agency takes your details, skills etc, and calls you when jobs come up. There is stacks of temp work available, especially if you have some secretarial skills. I only had basic typing but I have a good phone manner, and I pushed a bit! You earn a bit more temping than doing bar work, and you get to mix more with English people.

'I could survive on the wages, but that wasn't the incentive. The big pluses for me were working in one of the biggest media centres in the world, meeting people in more than a superficial way, and being able to go off to Europe or the rest of Britain on weekends.'

Christine
Nanny – London, Europe, the USA
'I'd been travelling in Europe and I ran out of cash, so I decided to try to work in London as a nanny. I had a one-year working visa which I'd got before I left Australia. I

applied to some agencies – anyone can join – and was placed with my first family a few days later. They were rich and seemed nice. They interviewed me over lunch and liked me, so I moved in the next week.

'I didn't have any specific training in child care, just common sense. But I was clean, well presented, well spoken, and I knew how to sell myself. You have to come across as loving children, being practical and down to earth, and willing to give up your time and freedom. In the interview, forget your pride – get on the kids' level, play with them. If you can do that, it helps. Apart from that, they usually want you to have an International Driver's Licence and some character references. They prefer it if you only drink on your days off, and they don't generally like boyfriends. Skills in nursing, cooking, languages, teaching or special nanny school qualifications are all sought after.

'European and American families love Australian girls because they're straightforward and prepared to work hard. There's not a lot of money in it, but you don't pay for accommodation or food. You may only get to travel occasionally, so you just break even and you often have to put up with a lot. The British, especially, tend to be strict and formal: it's more of a servant-master relationship, where you're housekeeper, dogsbody, everything. In America, it's far more relaxed: you don't have to do much housework, you're treated like one of the family, and the pay's better – it can be fantastic.

'The richer the family, the more money, travel and perks you get. With one of the wealthy European families I worked for, I got to eat Christmas dinner on board a private 747 jet, with food flown out from Harrods and guests like Robin Williams the actor. I got presents; I got to travel all around Europe; I could call home when I liked. I met some very important people. And the kids were wonderful, too. It's not always that good.

'About half the girls who start off as nannies in England

end up in America, but it can be hard to get a permit to work unless you know people there and can arrange jobs and papers well in advance. Without a legal contract, you have to choose the family very carefully, because if something goes wrong, or you want to leave, you're at their mercy. If you do have trouble, stick up for yourself! And make sure you clearly sort out things like duties, days off, and whether the kids get to travel, *before* you start: it's much harder afterwards.

'I was prepared to compromise, for the experiences and the travel. It's exciting and challenging. Even when it's horrible, it's an experience. You have to look at it in perspective. Having worked as a rich family's nanny was a huge asset when I got back to Australia: I had no trouble getting jobs, especially in the hospitality industry, because I had heaps of confidence and poise. Because of everything I'd seen, all the important people I'd met, everything was a piece of cake. I guess I'd become "worldly". You soon come down to earth, but it certainly helps you get any job involving self-promotion.'

Deborah
Journalist — Israel

'On my second trip to Israel, I wanted to get beyond the superficial tourist impressions. I thought the best way to do that was to work there. I chose Israel because I'd lived there for a while as a child and have a strong affinity with the place. I also speak Hebrew and had a few skills – an arts degree and some experience in uni newspaper and radio – so I knew I wouldn't be limited to unskilled jobs.

'I didn't know what sort of work I was going to do but I was interested in media and writing, so I arrived with my references and CV and started making calls. I had contacts through family but none of them could help me. Then I met a girl who was sub-editing on the English-language tourist paper *Jerusalem Post* in Tel Aviv. They needed someone bilingual to do interviews. I was lucky: I wouldn't have even heard about the job if I hadn't had my tentacles out. It was also an advantage to be a new face, with a fresh perspective.

'It was difficult work, because I wasn't really qualified. The pay was terrible. I had to work very hard, and I learnt fast, the hard way. The language wasn't a problem for me, and it wasn't dangerous – they didn't give me those sorts of assignments – but getting around a strange city was a challenge! It's one of the best ways to get to know a place, though. And I learnt so much. Now I have the journalistic skills, I can take them anywhere.'

STUDY

If you want to broaden your mental horizons at the same time as you expand your physical ones, consider studying at a foreign school or university. Not only will you meet some of that country's most dynamic young people, you'll also gain valuable educational qualifications and experience.

An increasing number of opportunities exist for Australians to study in foreign countries, at secondary, tertiary undergraduate and postgraduate levels. The variety of study options, courses and destinations available is enormous – and if you can't afford the expense, a range of funding schemes have been set up to help finance your study program, from grants and scholarships to private corporate assistance.

You may choose to do a six-week, on-the-spot crash course in French, German, Indonesian or Thai, or to spend up to three years pursuing more comprehensive knowledge. Major universities in many non-English-speaking countries provide courses conducted in English.

Most overseas study schemes require you to meet certain criteria so you should apply well in advance. If you need financial backing, you'll have to allow even more time so that you can explore funding options.

For information on programs available to secondary school students, consult your careers guidance officer, or apply directly to an overseas school.

Overseas tertiary study programs operate at both undergraduate and graduate levels, although more opportunities exist for students who have completed a degree, especially if you need financial backing. Some overseas undergraduate courses can be used as accreditation for your course at an Australian university.

Resources

Look for information on overseas tertiary study schemes in university or college libraries and career centres, or talk to your campus careers officer. Publications that may be of use to you in your search are:

- *Awards for Postgraduate Study Overseas* (Graduate Careers Council of Australia), available from GCCA, PO Box 28, Parkville VIC 3052, ph (03) 9344 8247 – gives details of study grants for overseas students
- *Study Abroad* (UNESCO Publications, ph (02) 9905 0307) – lists over 200,000 courses and scholarships offered internationally
- *The Grants Register* (Macmillan) – a biannual publication containing details of financial assistance for overseas study offered by government and private organisations
- *Philanthropic Trusts in Australia* (ACER, ph (03) 9277 5555) – contains details of financial assistance schemes operated by non-profit, non-government organisations
- *International Handbook of Universities and Other Institutes of Higher Education* (Macmillan) – a guide to universities in 108 countries other than the Commonwealth, the USA, Ireland and South Africa.

BUSINESS TRAVEL

When you're travelling on business, you're usually tied to a fixed itinerary and a tight schedule. You have to be on the ball and alert if you're to do your job effectively. As a businesswoman, you're expected to be punctual, polite, and to present a polished corporate image. So it's crucial that you plan your trip with these considerations in mind.

Make sure you're on the ball, and try to be especially well organised – it's hard enough doing business in a foreign country without having to fix up errors or chase after loose ends.

> 'At home, I like to leave things here and there: you should see my office. But when I'm travelling, I'm so ordered. I know exactly where everything is, know what I'm doing, where I'm going. I'm a different person when I'm overseas. As soon as I get on that plane, I just head forward and take control of myself.'

Accommodation and transport

Save yourself time and trouble by pre-booking accommodation and transport. Go for comfort, facilities and convenience, even if it means higher costs. You need to have a base that allows you to operate efficiently during working hours, sleep comfortably at night, and impress your business contacts. Most of your expenses should be tax-deductible, so keep all receipts.

> 'The five-star hotels are really your lifeline. If you need to do the dry-cleaning or see a doctor, they can arrange that for you. Because in a lot of places, you can't read the street or shop signs, so it's more difficult to do simple things like changing money, putting luggage somewhere, making a telephone call, getting a taxi, reading a map . . .'

> *'I always stay in five-star facilities. It's really important,
> especially if you're doing business in Asia. If anyone is
> sending you there – that is, if you're working for a
> company – you should demand five-star accommodation,
> and if the company can't afford it, you shouldn't go.
> Because when you're on the road, you don't have an
> office, you don't have a corporate identity, you're in a
> strange country – the only stature you have is the hotel
> you can afford, your business cards, the clothes on your
> back: that's what you're presenting. They don't know who
> you are, whether you're a major blue-chip company or
> your own business. So if you can only afford to stay in a
> poor hotel, you're better off saving your money and not
> going away. It's fundamental to the impression you give.'*

Look for accommodation that has the sorts of in-house
services you'll need: modern phone and fax facilities, a
conference space, self-catering, laundry and dry-cleaning,
and so on. Five-star hotels, no matter where you are, provide all the business basics, but if you shop around you
may get more services or a better deal.

> *'Access to phones in big cities can be difficult. London's a
> bitch for phones – finding phones, tolerable ones, where
> you can have a conversation, that aren't insecure. In some
> countries, the phone system's just strange. It makes such a
> lot of difference to be staying somewhere where the staff
> speak English and where there's a phone in your room.'*

> *'You have to expect to spend at least the value of your
> hotel room again on telecommunications and business
> facilities. I travel with a laptop, GSM, mobile. On the
> road, I'd probably get 50 pages of faxes a week.
> Telecommunications aren't anywhere near as reliable as
> you'd like them to be: in a lot of countries – you're
> pushing to get out on a phone line. So you've got to expect
> to use fax. E-mail's lovely if you can get it, but a lot of the*

Cut down on commuting time by choosing accommodation that's close to where you'll be doing most of your
business. If you plan on spending part of your time sightseeing, or going out after hours, you may prefer to stay
somewhere in the tourist centre. Use taxis or hire cars with
drivers rather than trying to negotiate unfamiliar public
transport systems – it's a stressful and unreliable way to
get to work.

'You do things differently when you're on a business trip.
For example, I'd catch a taxi from the airport, regardless
of the expense, because I believe it's more important for
me not to go through the stress of having to catch public
transport into a city. It's worth $50 to me to catch a taxi
in from JFK airport rather than spending three hours
lugging my bags around, maybe getting something ripped
off. You have things in your bags that are vital.'

'When I'm going to a meeting, I always take a taxi. When
I organise meetings, I ask them to fax a copy of their
business card over and I carry it with me. I can usually tell
the taxi driver which main roads to take, where to turn
left or right and stop, and pay, and get to where I want to
go, in Mandarin. But if you start to give that much
Chinese, the driver starts to speak back to you and say,
"Well, what if I take this shortcut?" or "How about we
stop for noodles on the way?" and then you have to say,
"Sorry, you've lost me – I can't speak this much Chinese."

So it's good to have the address of the place you're going with you, along with the card from your hotel.

Scheduling meetings

Where possible, schedule important meetings in advance, but don't overload your schedule – allow for transport delays and orientation difficulties and traffic jams, especially if you're unfamiliar with the area.

'Make sure you have an itinerary – have at least one meeting every day that's officially arranged. Don't have more, 'cause you need time free to schedule in other meetings, but you also don't know how long it's going to take to get there, you don't know what the traffic will be like.'

'I went to Seoul for a meeting, after coming straight from Beijing. I got up at 6 a.m. and it took me two hours to get to the airport out of Beijing. Then there was a traffic jam at the airport; I was sitting on the plane for an hour and a half before we took off. When the plane arrived, a nuclear submarine had just surfaced in Seoul with 11 North Koreans on it who had all disappeared somewhere in the city, and they were checking every single car. It took two and a half hours to get from the airport to that first meeting. So in that day, I went to two meetings and it took all day to get to them. You can never assume things will go smoothly.'

'I went to India on business and I had five meetings scheduled per day. It was a joke. You just can't do it. And when your business is done, people want to eat with you, or entertain you afterwards. So if you have to rush off afterwards, it looks really bad.'

Clothes, dress and hair

Pack a smart, sensible, conservative work wardrobe (see pages 63–7) and get a chic wash'n'wear haircut. Trousers and pantsuits may be acceptable for working women in some countries but are considered inappropriate in others.

'I'm a business executive and I need to look my best from first thing in the morning to late at night. I pack conservative clothes in smart combinations; I take a lot of navy, cream and black. Microfibre suits are great 'cause they don't crush. And skirts rather than trousers, especially in Asia.'

'I twirl my hair, which is a bad habit in business – it can look provocative – so I need to have short hair. I wear dresses, mostly, just straight, classic business stuff. I wear pants when I'm out walking. They are a little more conservative in Asia – all the doors open for you and everyone tells you you're very beautiful, which I like. I just say, "Oh, thank you".'

'I always take dirty laundry with me when I travel and get the hotel laundry service to wash it. I take three complete outfits, top, skirt or pants and shoes – and a jacket, and something formal, and something for the pool. I travel in this shoulder-to-ankle-length T-shirt thing and then I put a shirt over it, so my arms are covered but I'm comfortable for the plane. The real test is when you have to travel in Beijing's winter, and suddenly you have to take five bags because you need so much clothing. You just try not to do it.'

Language

Learn common phrases and basic courtesies in the local greetings, and know the correct greetings, gestures and formalities. When in doubt, follow the lead of those around you, and notice how superiors and inferiors, men and women interact.

> 'One thing that's good to do is to learn the way in which people of a particular culture confirm – those "nodding" words – they change in different languages. So a Chinese person could be speaking to you in English but you can use those confirming Chinese words and gestures back. I really only have the basics, even in Mandarin. But that's all you need for business, 'cause almost all of it is conducted in English.'

Practicalities

As a business traveller, you may need to make special preparations, and you'll have to be especially well organised. It's important to make sure all your documents are in order – the last thing you want is to be held up in transit by red tape or distracted and inconvenienced by bureaucratic hassles.

Check that you have all the necessary visas (preferably multiple re-entry ones for maximum flexibility), sufficient funds (plus access to instant cash advances and prompt replacement of lost credit cards, travellers' cheques or tickets) and appropriate insurance (including insurance for computer equipment and important goods or documents). Reconfirm all flights, accommodation bookings, meeting times and arrival arrangements just before you leave. Make contingency plans with colleagues in case of transport delays. Consider carrying a laptop computer with fax modem and e-mail facilities, and/or an internationally usable mobile phone for ease of communication.

> 'You can do so many things everywhere nowadays. You can book hotel rooms across the other side of the world from your laptop, send faxes or e-mail anywhere, get money by phone. You can take on a travel insurance policy where they'll give you money instantly to go out and buy a new wardrobe if your stuff gets stolen – which you need if you're on a business trip.'

> *'The first thing to do is get the longest possible visa, 'cause if you're sent on one trip to a country, you'll probably be sent on 20. As soon as you start to go there on business, you're going to get work and have to go back there.'*

Streamline your luggage to ensure you look smart and well presented, make transits simpler and minimise your chances of losing vital documents en route. If possible, travel with carry-on luggage only, use wheeled suitcases, mark luggage clearly and keep important goods and documents on you while travelling.

> *'Never, ever travel with more luggage than you can carry. Because it's not acceptable in a business context to have backpacks – you've got to streamline your luggage so you can move around and not look like a dickhead. Internationally, try not to have to put anything in the hold, because a normal business trip might involve five or six connections. If you're in countries where the booking systems are different, the bar codes on luggage are different, you can guarantee you'll lose or misplace a piece of luggage along the way. It's really sensible to try to carry everything on board if you can. And have wheels on your bag, like the bags that pilots carry. So you can actually carry files in the outside pockets.'*

In transit

When you're travelling on business, it makes sense to fly business class, hire drivers for internal trips, and take first-class reservations on trains if you need to catch them. While a holiday-maker can afford to get drunk on her way from A to B, the last thing a working woman needs on top of jet lag or train lag is a hangover. It's imperative that you use transit time to relax and prepare. Smart business travellers spend their journeys sleeping – or at least resting – whenever possible. Eat only what's not going to give you indigestion and drink alcohol, if at all, in moderation and with meals. If your seatmate is bothering you with idle chatter, request a seat transfer.

If your work involves lots of travel and lots of stopovers, it pays to join airport clubs so you can escape enervating, time-wasting transit lounge waits. Airport club lounges are relatively quiet and comfortable, and most provide useful facilities such as fax machines, places to plug in your laptop, telephones and showers, along with refreshments and streamlined ticketing services.

'I always fly business class. If you fly economy, you've just got to be prepared to get up as quickly as you can after the seatbelt lights go out and go off and find an aisle seat. I tried not drinking on flights, and I tried drinking on flights – everything. Now I just eat and drink whatever I can get my hands on, and have a massage when I arrive. I look forward to that.'

'Joining the airport clubs is a good idea – you have to pay about $600 a year for membership but it's really worth it, especially if you're spending a lot of time in transit. And you have to count on flights being delayed. They've got a bar, food, newspapers. You can do your faxes, telephone calls; you can have a shower. And they reconfirm your tickets and all that sort of stuff. If I had to sit in the main airport lounge I'd go out of my mind. It's OK in Australia, but in most major airports, especially in Asia, you're just on the floor. The club lounge is a much better alternative.'

'When I'm away on business, the thing I'm always most scared about is losing my business material, my briefcase or my laptop – the idea of getting there and botching the whole show because you don't have your information. So I'm always super-careful in transit.'

Orientation

Again, doing a little advance research can greatly improve your ability to find your way around a foreign city. Being orientated and feeling 'at home' in the place where you're doing business helps you to feel relaxed and confident, and ups your chances of arriving at meetings and conference venues unruffled and on time.

> 'If you only have three or four days in a place, you have to do business pretty much as soon as you land – you've got to try and get an impression of the place. So I go to a supermarket and the local market to get a look at the prices and get a feel of what everyday people are buying and doing, and what the market's like. I read the newspapers. I catch public transport. I go to a nightclub, go to a bar, eat local, eat at a street stall. I really try and welcome the local food and get a feel for the things I like to eat. Because everyone wants to indulge you if you know a special local food.'

If language is a problem, and especially in places where foreign scripts make street signs and names indecipherable, you may need to enlist the services of your hotel staff, workmates and drivers. Make sure you have names, addresses and directions clearly written out for you in both English and the local language, so you can ask taxi drivers or passers-by if you're not sure of where you are (or what office you're meant to head for when you get there).

> 'I have a little plastic business-card holder with me, so I can carry the business cards of everyone I'm doing business with in that city with me. They usually have their names and addresses in English on one side and Chinese or Korean or whatever on the other. I carry that in my bag, so I can show the driver the address.'

Eating, drinking and entertainment

Leave time in your schedule for work-related socialising – it's often the place where deals get sealed. Try to stick to mineral water or fruit juice rather than alcohol at business dinners, and don't party too hard after hours (or wade through the hotel minibar). When you're hung over and stressed out, you're more likely to make costly errors of judgement. Instead, have nights in, or plan early-finishing outings like films, concerts or dinners.

'The entertainment in most of Asia consists primarily of banquets, although you get taken to the occasional nightclub. In Korea they're big drinkers, but in most places in Asia they're not, such as Indonesia, Malaysia, Singapore, Hong Kong and India. In Northern Asia, they drink. And they expect you to get drunk with them.

'In Korea, they have this tradition where one of the people you're drinking with sculls their cup, then they put it down in front of you and pour it, and you have to drink their cup. And then everyone at the table will follow suit. So everyone at the table is swapping cups. If you don't drink the cup that's offered you on the spot, you will accumulate cups about you. The force of the masses means that eventually you're up for eight big ones!

'And the alcohol level of some of the drinks is very high. It's like a sake, 50 or 60 per cent proof – vodka's 27 per cent. I've been to do's in Shandong where I've had to throw drinks discreetly under the table just to get through the "salutes". In some places, a number of the people at the table won't drink, but in Korea, they all do.

'Business is over by six, and people then sit down to a business dinner. In fact, anywhere on business it's like that: you do a full day's work and no-one goes back to their hotel – you go from meetings to dinner. Afterwards, people tend to know that everyone wants their private time. But it all tends to finish pretty early – China's in bed by 10.30 at night.

> 'You still get time to yourself, because you're staying on your own: you get to eat breakfast alone, and evenings usually wrap up early. When I have time, I like to go to the movies. I tend to go out after dinner. I play pool a lot, too. I'll go off with one or two of the interpreters, have a game and learn a few words of the local language at the same time.'

Staying healthy

If you're on the road a lot, try to maintain a health and fitness routine. Relax between meetings or at the end of the day by having a massage, scrub and sauna, meditating, working out or swimming laps. Take vitamin and mineral supplements to keep you operating at peak efficiency. And if you're exhausted, don't push it: put your feet up, order room service and watch cable TV or read a novel.

Sexism and harassment

Although sexual overtures and sexist remarks or behaviours are usually less prevalent in the business environment than they are on the streets, harassment of female foreigners on business is not unheard of. Minimise the likelihood of your being viewed as a sexual 'target' by observing the business dress codes, behaviours, formalities and courtesies of the countries you're visiting (if in doubt, ask your overseas colleagues in advance). Don't encourage intimacy with business associates who may misinterpret your friendliness, and curb your urge to party with male colleagues till all hours, especially if you're the only woman present. Remember that people do business differently in different countries – what's acceptable in your workplace at home may be viewed as odd, rude, or even provocative somewhere else.

In some cultures, sexism as we have come to view it in the West may be considered 'normal' behaviour. Courtesies we see as old-fashioned and perhaps patronising are still accepted as simple politeness in more conservative countries, particularly by older men. And in an environment which, in most places on earth, is still male-dominated, the mere presence of a female may be cause for excitement, embarrassment, concern or amusement. Try not to let it faze you, and attempt to keep a sense of perspective and humour. While it's no fun to be ignored, insulted or patronised, a humourless, pedantically PC reaction won't endear you to your business associates, either. Be warm and courteous but firm in your responses to sexist behaviours and remarks. There are ways of putting chauvinist pigs in their place without damaging business relations or alienating all around you. Find them.

If you are sexually harassed, you may feel uncomfortable about complaining – after all, you're a stranger, unfamiliar with local behaviours, laws and business etiquette. If you appear too compliant or naive, unscrupulous colleagues may take advantage of your ignorance or exploit your desire to 'fit in'. To prevent this from happening, do your homework: in particular, talk to female colleagues about what sorts of behaviours are expected, and what is and isn't acceptable in the work/business environment. Make sure you're not alone with the harasser (or any man you perceive as a potential harasser) unless absolutely necessary. Stand on your dignity, and make sure you're not unwittingly conveying sexual messages with your clothes, hair, behaviour or body language.

If sexual harassment is clearly a problem and you're afraid to assert yourself for fear of bringing reprisals, losing a client, blowing a deal, or causing offence, ask a trusted colleague to approach the harasser on your behalf. If the behaviour persists, you may have to talk to the offender yourself, or go to the authorities.

'I've never had any problems with sexual advances or expectations. In the business I'm in, the environment is

really structured: transport is arranged for you to where you're going and back home, and the structures are formal once you get there. Even the drinking sessions are conducted in a formalised way.

'The most restrictive country I've had to do business in is probably Malaysia, because of the Islamic culture, and the hostility towards Australians. In Indonesia, too, but in a much less overbearing way. You see a lot of women all clothed up in Malaysia, whereas you don't see that in Indonesia. I don't wear scarves or anything on my head, but I wear long skirts: one chiffon skirt and one wrap skirt, long and flowing. And that's fine.

'Most of the people I do business with are men, but I do meet women as well – hotel staff, wives, interpreters. In some contexts, you'll meet more women: in China, women tend to be more active in public life.

'In every group, there are the dull people and the exciting people. There are always three or four exciting people. You have a great time, it's usually very easygoing. You just can't let yourself get irritated, you have to laugh and relax.'

Gifts

In some cultures, the giving of gifts to your hosts, business colleagues (particularly your superiors) and people who take you out or do you favours is expected; in others it's unimportant. Appropriate gifts – along with the way in which and the occasions on which you give them – vary according to the country, the relative positions of you and your host or colleagues, and the favours or hospitality you're 'repaying'. Too much can be embarrassing, too little, insulting, and a gift that's inappropriate may be both.

To get an idea of what's expected and appropriate, consult colleagues who've done business with the people or in the countries you'll be visiting; ask natives of those countries; or call the relevant embassies, consulates or the

Department of Foreign Affairs and Trade and get their advice. Bring a few extra gifts for unforeseen occasions, and don't forget to bring something for the wives and families of your hosts and associates. A good failsafe is to stock up on high-quality duty-free goods (alcohol, perfumes, cigars and the like) in transit. Things that are difficult to obtain, coveted or expensive in the countries you're visiting are usually appreciated, as are goods that are strongly associated with your culture or available only in your country.

> 'I carry currency from Australia with me to show local people, because it has pictures of our native animals on it. For gifts, I don't tend to go to too much trouble getting Australian-made products or anything. I usually just buy duty free: cognac is a favourite.'

Reading matter

Along with work-related material, it's sensible to carry a guidebook geared to your interests and income level, plus at least one readable, relevant novel for times when you need to relax.

> 'I always take a guidebook, for a new place. I usually take a Lonely Planet guide. And it's good to read local fiction, and the biographies of the leader or the heroes of that country. They don't expect you to know about their country or people, but are very flattered when you do.'

WOMEN WITH SPECIAL NEEDS

LESBIAN TRAVELLERS

Some cultures are more tolerant of homosexual behaviour than others. In many countries, physical affection between people of the same sex is considered quite normal and acceptable. Women friends go hand in hand, hug, kiss, and even sleep in the same bed without anyone raising an eyebrow. This may be a relief – it certainly makes it easier to act naturally if you're travelling with a lesbian partner – but it doesn't mean that the culture is tolerant of homosexuality. So don't get too free and easy unless you're sure you're in a lesbian-friendly zone.

> 'In Indonesia, boys hold hands and girls hold hands, but the sexes don't intermingle. You get lots of friendly offers from girls, which is cool. But they're not sexual offers. They're very innocent, platonic offers.'

Booking a double hotel room usually isn't a problem, but if it's causing raised eyebrows or refusals, try booking in advance, getting a room that has a double and a single bed in it, pushing two single beds together, or just cuddling together in one bed, then going off to sleep separately.

If you have friends or contacts living overseas, get in touch and ask them about local women's resources, lesbian clubs, bars and hotels, and gay-friendly accommodation. Or consult the guides and contact groups listed below.

Information and resources

For travel advice and accommodation tips, talk to returned women travellers, especially lesbians, about their experiences. Get as many contacts as you can. Join international gay organisations. Check the Internet for women's groups and make cyber contact with like-minded women in the destinations you plan to visit. And get hold of at least one lesbian-friendly guidebook.

Useful references include:

❑ Virago's *Are You Two . . . Together? A Gay and Lesbian Travel Guide to Europe* by Lindsy Van Gelder and Pamela Robin Brandt (Random House, 1991)

❑ the annual *Ferrari for Women* (Ferrari Publications)

❑ *Fodor's Gay USA* by Andrew Collins (Fodor's, 1996)

❑ *Inn Places: Gay and Lesbian Accommodations in the US and Worldwide* by Marianne Ferrari (Ferrari Publications, 1995)

❑ the gay and lesbian sections of UK-based *Time Out*'s city guides and the American-based Berkeley guides

❑ *Out in the World: International Lesbian Organising* by Shelley Anderson (Firebrand Books, 1991).

Read relevant travel magazines, such as:

❑ *Our World: International Gay Travel Magazine*, 1104 North Nova Rd, Suite 251, Daytona Beach, FL 32117, USA (ph 1-904-441 5367)

❏   *Women's Traveler*, PO Box 422458, San Francisco, CA 94142-2458, USA (ph 1-415-2550 0404).

Contact organisations that are geared for gay travellers, such as:

❏   International Gay Travel Association, PO Box 4974, Key West, FL 33041, USA; ph 1-305-292 0217; fax 1-305-296 6633

❏   International Gay and Lesbian Association (IGLA), c/- RFSL, PO Box 350, Stockholm, Sweden; ph 46-468-834 8050.

NON-CAUCASIAN TRAVELLERS

Travellers who come from distinctive ethnic groups may experience special problems or attract particular attention on the road. The fact that you're a traveller but you're not white may be enough in itself to make you a curiosity. In areas where non-white tourists are a rarity, expect lots of stares and questions.

Try not to jump to the conclusion that all this attention is negative attention. It's easy to get paranoid when you're in a foreign culture and can't interpret people's words or gestures. Adopt a positive, friendly attitude, rather than overreacting and mistaking innocent curiosity for racism or harassment.

On the other hand, you don't want to be complacent. Racism is alive and well in many parts of the world. To avoid being rudely confronted by bigoted behaviour or racist attitudes, know what to expect in the cultures you plan to visit. Guidebooks and returned travellers can alert you to possible problems, give advice on how best to deal with local forms of harassment, and help you to find suitable accommodation in safe areas.

Contacts and resources

Use your personal network, international friendship groups or the Internet to put you in contact with people who can help you to feel at home in the destinations you'll be visiting.

For inspiration and tips, read the entries from black and Asian women in *More Women Travel*. Some guidebooks (Rough Guides, Lonely Planet and Berkeley guides) give information on attitudes to ethnic minorities. Also look out for a new American book, *Go Girl!* (Eighth Mountain Press, 1997), a travel guide for black women.

OLDER TRAVELLERS

You've retired, your children are raised, and you finally have the time and money to go. It's not surprising that older women are big travellers. And they usually have a wonderful time on the road. Some older women don't mind paying a bit extra for added comfort, convenience and security, others are quite happy to 'rough it' – staying in hostels, catching local transport and venturing off the beaten track.

> 'When I was 50, I went to Europe for four months on my own, 'cause my husband couldn't get time off work. I made my base in Poland, where I have family, then travelled from there to places all over Europe. I did it on a budget and stayed in hostels, where I met lots of lovely people, most of them younger than myself but very pleasant and accommodating. I loved it. It was a testing time, but overall, it made me a stronger person. It made me really analyse my life and put it into perspective.'

Physically, older women may be a little more fragile and less agile than their younger sisters, but there are advantages to being an older woman. The most obvious one is that you're likely to be treated with greater courtesy and respect, especially in more traditional societies where elders are looked up to by everyone in the community.

It's common for older women to receive offers of hospitality, help and guidance from local people. If you're struggling with bags, you're more likely to get assistance from passers-by. On transport, there's a good chance that someone more able-bodied will get up or squeeze over to give you a seat. It's easy to shame anyone who's harassing you by reminding them of the need to respect their elders – but chances are, someone else will do it for you.

Your age may make you a target for bag-snatchers or pickpockets, but provided you keep valuables hidden under your clothes and your bag strap diagonally across your body when out and about, you should have no trouble foiling would-be thieves. Avoid isolated or badly lit streets at night, and wear sensible shoes so you can walk (and run) comfortably.

Make sure you're in good health before you leave. And take any physical limitations into account when planning your activities and itinerary. Talk to your doctor about health risks, preventative care, and medications you may need for ailments en route. If you plan to go off the beaten track or engage in unusually strenuous activity, increase your exercise levels before you go.

You may find travelling more exhausting and stressful than you expect, especially if you're in a tropical climate or are travelling through unfamiliar territory. Even if you don't normally rise early, it makes sense when you're travelling: temperatures are cooler in the early morning, the pace is more peaceful, and people are less likely to harass you. If you feel tired or under the weather, don't push yourself – relax with a good book, hire a car (with driver) and take a leisurely tour of the area, sit by the hotel pool, or lie down and take a nap. When you've regained your energy, you can go exploring again.

'My mother really loved the trip. It was interesting. We met lots of women travelling on their own, particularly Europeans, and three or four of them decided they were going to bring their mothers to Bali as well. You see things so differently – I'm blasé about a lot of things, whereas mum gets so excited about things I wouldn't normally get excited about, so you get to see it through different eyes.

'Mum was treated with a lot of respect. She was always viewed as "the mother". We were in Lavina, in the north of Bali, staying at a losmen, and she became not only my mother but everyone else's. There were a whole lot of European backpackers there, and they all became her surrogate daughters. They were drawn to her. They were telling her things they couldn't tell their own mothers because they would have been too worried, but because she was there, doing it, she was different, she was interesting. She'd embarrass me, telling them stories about me, but she entertained them at the same time.

'It was a dream come true for my mum. We stayed in Ubud four days, and she was fascinated by it. We stayed in a homestay, with a family, and all the blokes would come and talk to me, but the women would come up and talk to mum or touch her. In shops, the older women would pay particular attention to her – they'd come up and say, "This dress'd be really nice for you." The older women were definitely drawn to her more.

'She also had older men interested in her: she's in her sixties, but these men would sit and talk to her, and one or two of them got a bit friendly. She was all very, "Oooh, no, I'm married, and my daughter's married too", but she loved it, she had a ball.'

Contacts and resources

Take inspiration from *A Foxy Old Woman's Guide to Travelling Alone* by Jay Ben-Lesser (The Crossing Press, 1995). Or consult travel guides geared to the mature-aged traveller, male or female: try *The 50+ Travellers' Guidebook: Where to Go, Where to Stay, What to Do* by Anita Williams and Merrimac Dillon (St Martin's Press, 1991); Gene and Adele Malott's *Get Up and Go: A Guide for the Mature Traveller* (Gateway Books, 1989); *Elderhostels: The Students' Choice* by Mildred Hyman (John Muir Press, 1991); or *Unbelievably Good Deals and Great Adventures that You Absolutely Can't Get Unless You're Over Fifty* by Joan Rattner Heilman (Contemporary Books, 1995).

If you're over 60 and are interested in arranging a one-week homestay along with two weeks of scheduled classes and field trips in one of 10 countries, contact World Learning's Elderhostel Homestay at 75 Federal St, Boston, MA 02110, USA; ph 1-617-426 8058.

To link up with like-minded companions on your travels, contact US-based organisations Elderhostel (see above); Golden Companions, a travel network and newsletter (PO Box 5249, Reno, NV 80513, USA; ph 1-702-324 2227; fax 702-324 2236); or the international women's link-up organisation Women Welcome Women (88 Eaton St, High Wycombe, HP11 1LT, UK; ph/fax 44-01494-46 5441).

PREGNANT TRAVELLERS

You can travel safely and enjoyably while pregnant. Whether you choose to depends on how you feel in yourself. If you do decide to travel while you're pregnant, plan your trip to take account of your health and well-being.

Take a reputable book on pregnancy that includes a comprehensive section on health in pregnancy, so that you can monitor developments and know what to expect at various stages. That way, you won't panic over something that's perfectly normal or ignore a problem that needs attention.

If you have the choice, travel in the second trimester (between the 16th and 30th weeks of pregnancy). At this stage you won't be uncomfortably big, should still have lots of energy, and are less likely to feel nauseous. It's also the safest time, as your risk of miscarriage drops after week 14 and you're unlikely to go into premature labour before week 30. It's smart to minimise travelling during the final month – besides, airline regulations make it very difficult to fly after the 35th week.

While travelling, listen to your body and don't push yourself too hard. Take things easy and don't pack in too many long, hard trips: you may tire more easily than normal, especially in the first three and the last two months of pregnancy.

When packing, remember to include clothes that can accommodate your changing body shape comfortably, especially if you'll be travelling past week 20: choose loose clothes, elasticised waists and comfortable shoes with a bit of extra room.

Diet is especially important during pregnancy, and you may have to go to special lengths to make sure you get the nutrients you need. You may wish to take iron, calcium, folic acid or other nutritional supplements with you if you're not sure whether certain foods will be available locally. If you're taking anti-malarial tablets, you should also take folic acid supplements. Use iodised salt on your food if it's available, especially in places where the local produce is iodine-deficient.

Make sure you drink lots of fluids and eat a balanced, fibre-rich diet to minimise your likelihood of getting constipated (often a problem for pregnant women). If you're feeling nauseous – or just peckish – snack often during the day. Be careful about using iodine to purify water: boil it instead.

You may feel the need to urinate more frequently, especially during the latter stages of pregnancy. When planning journeys or tours, take this into account. You may decide it's worth paying the extra for a private berth or first-class seat with access to clean toilet facilities.

You may also find that your feet and ankles are more prone to swelling on flights and in transit: to minimise this, try to get up and stroll the aisles once every hour or so, if possible.

Resources and contacts
Unfortunately there are few resources for pregnant travellers, but most women's travel guides include information that's relevant, as do travellers' health guides. Beyond that, your best sources of useful information and travel tips are other women who've done it.

TRAVELLERS WITH CHILDREN

Travelling with a child is a mixed blessing. While kids may not be able to provide the practical support and intellectual input that an adult companion gives, they do bring companionship, amusement and a delightfully fresh perspective on the world and its wonders.

At times, travelling with a child can be more difficult and stressful than travelling solo. Not only are you solely responsible for all the arrangements – finding accommodation, making bookings, ensuring your security – but you also have someone else to look after. Taking your child with you on your travels can be an immensely rewarding experience, but don't expect it to be simple, or to satisfy all your personal holiday needs.

Before you go . . .
Get passports, visas, vaccinations and health checks handled well in advance of your departure date, in case anything needs to be followed up. Remember that if the

child's father's name appears on his or her birth certificate, you'll need his written permission before you take the child out of the country. You don't need a separate passport for children under 12 years of age, but the child's details must appear on your passport.

Pack carefully, because your ability to run around finding things you've left out will be somewhat restricted once you're on the road. You may want to include some or all of the following:

❑ A medical kit that includes medicines (and prescriptions) for any ailment your child is prone to, as well as pain relievers, stomach upset remedies, antiseptic, Band-aids, and so on. You don't want to have to leave a sick child in order to go rushing off to pharmacies, so taking extra supplies is worthwhile.

❑ Any equipment you'll need for feeding, sterilising bottles, changing nappies, and so on, if you're travelling with an infant. You can now buy disposable nappies almost everywhere, but bring a couple of cloth ones just in case. Try to ensure that baby items are made of lightweight, unbreakable materials, such as plastic. You can buy basic baby-care supplies in larger towns almost everywhere. Getting boiling water for sterilising usually isn't a problem, but you may want to carry a small immersion heater to save hassles.

❑ Your child's favourite cuddly object or toy. Forget to pack it and you may be subjected to endless whining and fretting.

❑ Comfortable, wash'n'wear outfits in easy-dry fabrics for both of you, plus a sunhat and sunblock for your child if travelling in hot climates.

❑ A foldable, lightweight stroller may be handy if your trip includes a lot of city legs; otherwise, consider a pouch-style carrier that you can wear in front of your body or sling on your back. A long, strong leash is useful for keeping track of junior while you shop, sightsee or queue.

❑ A couple of storybooks that will stand up to some re-telling.

Ensure that you have access to sufficient funds to see you through an emergency, and that your insurance policy adequately covers both you and your child.

Where possible, pre-book accommodation and reserve seats or berths for long trips – you don't want the hassle of traipsing around from hotel to hotel or having to queue for tickets with a child in tow. On overnight train trips, get a sleeping berth – you can usually share it with your child.

Build sufficient relaxation time into your itinerary. You may be able to cope with a gruelling schedule, but your child is bound to become tired, stressed and bored if there's too much time spent in transit. Go for quality rather than quantity. Choose places where kids won't find the going too rough, the climate exhausting, or the activities boring. You may have always wanted to tour Europe's art museums or trek the Andes, but that doesn't mean it's a four-year-old's idea of a good time. And if your child's not having fun, there's a good chance you won't be either.

En route . . .
Keep your child close to you while you negotiate customs, queues, airports and public transport – surveillance is most difficult when you're in transit. Infants may be safest and most comfortable in a pouch-style carrier that leaves your hands free to handle bags and documents. For children who are mobile, a leash may be the most practical solution. Often, others will shunt you to the head of the queue if they see you struggling with youngsters.

'I did get more sympathy travelling with a child. Especially going through customs. I'd arrive and my son

would be asleep, sprawled out on a suitcase, and I'd be at
the end of the line, having struggled out of the aeroplane
with all the luggage and him asleep. People would always
let me go through first. That was great.'

Be prepared to spend more than you would if you were doing the trip on your own. Although your costs are unlikely to be double – kids often get to stay or travel free – you may pay more for better-quality accommodation, taxis, occasional room service, special tours and other 'luxuries'.

Choose your accommodation carefully. Usually, the most child-friendly places are family-run hotels, resorts geared for families and campgrounds. Here, you may also find it easier to tee up formal or informal child care. Useful facilities include an on-site laundry, a good in-house restaurant (or at least breakfast) and an enclosed garden or safe communal area. Entertainment facilities, such as video, table tennis tables or a swimming pool (provided you're there to supervise), can be a boon. At family resorts and larger campgrounds in summer months, you'll often find there's a whole program of activities for kids.

Be careful about what your child eats and drinks – children's stomachs tend to be more delicate than adults', and their immune systems aren't as strong, so they're more susceptible to stomach upsets and infectious diseases. In restaurants, avoid ordering hot and spicy foods if your child's not used to eating them, and make sure you follow the hygiene rules outlined on pages 283–6. If restaurant food doesn't agree with your child, buy fresh produce from local markets and concoct picnic meals, or cook in your hotel room if you have the facilities. If you're worried about local hygiene standards, have food and drinks prepared before leaving your child with local babysitters and remind childminders that you'd prefer it if they fed your child only what you've provided. Make sure your child doesn't accept food or drink from strangers, however well-meaning their offers may be.

> *'I had to be very careful with my son in Bangkok. People were always saying, "Let me take him and buy him a drink", or wanting to touch him, to hold him. I could have lost him so many times.'*

Stop your child from playing around in unsavoury-looking places or patting local animals – in addition to fleas and lice, dogs, monkeys and even squirrels can carry rabies and other diseases (see page 282). Even seemingly friendly creatures can and do bite, and such bites can become infected easily, especially in tropical climates.

If your child becomes ill and you're not sure how to treat the condition, contact an English-speaking doctor through your hotel or embassy, or call a travellers' medical hotline (see pages 291–6). Children may be unable to communicate to you just how sick they feel, and some illnesses can progress rapidly from mild to severe, so it's important not to let an unidentified ailment go unchecked.

If you become ill, phone a doctor and arrange for a hotel visit. You can't afford to sit it out when you have a child to look after. If possible, organise some child care: your hotel or local tourist office should be able to help you arrange for a suitable babysitter. Even if you're not ill, you may need to take a few hours out every once in a while. Don't feel guilty or worry unduly – good, reliable childminders can be found all over the globe, and if you're staying in a village, it's likely that local people will look after your child automatically, along with the rest of the kids.

Note that in more conservative societies, locals' attitudes to single motherhood may be moralistic. To some people, the absence of a father may imply that you're sexually loose or unable to keep your man. Counter such impressions by behaving in a courteous and conservative manner. If you are a single parent, you may feel more comfortable if you 'invent' a husband, and a story explaining why he's unable to travel with you.

Resources and contacts

If you're planning to take your child travelling, check out one of the many guidebooks for parents, such as Maureen Wheeler's *Travel With Children* (Lonely Planet, 1995), *Innocents Abroad: Traveling With Kids in Europe* by Valerie Wolf Deutsch and Laura Sutherland (Penguin, 1991), Nan and Kevin Jeffrey's *Adventuring With Children: The Complete Manual for Family Adventure Travel* (Menasha Ridge, 1995), *Traveling With Children and Enjoying It: A Complete Guide to Family Travel by Car, Plane and Train* by Arlene Kay Butler (Globe Pequot Press, 1991) or *Take Your Kids to Europe* by Cynthia W. Harriman (Mason-Grant Publications, 1995). You can now buy kids' guidebooks, too: look out for the Kidding Around series (John Muir Publications, 1990).

TRAVELLERS WITH DISABILITIES

Travellers whose mobility is impaired may find it more difficult than most to get around, particularly outside of cities and in the developing world. But this doesn't have to stop you from travelling safely, enjoyably and comfortably. You'll just have to plan things more carefully. Fortunately, there are now guidebooks, groups and tour companies geared to assist travellers with special needs.

Contacts and information

For disabled travellers wanting useful information and travel tips, there's Rough Guides' *Nothing Ventured: Disabled People Travel the World*, *World Wheelchair Traveller* (The Automobile Association, UK) or FT Publishing's *Smooth Ride Guides* to Australia and NZ, the USA and Canada (with more destinations to follow).

If you're looking to work or study while you're overseas, get hold of a copy of *A World of Options for the '90s: A Guide to International Educational Exchange, Community*

Service and Travel for Persons with Disabilities by Mobility International USA.

For inspiration, turn to *Nothing Ventured: True Stories by and for People with Disabilities*, edited by Alison Walsh with Jodie Abbott and Peg L. Smith (Rough Guides, 1994).

The global travellers' information exchange, Travelin' Talk Network, helps travellers with disabilities to locate all sorts of services, from tours to accommodation, wheelchair hire to vans with chair lifts or medical escorts. The membership fees are on a sliding scale. Contact Travelin' Talk, PO Box 3534, Clarksville, TN 37043, USA (ph 1-615-552 6670; fax 1-615-552 1182).

If you're after an adventure tour that caters to people of all mobility levels, try one of these US-based companies:

❑ Environmental Traveling Companions provide outdoor adventures such as white-water rafting, kayaking and ski trips for those with special needs. Contact them at the Fort Mason Center Building C, San Francisco, CA 94123, USA (ph 1-415-474 7662; fax 1-415-474 3919).

❑ Wilderness Inquiry offers canoeing, kayaking, raft and dog-sled trips for people with mobility impairments, and may be able to help you out with finances, too. Contact them on 1313 Fifth Street S.E., Suite 117, Minneapolis, MN 55414, USA (ph 1-612-379 3858).

The ACCESS Foundation for the Disabled can provide you with travel information and services, including a global home exchange program for people who have mobility impairments. Contact ACCESS in the USA on ph/fax 1-516-568 2715.

MAKING THE MOST OF YOUR TRIP

All journeys end eventually. Even if you're looking forward to going home, making the transition from travel mode to settled mode can be difficult. Many women experience culture shock on their return. After the initial excitement, you may feel let down, lethargic, even depressed. The longer the trip, the more exotic the destinations, the more time you'll need to readjust to 'normal' life. Take these steps to make the transition easier:

❑ Give yourself time to rest and relax – don't schedule a hectic social schedule or plunge straight back into full-time work.

❑ Request tolerance – and privacy – from those close to you, at least for the first week or two.

❑ Avoid making major life decisions till you've had time to settle.

❑ Be cautious on the road, especially if you haven't driven for a while. Remember that local traffic conditions may be very different from what you've been used to overseas, so even as a pedestrian, you should pay special attention till you readjust.

❑ Monitor your health, especially if you've visited a region where disease is prevalent. Continue taking anti-malarial medication for the prescribed period after leaving a malaria-prone area. Check yourself for signs and symptoms of illness or parasites, and get a medical examination from someone who's familiar with exotic ailments if anything seems amiss.

❑ Appreciate the things you enjoy about your own culture – healthy food, comfy beds, flush toilets, having your own things around you, family support and friends.

DEALING WITH CHANGE

You've changed as a result of what you've seen and done, and it can take time to assimilate those changes into your daily life. You may find it hard to get used to the fact that you're no longer the special one, the foreigner. You belong here, just like everyone else. And everyone else may not seem so great any more.

It's common for returning travellers to feel as though those they left behind are stuck in the same old rut. To point this out isn't generally a good idea – your 'helpful advice' is likely to be perceived as presumptuous and annoying. Let people know – by your actions and attitudes, not by lecturing – that you're a different person from the woman who went away, and that the changes are for the better.

You may feel as though friends and family fail to acknowledge the new you or to understand the changes you've been through. If you're feeling alienated, it can help to spend time with people who sympathise with your situation. People from other cultures and people who've spent a lot of time travelling may be good sources of support at this time. Keep the connection with the new places you've discovered by joining a cultural, aid or friendship group.

APPRECIATING WHAT YOU'VE LEARNED

One of the most rewarding things about travel is the way it changes you. You may have grown in many ways, but often you don't realise it till you get home and look back on your experiences. Here's what some women say:

'Travelling alone makes you grow as a person. It really develops your social skills. You get a deeper understanding of what you want out of life, and a better appreciation of the things that are going on around you.'

'You become more broadminded and have more get up and go. You get a lot more confident and you're more willing to try new things. When I left, I think a lot of people thought I'd be back in a couple of months, but it's been two years now and I'm living in Australia with no plans to go home. When I go back to visit, people are still in the same houses, in the same jobs, taking two-week holidays to Spain once a year. And they assume they're stuck. But you don't have to be. I nearly did the same. I had a job and a mortgage, but I left the job, rented my place out and went. And it's the best thing I ever did.'

'You don't know until you try. I have a friend who's 40 and had been working in a florist's and living with one guy for about nine years. She went away six months ago on a world trip. She used to be so timid, and she'd always thought, "It's too late for me to travel", but once she got out there, she thought it was the best thing she'd ever

done. It's never too late. She's been all over Asia, Australia, the States: she's planning to go to South America now.'

'Travelling teaches you to appreciate little things more. You can be quite materialistic but then you go to places like Indonesia and see how basic things are, and you realise you can do without comforts and still be happy. These days, I don't ask for much, materially, even now I'm in Australia where you can get all the mod cons. Things like stereos and groovy clothes aren't that important – there are other things in life.'

'I learnt things that I can't even put into words by travelling on my own. To me, travelling is the greatest education anyone can ever have. You're in another culture where you may not read or understand the language. It makes you use your basic instincts. It pushes you into another realm, into a situation where you have to survive, and you are going to survive.'

'Travelling is a growth thing. Handling so many different situations gives you a lot of confidence. It showed me what I was capable of and taught me not to be scared of making decisions, or of making wrong decisions.'

'I came away from my trips with a huge education. I was burning to learn – I wanted to know everything about the cultures I possibly could. But I also learnt that I was someone who could get scared, and that I was someone who could get lonely.'

'Travelling solo forces you to get out and do things on your own; it forces you to build up your confidence. You do things that you probably wouldn't have thought of doing in your own country. Then having done it in a foreign country, you can come back and do it in your normal life.'

> 'I learnt a lot from my solo travels. It was like growing up all over again for me. How totally sheltered and naive I was before! I'd write letters to my friends describing these blow-out experiences – and I feel a bit embarrassed now, but that was what I was going through. It was so amazing.'

> 'For me, it was truly inspirational to travel on my own. Travelling with other people was fine, sometimes it worked and sometimes it didn't – but there was never a time, ever, when I felt so good as when I was on my own. I think it's because of that confidence: that feeling that I'm here, I'm all alone somewhere completely foreign to me – and I've done it.'

REVIVING YOUR TRAVELLING SPIRIT

Work to develop the outgoing, curious, confident, assertive, directed personality you manifested when you were travelling. Such qualities are useful in any environment. Don't let your trip become a fading memory or lose the skills you acquired on your journey.

Keep your travel experiences alive by:

❏ phoning or writing to thank friends or family members you stayed with on your travels, and to update your contact details

❏ making a list of all the people you met and vowed to keep in touch with, then writing to them and sending any photos or gifts you promised

❏ developing your photos. Label them all so you never forget, and get duplicates of ones you want to send to friends. Blow up the best ones and frame them.

❏ hosting a travel slide night. Only use your best shots, be selective, and script a travelogue to accompany them. If you have friends who've

travelled, hold a group showing and compare travel
tales afterwards.

- ❏ recreating your journey in your mind – for pure
pleasure, and to gain new insights and perspectives.
Re-read your diary. Look at photos, postcards,
mementoes. Relive the highlights of your trip.
- ❏ thinking – about how you've changed, what you've
learnt, as a result of your experiences and
encounters; about what you can do to counter the
problems and alleviate suffering you witnessed on
your travels
- ❏ following up interests or maintaining skills
acquired on your travels – photography, scuba
diving, art history, Thai cookery, playing the
Japanese flute, riding a motorbike
- ❏ maintaining good habits. If you got really fit
walking around Europe or trekking in Peru,
meditated every morning in Thailand or became a
vegetarian in India, don't drop the healthy habits
just because you're home.
- ❏ hanging on to your traveller's instincts. Remember,
you're the woman who backpacked around Asia,
lived on your wits in London, handled the hustlers
in Morocco. Keep those survival skills honed by
practising them whenever the opportunity presents
itself on home territory, and you'll be better
prepared for future journeys.
- ❏ developing travel-related skills. Learn to speak a
language, defend yourself, administer first aid or
take better portraits: skills that will come in handy
next time you travel.
- ❏ getting a job that puts you in contact with people
and events in other countries. Train for a job in
tourism or travel, or in one of a range of
professions (including civil engineering,
accounting, teaching and nursing) that are in
demand in developing countries. Join an

international company and you may get opportunities to transfer to an overseas position further down the track.

❑   doing your bit to help. Sponsor an aid project or foster a child in need. Do voluntary work for an international aid or environmental organisation: preferably one that helps local people to generate skills and initiate community projects.

❑   supporting women worldwide. In strongly male-dominated cultures, women and female children may have limited or no access to education or assets unless they receive support from outside sources. Often, women are the backbone of family and community, and projects that advance women's knowledge and skills generally have positive repercussions for the whole community. Your support could take the form of fostering a female child (and ensuring she gets an education), donating to a women's aid or community project, starting an Internet site for female travellers, or just keeping in touch with all the wonderful women you met on your journey.

But perhaps the best way to keep that travelling spirit alive is to start planning your next journey. You may decide to follow up friends you made on your last trip by visiting their homelands (do check with the people concerned before deciding to land in on them, however). You may wish to return to a favourite place or to spend more time in a country you rushed through last time. You might have the urge to do something more adventurous or mind expanding (such as a jungle or desert trek, a meditation retreat, a dance festival or a course of study). Or you might want to explore totally new territory.

Whatever you choose to do, wherever you choose to go on your next trip, the mere fact that you're making plans will help you forget about being stuck at home, give you lots to get excited about, and provide you with a great reason for talking with fellow wanderers, attending travel seminars and slide shows, and reading about exotic places – because, as every traveller knows, the next best thing to *having* a big adventure is looking forward to one.

INDEX OF DESTINATIONS